# The Most Awkward Man in Japan

Dispatches from a Philosopher Abroad

Robert Gressis

Copyright © 2024 by Robert Gressis

All rights reserved.

No portion of this book may be reproduced in any form without written permission from the publisher or author, except as permitted by U.S. copyright law.

While the publisher and author have used their best efforts in preparing this book, they make no representations or warranties with respect to the accuracy or completeness of the contents of this book and specifically disclaim any implied warranties of merchantability or fitness for a particular purpose.

The author expressly prohibits any entity from using this publication to train artificial intelligence technologies to generate text including, without limitation, technologies capable of generating works in the same style as this publication.

Some names and identifying details of people described in this book have been altered to protect their privacy.

# Contents

| | |
|---|---|
| Dedication | VII |
| Introduction | 1 |
| DECEMBER 28, 2022 | 7 |
| 1. Flyer's Remorse | 8 |
| DECEMBER 29, 2022 | 15 |
| 2. A Japanese Obstacle Course. No, It's Not Sasuke | 16 |
| DECEMBER 30, 2022 | 21 |
| 3. One Man's Treasure ... | 22 |
| 4. The Three C's | 26 |
| 5. Scramble On | 29 |
| 6. Staying Married Around Unmarried Mari | 38 |
| 7. Eat, Drink, and Be Mari | 45 |
| DECEMBER 31, 2022 | 60 |
| 8. The Most Absorbing Thing | 61 |
| 9. Kapitel 9: Spazieren Gehen und Zweimal Essen | 74 |
| JANUARY 1, 2023 | 83 |

10. Welcome to 2023 — 84

## OH SHIT I HAVE TO GO BACK TO DECEMBER 31, 2022 — 89

11. Imagine if a Shopping District Was Designed by a Stage 5 Hoarder — 90

## JANUARY 1, 2023, MORE FOR REAL — 96

12. Bullet Train: Fine, and Better than Bullet Train — 97
13. Frankenstein's Monster's Master's Servant's Hotel — 103
14. In Which I Really Make a Meal Out of This Dinner — 109
15. Gates Are Only Fun When They Lead to Somewhere That Is Not Just Gates — 127

## JANUARY 2, 2023 — 131

16. In Which I Look My Gift Horse in the Mouth and Enjoy Its Mouth (the Ritz is the Gift Horse) — 132
17. Public Displays of Religion — 138
18. A Walk That Walks the Walk — 145
19. A Palace Fit for a King — 151
20. Tasting the Sights — 160

## JANUARY 3, 2023 — 174

21. The Platonic Form of Averagosity — 175
22. A Staggering Work of Hirsute Genius — 181
23. The Constant Garden — 185
24. Checking on Checking in — 201

| | | |
|---|---|---|
| 25. | Making a Mountain Out of a Monkey Hill | 207 |
| 26. | Bamboo Forest, But Boo, Not For Us | 213 |
| 27. | The Reward at the End of the Quest | 218 |
| 28. | The Very Definition of Romantic | 222 |
| 29. | Beef over Fish | 227 |

## JANUARY 4, 2023     240

| | | |
|---|---|---|
| 30. | You Can Notice a Lot of Stuff if You Just Read about It Months after You See It | 241 |
| 31. | Traduttore Traditore | 245 |
| 32. | The Pre-Show | 251 |
| 33. | A Very Small Part of My Life Has Been a Lie! | 262 |
| 34. | A Sad Ending, an Embarrassing Beginning, and an OK Ending | 268 |
| 35. | I Went to Wrestle Kingdom 17, and All I Got Was One of the Most Thrilling Nights of My Life | 273 |
| 36. | Above It All, Except for Drinking Alcohol, Which I Was Not Above, Except for When I on the Second Storey of a Bar, at Which Point I Was Above It All | 286 |

## JANUARY 5, 2023     291

| | | |
|---|---|---|
| 37. | Fancies Don't Let Me Down | 292 |
| 38. | Mate for an Hour | 305 |
| 39. | The First Rule of Flight Club Is That You Brag to Everyone about Flight Club | 310 |

| | |
|---|---|
| 40. My Master Theory of Japan: No Masters! | 322 |
| APRIL 1, 2024 | 331 |
| Coda: Answering the Question | 332 |
| About the author | 344 |

To my wife, without whom this dedication would not exist.

# Introduction

My wife told me this book needs a hook.

I didn't know what that was, so I asked her. She told me that a hook is something that gets readers to read the book.

But won't the cover do that? Apparently not; all the cover does is get people to *open* the book. A hook is supposed to get people to start *reading* the book. In other words, the cover is the lure—the worm that attracts the fish—while the hook is the part of the book that rips in to readers' flesh and pulls them forcefully against their will to a giant who will beat them to death or suffocate them, cook their bodies over an open fire, and then devour them.

If you've read this far, maybe I've already hooked you. If not, then I promise you this: one day, I will find you. After I find you, I will grab you by your lips, I will pull you onto my boat, and then I will watch as you flail around, trying to breathe life-giving water into your gills, to no avail.

How's that for a hook?

OK, let me tell you about what you're (still, God willing) reading. One day—I don't know when, but I'm 95% sure it was in the past—my wife Shawn promised me that we would go on an all-frills trip to Japan from December 28, 2022 to January 5, 2023. She did this for three reasons.

First, we hadn't had a vacation with just the two of us since our son Briscoe was born in 2014. Living together in southern California was getting suffocating and monotonous, so we needed to live together for a shorter time, in a smaller room, in a place where we didn't understand the language.

Second, she loves planning things: no single word scares her more than "surprise." By contrast, no octet of words lifts her spirits more than "surprise inspection planned by Shawn at taxpayer expense."[1] Meticulously planning each step of a nine-day trip to a foreign country lightened her heart in the same way that most contemporary Americans' hearts lighten when they learn that someone they have political disagreements with has just died.

Third, and most significant of all, she wanted me to go on this trip so that she could exert power over me. If you've ever been married before, had a roommate, or owned a cat, you probably get what I mean. But if not, then let me go back to my past.

See, OK, my mom has a Ukrainian friend, Polina, who told me that marriage is about balancing power. That is, there is a total of 100% power in any marriage; if someone has 80% of the power, that means the other one has 20% of the power. The only way to have a successful marriage is to get your power level to 100%. Once you do that, you can kick your spouse out of the Donbas region and fruitlessly bicker with him until you're both so tired that you die.

Anyway, I wasn't going to let Shawn use this trip to benefit me, thereby upping her power level in our marriage from 90% to 92%. So I thought to myself: "how can I transform this trip from a gift to me into a delight

---

1. Shawn works for a government agency, one that inspects things. I don't want you to have any negative preconceptions about her, so let's just say she works for ICE.

for Shawn?" Once I put the question to myself, the answer became clear: think and talk only about myself![2]

It wasn't enough, though, just to think and talk about myself; I do that all the time, for free, and to my great psychological detriment. Although I compulsively perseverate, I also covet validation, so I decided I would chronicle Shawn's and my time in Japan by writing electronic missives to my friends and family back home.

My master plan paid off: the emails were well-received, I managed to pass off my various (self-diagnosed) mental illnesses as me "just being funny", and, most importantly, I made it look like I was repaying Shawn for her efforts, thereby arresting her ever-growing control over our marriage. I would remain the RC to her Coca-Cola.

At first, I sent emails about my time in Japan pretty regularly—maybe once a week. As time passed, though, my memory weakened, and I had to consult my notes and pictures for ever-longer periods of time until, finally, my job responsibilities started to pull me away, and I had to move writing these emails to the back-burner. For you see, my job is very noble, and very important: I am a philosopher.

Well, technically, I'm not so much a philosopher as I am a professor of philosophy.[3] But I still see myself as part of that noble tradition of thinkers who were so annoying that their countrymen would either execute them (Socrates), banish them (Aristotle), excommunicate them (Spinoza), or not have sex with them (Kant).

---

2. It's what every woman wants!

3. Philosophers love making distinctions. Also, I'm pretty sure we invented the phrase, "well, technically...". Well, technically, we didn't so much *invent* it as *popularize* it. That's an important distinction, you know.

Anyway, once the semester started in earnest, I had to focus on teaching students and not so much on writing funny emails. My dozen of fans started to get restless. "When is your next entry? Why do you still keep on teaching when you're so bad at it?" are the questions they would ask me.[4] Realizing that my memories of my once-in-a-lifetime marriage-power-reversal would wither and die if I didn't come up with a rationale to keep on writing, Shawn proposed that I turn my emails into a book. And because she is nothing if not a team player, she promised me that she would not only continually harry me into writing more, but she would also entertain unrealistic fantasies about my notional book's success, such that if this book didn't earn $500,000, she would divorce me.

How's *that* for a hook?

Once I had this organizing principle, everything fell into place. Rather than try to give my readers just the gist of my experiences, I would marry an insurance adjuster's eye for detail to a court stenographer's completionism to an insurance adjuster's descriptive prowess. Rather than use my friends' and family's real names, I would devise pseudonyms that were both demeaning and also complete failures at pseudonymity.[5] And rather than go easy on the philosophy, on the grounds that my loved ones already know I'm a philosopher and are unhappy about it, I would inject just enough philosophy to prove to you that I know what I'm talking

---

4. My fans focused more on the first question. It was more my students and colleagues who offered me the second one.

5. *E.g.*, the real name of the person I call "Shawn" in this story is "Shawn", the real name of the person I call "Scotty" in this book is "Scott", and the real name of the person I call "Chewy" is actually "Chewbacca." Chew story!

about, while also being bad enough at it to make you feel good about yourself when you easily dunk on me.[6]

In theory, by reading this book, you could learn something about Japan. But that's only if your narrator were reliable. Unfortunately, he's not. See, when it comes to writing, my approach is the same as John Irving's: start writing about yourself, then at some point just start lying.[7] That means that many of my observations and stories about Japan are a little bit, um, heightened.

So that's one reason you shouldn't trust me: I'm untrustworthy. Another reason, though, is that going in to this trip, I didn't know anything about Japan. I mean, that's a bit of an exaggeration, but unless you're educated about Japan, like my colleague, Dragon,[8] I know no more about it than you. Having little prior knowledge about Japan adds authenticity to my scrutiny, enabling me to spot noteworthy aspects, but it also makes it somewhat naïve. Point is, if you learn about Japan by reading this book, it will be accidental.

Really, the thing you most learn about by reading this book is me. You learn about my fears, my worldview, my insecurities, my personal history, my anxieties, my favorite foods, and my top three worries (people yelling at me, accidentally hurting someone, and locked-in syndrome). I realize I'm not important, but neither are most people. So really, by learning all about me, you learn all about humanity. And by learning all about

---

6. My philosophical research is on being a philosophical mediocrity. It's a passion project.

7. He never said that. Which makes my approach all the more true to his spirit.

8. Real name: Drake.

humanity, you'll inadvertently learn about Japan, a country full of many people who are as terrified about things as I am.

How's *THAT* for a hook?

# DECEMBER 28, 2022

# 1

# Flyer's Remorse

I've known for about six months that I'd be going to Japan. My wife, Shawn, has visited the country three times before, in 2018, 2019, and 2020. She, like my friend Scotty, is a great enthusiast for the place. What's strange, though, is that it's very difficult for me to understand why Scotty and Shawn like it so much. It's not that they like something that I find off-putting; that would be normal enough. No, the weird thing is that they seem unable to articulate what's so good about Japan.

Don't get me wrong; they've tried. Near as I can tell, what (they think) makes Japan so great is that it's very competent and introverted. Not only do Japanese people do their jobs well, but, even better, they're not interested in you. This observation from travel writer Pico Iyer captures their sentiment well:

> If nothing's personal in public Japan, you may conclude that Japan is an impersonal place. But as the woman in the tiny patisserie flashes you a beautiful smile and spends many long minutes placing your $1.50 éclair in a pink box, enclosing a bag of ice so the pastry won't melt on the long way home, wrapping the box in seasonal paper and appending a bow (pick any color) under a badge to keep the box shut, you're

really in the realm of the transpersonal. Everything is deeply personal; it just has nothing to do with you.

A Beginner's Guide to Japan, pp. 16-17

Now, if you're an introverted tourist interested in excellence, I can see why such a place excites you. Not only does their lack of interest in you put you at ease, but their skill means that things are unlikely to go wrong, further reducing the chances that you'll have to interact with anyone more than is absolutely necessary.

But me? I'm a forgiving extravert. I quite enjoy talking to people. Some of my friends tell me that my style of conversation is that of an endless first date: I'm always asking questions like, "do you wish that you had been shot, but have now gotten over the physical and mental trauma of it, so that you can brag about it to people at cocktail parties?", or, "if you had to be a werewolf, vampire, or ghost, which would you be? I'd be a mummy."

The point is, I enjoy talking to people to the point that if I don't hang out with one of my friends for over two days, I get antsy and depressed. But Japan doesn't seem to welcome that kind of vibe. It's not Ireland, where strangers will go up to you and tell you about their grudges against people who are long dead. No, from what I've picked up, Japan is like Eastern Europe, in that everyone is cold, but it's not like Eastern Europe, in that everyone is also embarrassed.

Not only am I extraverted, but, as I mentioned above, I'm forgiving. If a student turns in work late, I usually accept it with a small penalty, no questions asked. If someone forgets that we had lunch plans at 12:30, and I end up sitting by myself at Kebab Stop for forty-five minutes, it's no sweat—I brought a book! And if someone accidentally spills his champagne on me, I apologize to him for not going better with champagne.

I get the sense, though, that the people in Japan are not so forgiving. If someone messes up, then this is, like, really bad. Everyone is embarrassed. And even if the person who messes up is you, because you don't speak Japanese or have never been there before, well, that's no excuse. You should have read a travel book.

I'm not saying, of course, that this is what Japan is *actually* like. It's a country with a rich history and with over one hundred and twenty million people; few informative generalizations will be completely accurate. I am saying, though, that this was my *sense* of what Japan was like. Consequently, when I woke up at 6 AM on December 28, my chest was tight, and I had trouble breathing.

This tightness was not, as I feared, Covid-19, finally coming to kill me four years after it was invented by a bat in a Chinese lab; no, it was anxiety. My body realized I had no escape. I was finally going to Japan.

I should mention one more thing, because this also has a part to play in my anxiety. I was going to be gone for roughly nine days from my house and, *ipso facto*, my homebody of a son, Briscoe. He would be in the caring hands of his grandmother, and his maniac friends would visit him while Shawn and I were away, to keep his spirits up. I feared two things: being apart from him for longer than I've ever been apart from him; and his reaction to my being apart from him for longer than I've ever been apart from him.

In my head, I imagined him weeping profusely as I left (while ignoring his mom). And then, I would also cry, and we would have to be forcefully separated. Finally, I would make it to LAX, and as my plane lifted off to Tokyo, I would tearfully look out the window and see him hanging on to the wing, like the monster from The Twilight Zone that menaced both William Shatner and John Lithgow.

Instead, what happened is that his mom and I left at 7:15 AM and he cheerfully yelled "bye!" while looking at YouTube.

Still, my chest tightness remained. One of my worries didn't come to pass, but there was still all the other stuff about the taciturn Japanese people, my longing for my friends, and my messing up and possibly getting incarcerated in a Japanese prison. (I didn't actually mention that earlier, but I don't know what the penalty is for, like, accidentally cutting in line. It could be prison, what do I know?)

It's at this point that I should say that Shawn did all the planning for this trip. She was very excited to do it and we had accrued many, many frequent flyer miles over the Covid-19 lockdown. So over the last week she has promised me that I would, alternately, "drown in class", "vomit luxury", "suffer a spinal tap of lavishness", "piss comfort", "get stabbed by sumptuousness", "ooze opulence", "burn to an extravagant crisp", "lactate lavishness", "be poisoned by indulgence", "ejaculate wealth", and, finally, "get kidnapped, tied up, and beaten within an inch of my life by splendor."

Now that I think about it, I'm starting to wonder whether this whole trip is an elaborate way of telling me that she wants to violently murder me.

That speculation aside, after leaving home, we made our way to LAX. I won't bore you with most of the details, but after a little bit of time, we found ourselves on the first luxurious leg of my luxury trip to Japan: the Qantas first-class lounge. It was, then, upon seeing this beautiful place, that my chest loosened up and my anxiety dissipated.

It's a quite pretty lounge! Pictures don't do it justice. At least, not pictures I'm capable of taking. In addition, my strengths as a writer don't lend themselves to descriptions of physical objects, so I can't really describe it either. Here, for example, is how I would render the lounge if forced to: "there was a long bar made of some material, but it wasn't shiny. It was the opposite of shiny. Matte? I think that matte is the opposite of shiny. There were a lot of glass shelves behind the bar showcasing the alcohol. The carpet underneath the tables had a crisscross pattern, and there were lots of tables where people could sit and eat. There were two stations with free alcohol. There was a kitchen in the back where you could, if you wanted to, sort of see people cooking things. Like, I saw people in white clothing, as if they were cooks."

You get the idea. I mean, you don't get the idea about what the lounge looked like. But you do get the idea about my ability to describe the lounge. Look, I'm a philosopher. I'm not good with matter.[1] So let's just get straight to the airplane.

Since I was traveling in business class on Japan Air Lines (JAL), I thought of this as potentially my first taste of Japan. Thus, I kept my eyes peeled for any differences between Japanese and American air travel. The first difference wasn't hard to spot at all—you had to wear your mask on the plane.

Shawn had told me that, since Covid, Japan has been very into masking. I mean, on any given day before Covid, 30% of Japanese people would be wearing masks, but after Covid, something like 90% of people wear masks wherever they go. Keep in mind, though, that this was at the beginning

---

[1]. I owe this observation about philosophers not being good with matter to an undergrad professor of mine, Kurt Mosser. Unfortunately, in much of the rest of this book, I have no choice but to try my hand at describing the physical features of things. While I am proud of how much my ability to describe things improved over the course of the writing of this book, I am ashamed that, even by the end of this book, my ability to describe, say, a table is worse than my ability to make friends with a stranger's corpse. "This inflation is a real killer!", I'd say to it.

of 2023. I suspect that by now, in 2024, the only people in Japan masking is the 30% of the population that is constantly ashamed.

The second difference was that I hadn't experienced such a cramped layout in the business class section before. Flying internationally in business class on an American airplane, I wouldn't expect to get my own private pod. I mean, I would be entitled to one, but I wouldn't expect to actually get it—I would assume something would go wrong at the last minute and I'd have to give up my seat for a banker. By contrast, in the JAL plane, I got a pod, but it came with a cost: it was tight in there! Getting to my window seat required me to navigate a tight passageway as though I had been painted by Picasso or was an Egyptian hieroglyphic (I was all to the side, if you get what I mean). They gave me a lot of stuff, too—a night mask, a toothbrush, a pillow, a blanket that was too short for me (I'm a little shorter than six-foot-one), and slippers that were also too short for me (my feet are size 12). When I turned on the lie-flat feature of my seat to take a nap, I couldn't fully extend my body. The Japanese airline industry just doesn't build things for 6'1" pears.

The third difference was the service. Similar to most flight attendants, the JAL flight attendants were highly attentive (it's literally in the job title!), but they were also more officious. When I sat down, they took my coat. That was nice! But I didn't know where they put it. They also gave me a bottle of water and told me, "hold this until we are in the sky." I did want the water, so that was nice, but since there was no place to put it without it shooting across the plane during take-off, I didn't actually want to hold it right then and there. Also, later on in the flight, they gave me an eye-steamer! I had never heard of such a thing. I put this blindfold-like thing over my eyes, and then it heated them up. It felt amazing, but it made me fear the next evolution of masking in Japan, which would involve universal hot-blindfold-wearing while everyone gets led around by robot dogs.

Most confounding of all, after about eight hours (it was a twelve-hour flight), my wife and I were talking, and an attendant told us to keep it down! I mean, not so brusquely. She was exceptionally pleasant about it. But it's not like we were yelling. We were talking at what I would call a normal conversational level. (That said, my voice is extremely resonant. This helps with opera singing, which I like to do, but it also cuts deep into the soul of the Japanese ear.) Shawn told me, though, that this was a thing in Japan. Universally, people don't like to hear strangers talk, but rather than a norm emerging of sucking it up (like in America), the norm that developed was shutting it up.

When we landed, at 5:30 PM on December 29, everyone very quietly left the plane. The rest of my trip awaited.

# DECEMBER 29, 2022

# 2

# A Japanese Obstacle Course. No, It's Not Sasuke

After deplaning, the staff ushered us into a long line. The line worked like this: at its beginning, an airport employee handed you a half-sheet of pink paper with English writing on one side and Japanese on the other. The English told you to keep your mask on at all times, to wash and disinfect your hands a lot, and to avoid crowded spaces. It also included some QR codes that, if scanned, would take you to information about how to do those things. As I grabbed it, the page told me, "welcome to Japan. Please do not move." I mean, that's not what it literally said, but spiritually, that's what I picked up.

After we received the paper, we followed the course of the line, which wrapped around to where we started, but with a (literal) twist ending: we could now proceed forward in the airport. It appeared that, for the Japanese authorities, the most efficient way to give people information was to hand them a piece of paper and then have them walk in a circle.

Shawn, who was by now delirious, knew the only way to get me to help her survive the upcoming bureaucratic challenges without her succumbing to incipient brain fog was to pitch it to me like a Dungeons & Dragons campaign. Thereby described as "these obstacles three," I was told we had to survive three challenges: the quarantine, immigration control, and customs. What she did not predict was that we had to surmount them in eighty-five degree temperatures, all while we were wearing clothing preparing us for thirty-five degree weather.

Let me back up and elaborate.

Before you visit Japan, the Japanese government wants you to do a lot of things. Partly, this is because of Covid. Another part is that the Japanese just want you and everyone else to do a lot of things. The national motto, if I'm not mistaken, is "Japan: where we make make-work work!"

The quarantine procedure was one such bit of busywork. When you're in your home country, the Japanese travel authorities want you to use that time to get some chores out of the way. One of these chores is part of the aforementioned QR code business: the government wants you to show proof of vaccination against Covid. In order to streamline this for you, they enable you to upload the information online before you travel, rather than having to bring vaccination cards and then complete additional paperwork where you declare that your vaccination card is valid, and not given to you by a scheming tramp. So, the first obstacle was us showing an agent our vaccination information, which we would do for them via QR code. (Note: several people reported online that even after you do this, the authorities still make you fill out the paperwork that you uploaded beforehand ostensibly to avoid filling out the paperwork. The explanation given was that the Japanese love paperwork. Remember the national slogan: "make-work makes the dream work!" Luckily, this didn't happen to us.)

The second obstacle was to go through immigration. For this part, you had to take off all your headwear—mask, glasses, and hat—and then stare into a screen while putting your index fingers on a fingerprint-reading surface. You then saw an *extremely* unflattering photograph of yourself, after which the agent waved you on to the next challenge. The most difficult part of this obstacle was its forcing you to realize that you and everyone you love are ugly.

The final labor was to go through customs. For this, you had to declare that you had no food, vegetables, guns, explosives, or crossbows. In some places, while waiting for the customs agents, the airport signage would list only a few things that were forbidden. In other places in the airport, the signage listed many things that were forbidden. But one constant, in each case, was that you could not bring crossbows.

This, of course, raises many questions.

The first question is: how many people are bringing in crossbows, necessitating the state to specially designate that crossbows must be declared? Is Japan particularly attractive for crossbow-wielding South Korean math professors?[1] Second, if you're bringing a crossbow into Japan, what happens if you *do* declare it? Do they simply permit you to bring it in? Do they see how accurate you are with it? Or do you just say, "I'm here to hunt boar in the mountains of Shikoku, and will definitely not shoot bolts at judges?" Third, does the Japanese government secretly want people to bring in crossbows? Like, is this a subliminal message to foreigners to break the law in an antiquated way? Fourth, is it okay to bring in a regular bow? How about a ballista?

Anyway, we passed through customs without much incident, presumably because I've never touched a crossbow.

---

1. 26.1% of travelers to Japan in 2023 were from South Korea, and you know how South Korean math professors feel about their crossbows!

From there, we had to catch a train to Shinagawa (a part of Tokyo). Here's something neat I had never experienced before until this visit to Tokyo: you can install an app on your phone where, if you just pass your phone over a sensor, the gates will open and allow you to enter the train station. You don't even have to open the app! It just opens the gates and bills you. I mean, there are scary parts to this too, but in the battle between fears of surveillance and control and desires for safety and convenience, the desires for safety and convenience often win. They certainly won me over!

The trains in Japan always arrive when they're supposed to, and when you get on, you're supposed to be quiet. As I mentioned in Chapter 1, the Japanese really don't want people to bother other people, and if you end up bothering someone, you better believe you'll be on the receiving end of what Paddington the bear calls a "hard stare."

After arriving in Shinagawa Station, we took a bus to our hotel, the Tokyo Marriott. I should say, we did all this without a hitch. Not only had Shawn prepared both our phones before we arrived in Japan with the QR codes and train passes and whatnot, she also proceeded immediately to the correct train and subsequently to the right bus. I was quite impressed! But I was also feeling quite helpless. Here I was, forty-six years old, and arguably the fattest man in Japan, but I also was being led around, fully dependent, in a country where all the signs made no sense to me, and all the celebrities in advertisements were unknown to me. Why on earth should I want to buy your project if it's *not* recommended to me by Doja Cat? Like, what is Japan even thinking??

Finally, at 7:30 PM, we reached our hotel, and then our room. Like a kindly grandmother, the hotel was quite inviting after a long day of travel. And like a grandmother who turns out to be a witch who wants to fatten you up while locking you in a cage, the hotel room was as roomy as the trunk of a Fiat 500. There was almost no space in which to stow our belongings, there was a small table to write on, there was a TV (which dubbed over CNN International with Japanese), and, dominating 50% of the room space, was a bed that I think had previously been a marble kitchen counter. It was firm, is what I'm saying. Anyway, after staying up for about ninety minutes, I fell asleep, ready for, but wary about, my first full day in Japan.

# DECEMBER 30, 2022

# 3

# One Man's Treasure

...

Today was my first full day in Japan. And boy, was it full.

We awoke at 3:30 AM. Well, *I* awoke at 3:30 AM. Thanks to my snoring, her insomnia, her jet-lag, and her lack of sleep-assisting drugs, Shawn usually wakes up between half an hour and one year earlier than I do.

Side-note: you might wonder why Shawn is without her sleep-assisting drugs. Why not just take a couple of weeks' worth of tranquilizers and narcotics to Japan to help her fall asleep? Answer: Japan is weird about drugs. And by "weird about drugs", I mean silly stuff like, if you're caught with marijuana in Japan, they'll put you in prison for five years. Such goofs!

The point is, if you go to Japan and take too many drugs with you—and "too many drugs" to a Japanese customs official looking at an American is like "too much food" to Stalin looking at a Ukrainian—then bad things could happen to you. Now, when it comes to daily drug intake—caffeine, alcohol, sleeping pills, ashwagandha, stress relieving gummies, melatonin, allergy medication—every night for Shawn is like Elvis's last day on earth. Therefore, Shawn decided *not* to take her two suitcases full of sleeping pills with her, and this is also why her going to sleep at 8:30 PM after jetlag and a day of travel resulted in her waking up at 3 AM.

Anyway, *I* awoke at 3:30 next to a red-eyed, frazzled wife. "Well, what should we do?" I asked her. "Let's walk around the hotel garden", she suggested.

To the best of my knowledge, the Tokyo Marriott is not renowned for its garden. It's just a hotel in Shinagawa. But its garden blew me away! To give you a sense of how I was feeling, it would be like if a McDonald's in Silverlake had a small roller-coaster attached. You better believe I'll be riding that contraption while Filet-O-Fish scraps fluttered from my mouth, but the whole time I'll be wondering, "why is this here?!"

As I've said before, it is difficult for me to describe physical objects in a helpful way. But because Japan appears to put such a premium on beautiful architecture, I am honor-bound to try.

As we walked outside the hotel, we headed to a narrow path that circled the garden, which itself was situated below street level. Stone stairs descended into the garden's heart. A map at the entrance read "Gotenyama Trust City." To me, this name sounded dystopian; anything calling itself Trust City doth protest too much. In Japan's defense, though, what you get when you translate names into English will result in something fusty or stilted. So if Americans named a place "Trust City", they would know that this was to be taken ironically. By contrast, I would bet that Japanese people in such a place would simply try to be on their best behavior.

The entrance of the path featured two lamp posts wrapped in ribbons of bamboo. Bamboo cylinders, standing six feet high, lined one side of the path. Navigating the garden's perimeter, I followed the trail as it twisted, with the center of the garden on my left. Continuing on, I took another left (the garden was laid out in a rectangular shape) and noticed a ghostly light emanating from below. Looking over the railing, I observed dim lights casting a glow on a pond in the garden's center. However, from above, I couldn't tell what the lights and the pool were highlighting, because whatever the subject of the light was, it was directly under where I was walking; it looked like a shrine to a forgotten god, and it beckoned me forward to discover its secrets.

Not surprisingly, Shawn and I wanted to make our way into the heart of the garden to see what kept this natural-but-curated structure alive. The center, unlike its perimeter, was much less lit, giving the area an ominous feeling, as though there were dangerous nymphs and sprites lurking inside, ready to smuggle unwise travelers to the fey realms forever. Nevertheless, at around 4:30 AM, we descended to the garden's dark insides. Fortunately, we arrived at the entrance to the garden just as an elderly guard was unlocking its gates. We went inside, ready to see the abandoned hedge-deity.

Taking out my flashlight, we navigated the pathways until we arrived at the illuminated pool we had earlier seen only from above. Getting closer, we finally saw the shrine to what I assumed was going to be a revered ancestral spirit.

It was a trash can.

Well, that was disappointing.

Disappointing or not, it made me reassess my prior beliefs. Here I was, assuming that the Japanese people are forever reverent and tranquil, and that this garden served as a place of peaceful meditation for passersby, infusing them with renewed focus and attention. Instead, it was just a cute garden that someone made, and if you happened to have something to throw away, the designers wanted to make sure that you would put it into the garbage, and not onto the garden path. Also, the place was called Trust City because it was named after *a* trust, not trust itself. In other words, it was just named after a bank.

The Japanese do not always have their eyes pointed at the heavens. Sometimes, they just want to make sure you can throw your shit away.

# 4

# The Three C's

After we finished exploring the surprising combination of beautiful and utilitarian that was the garden in Gotenyama Trust City, we returned to our room to get ready for a 7 AM hotel breakfast.

Shawn eagerly anticipated the victuals; not only would they be good, they would also be free! This is what she has become after having been married to a(n ethnically) Jewish man for fourteen years. Regardless of the etiology of her lust for a good deal, I have to say: she was right. It was an excellent breakfast! They made me eggs benedict, there were delicious pastries (very croissant-like, but with fruit or cream in the middle), there was bacon, sausage, eggs made to order, salmon, rockfish, smoked salmon, Italian cold cuts, pork buns, shrimp dumplings, tofu, chicken curry, yogurt, strawberry and mango compote, and even more to list.

Two minor complaints about the breakfast, though. First, the bacon was not crispy; it was much more like strips of ham than the bacon I'm used to.

Second, they served us ridiculously small pours of coffee—I'm talking two to three ounces at a time. My coffee cup was never close to full. And it's not like the servers were constantly floating around, ready to refill your coffee cup up to the invisible two-ounce-line. No, they were milling about, but mainly to take your plates and relay inaudible communications to each other. If you got the staff's attention to inform them you wanted more coffee, they would evince a brief startlement, as though you had asked them to help you refinance your mortgage. They seemed at odds with themselves when you asked for more coffee: the impulse to meet your needs seemed to combine with a worry about your safety. But duty would win out over paternalistic concern, and they would refill your cup.[1]

I should say, the coffee thing was even weirder given the context of Japan. If three things unite Canada—ice hockey, single-payer healthcare, and cynical politeness—then the three things that you don't have to worry about as a tourist in Japan are (what my wife has described as) the three C's: carbs, caffeine, and cold. As in: Japan is *constantly* offering you carbohydrate-heavy food, caffeine-rich beverages, and environments that are warmed to at least 80° Fahrenheit. So, why so skimpy with the coffee, Tokyo Marriott? Why so surprised that we wanted more coffee, waiters?

One more thing, and I'll finish up this coffee-jag. Although cafes and coffee-vending machines are ubiquitous, the cafes don't really open until noon. If you take their approach to retail to reveal their preferences, then Japan thinks that freshly-prepared coffee is for afternoons, not mornings.

This is completely deranged. Maybe they think that coffee in the morning troubles your guts and overheats your brain, and that the only point of coffee is to power you through work in the mid-afternoon? I

---

[1]. I realize there is an almost zero percent chance this is what they were thinking; they were probably just trying to parse the English we chirped at them. That said, if *that's* what was going on, why did they seem so confused? I mean, we pointed at our coffee cups, said "please, more coffee, arigato" and made eye contact. There are other things we *could* have meant, but surely, even if you didn't understand any restaurant-English, this was the most likely meaning? Regardless, this is why I invented the florid interior monologue I offered above.

mean, yes, that is *one* of the points of coffee, but the *other* point is to trouble your guts and overheat your brain, so that you can start your work in a state of mental *and* rectal panic.

Once breakfast was out of the way, we had a lot of time to kill, so I wrote some of this book and then took a nap. Great nap. I want to memorialize this nap, because it was so good that it misled me into thinking that the best thing for me on my first day in Tokyo would be to walk for over fifteen miles. To paraphrase John Bradshaw Layfield,[2] I need to remember that the great naps make it look easy. Too easy, as you'll see.

---

2. If you've never heard of John Bradshaw Layfield, maybe this will help: he's one of the many assholes involved with World Wrestling Entertainment, aka the WWE.

# 5

# Scramble On

After this refreshing nap, we began my exploration of Tokyo. One of my goals was to inspect a Japanese university, because I love touring universities in general. This is not because I have an eye for architecture; I do not. Rather, I enjoy seeing how various educational institutions design space and structure to trick their students into thinking they're getting their money's worth, when really they're just learning useless nonsense. "Oh, you think a class on the epistemology of soda is silly? Well, if it's silly, then why do our buildings have ivy on them?"

Admittedly, I was told by Katashi, a Japanese colleague at my university, that, "compared to most university campuses in the U.S., university campuses in Japan tend to be small and cramped", but this did not deter me; if anything, seeing how much university a country can fit into a small space would itself be an interesting new wrinkle on university architecture. In the future, maybe we can run CSUN out of the stillborn Twisted Kilt on Nordhoff.

Because meeting Shawn's Japanese guide and friend, Mari, at 3:50 PM was the only time-sensitive thing on today's agenda, and because it was only noon when we started our trek, and because I was intoxicated by nap-energy (aka "napergy"), we decided to walk. First, we would go to Shinagawa train station to get some train tickets for our trip around town, as well as our tickets for the train to Kyoto, and then we would walk to Meiji Gakuin University.

It was at this point that I got my first exposure to Tokyo's architecture.

At first, it didn't seem like much; I found myself thinking, as we walked from the hotel to the train station, that, but for the Japanese signs, I could be in Germany, Greece, or Los Angeles.[1] I'm not saying it was nondescript, but it didn't seem particularly special. Shinagawa train station also wasn't striking. I suppose the only noteworthy thing was the ticketing situation.

Japan, as I noted earlier, loves make-work. More particularly, they love *paper*work. If Japan had another slogan posted via Sticky Note to their other slogan about make-work, it would be: "Japan: where our make-work is when we work our paper to work to paper you with paperwork!"[2]

Thus, even though Shawn had already purchased our Japan Rail passes (which allow you to ride on the bullet train ["shinkansen"] as well as an elevated train throughout Tokyo) and reserved seats for our shinkansen trip to Kyoto, it still took us about half an hour to pick up the passes and tickets she had earlier bought and reserved, because (a) we had to fill out some paperwork, (b) they had to compare the paperwork we had filled out against the record they had on reserve, (c) they had to redo some of the paperwork, because they mixed Shawn's and my tickets up, (d) the person

---

[1]. The fact that all these locations look the same to me should tell you both that I have extremely ecumenical sensibilities and that I have no idea what anything looks like

[2]. I assume this would make more sense in the original Japanese it never appeared in.

we were talking to had to talk to the other worker about the mistake she made, and (e) they had to give us paper tickets to hold everywhere we go.

Now that I think about it, Japan has a real yen for making people hold on to and carry things.[3] Recall, first, the flight attendant from Chapter 1 who had me hold my water on the plane as it was about to take off. She saw my hands were free and just *leapt* at the chance to occupy them with something.

Second, Japan loves paper, and wants you to bring around paper versions of things rather than just have an electric record. Don't get me wrong, they *have* electronic records, but it seems that, at the end of the day, the real thing is and always will be the paper. Maybe this has to do with how touch is the sensation we trust the most? For example, if you see something and try to touch it, but your hand passes through, you'll conclude it's visible, but not real. But if you touch something you can't see, you'll think it's real, but invisible.[4]

---

3. Maybe this is why some Japanese people seem to have such admiration, to the point of sexual arousal, for the deeply off-putting, alien, and delicious octopus. If Japan had a third slogan, one that Japanese bureaucrats yelled at tourists, it would be: "Hold on! You forgot to hold on to what you put on hold!" I'll workshop that one.

4. I first realized this point about the relationship between touch and sight back in 2006, when I read it on page 334 of philosopher Wayne Waxman's very dense tome, *Kant and the Empiricists: Understanding Understanding* (New York, NY: Oxford University Press, 2005). If you read nothing else from that book, read the last paragraph of the acknowledgements. I once had lunch with Wayne, and I asked him about that paragraph. If I recall correctly, he told me that including it was the primary reason he wanted to write the book.

The third reason to think that Japan is a holding-and-carrying culture is the situation with the garbage cans. I'll explain.

Earlier, I described my pilgrimage through a haunted forest to a rubbish deity. And I ended that by saying that, sometimes, Japanese people just want you to throw your shit away. Well, that's not entirely right. Indeed, foreigners in Japan who detail their experiences on Reddit inevitably mention the *lack* of garbage cans.

"Why aren't there any garbage cans?" they ask.

"Sarin" is the reply.

As everyone knows, back in 1995, Shoko Asahara and his Aum Shinrikyo goons dispensed poisonous sarin gas in a subway (supposedly from a trash can). This attack killed thirteen people, seriously injured fifty-four, and mildly injured up to 6,000 more. As a result, Japan cracked down on the real culprit: trash cans. Apparently, after the sarin gas attack, Japan would no longer publicly support waste bins. Now, there are still privately funded garbage cans, near vending machines in particular[5]; so the trash situation isn't *that* bad. That said, because this is Japan, it's not like people started littering more. No, they just held things for longer, and so, a norm was born.[6]

---

5. Shawn tells me that, for a time, the Japanese seriously frowned on eating or drinking while moving. So, despite the fact that there are as many vending machines as people, people were supposed to (1) buy their canned café au lait and red bean roll, and then (2) drink and eat them next to their vending machine of origin, lest they displease some gray-hair who fondly remembers the time when no one was brazen enough to eat food in public (while forgetting the part that people were starving, and so had no food to publicly eat).

6. Let's call this theory of mine an instance of "heightened sociology".

Having finished with our make-work paperwork at Shinagawa train station, we made our way to the next stop on our tour: Meiji Gakuin University. Meiji Gakuin was, indeed, cramped and small. It seemed to comprise about four buildings and a lawn. Despite this, it allegedly serviced the learning needs of 12,389 students. That's about as many as Yale, which, in case you don't know, is a comparatively gigantic set of gothic buildings full of squids cosplaying as humans.

Unfortunately, Meiji Gakuin was closed, so we couldn't explore its modest grounds. Instead, we went to our next stop, Happo-en garden. This was a significantly nicer garden than Gotenyama Trust City, but there was one catch: it was also closed.

It's not that December 30 was a special day; it's rather that we visited Japan during its most closed off season—Christmas to January 5—and many people have better things to do than to stay and work in Tokyo or wander through a garden.

Lucky for me, the trip to and past Meiji Gakuin and Happo-en (in the Shirokanedai neighborhood) introduced me to Tokyo's architecture, and as I mentioned earlier in this chapter, it didn't seem particularly special at first.

As we plodded on, though, things began to stand out. For one thing, people parked their cars in small garages without any doors securing them from the the public. If you wanted to, you could walk up to a car and milk its exhaust pipe. Moreover, there were belongings outside of their homes. Bikes, boxes, brooms, etc. I could have just taken a broom! Or a box! Who would have stopped me or noticed? It's open season on Japanese sundries!

More striking was the layout of the city. I recall reading somewhere that Tokyo was built in a labyrinthine manner to make it difficult for invaders to conquer it.[7] Hard to kill the emperor if all you keep on finding is cats licking drunks passed out at the ends of blind alleys. The effect on this modern American tourist (whom I'd like to think is *not* an invader) was delightful and dizzying: there were so many times when we would turn down what I thought was an alley, but it would be a full-fledged street, just exceedingly narrow. One time, we were walking and then, out of nowhere, an immense structure that looked like a giant anthill appeared. It gave me a presentiment of endless depths and hidden experiences.

After an hour more of walking, we visited another campus, called the Kokuaguin campus. This was a bit surprising, because we had, on Katashi's advice, entered the address for the Aoyama Gakuin University on Shawn's phone, but when we arrived, we just found this other university. This reminds me of another observation of Pico Iyer's:

> There are no addresses, it's said, in Japan—or, worse, there are collections of numbers, but sometimes they refer to the chronology of construction, sometimes to something else. When my daughter, my wife, and I write down the address of the flat we've all shared, each one of us inscribes a completely different street name.
> 
> A Beginner's Guide to Japan, p. 8

I'm not sure whether this story is true, but it captures my experience of the confusion of Tokyo's layout, and it dovetails with Iyer's experience of address-fusion.

---

7. "Before the West arrived, there were twice as many T-junctions and dead ends in Tokyo as there were thoroughfares. A castle town needs to confound invaders" (Pico Iyer, *A Beginner's Guide to Japan*, p. 8).

The Kokuaguin campus was both fuller and less closed than Meiji Gakuin University. There seemed to be a lot more to see, even though it only served slightly more than 6,000 students. By "a lot more to see", though, I mean it had about nine buildings. It's like if Cal Tech fell into a black hole and became infinitely dense (which I expect to literally happen to Cal Tech in about fourteen years, by accident).

After visiting Kokuaguin, it was time to go to Shibuya to meet Shawn's friend and our guide for the night, Mari. We had agreed to meet near Shibuya crossing, at the statue of Hachiko.

Hachiko, in case you don't know, is an Akita dog whose master would always meet him at the train station. One day, though, Hachiko's master died, but he didn't know that, so he would wait for his master to return to the train station every day, for years, because dogs are stupid. In honor of his loyalty, the Tokyoites made a statue for him, and it now serves as a meeting place for people who love to watch other people wait in line to take pictures of themselves in front of a statue of a dog.

Another notable fact about Shibuya is that it's home to the Shibuya scramble. The Shibuya scramble is allegedly the busiest intersection in the world. Gigantic masses of people pool around the intersection until the pedestrian signal turns from red to green, at which point, it's fucking *on*. Well, there's no way I wasn't going to take part in *that*.

Once at the Shibuya scramble, I felt an electricity as I waited to cross the street with a team of Japanese locals and tourists. It was like your roller coaster car slowly inching up the tracks until, BAM!, it drops, and then, next thing you know, you're 200 feet closer to a Seibu department store.

It's amazing to me that Japan can make something so exciting out of something that is so *pedestrian*.

*wink emoji*

Anyway, when we got to Shibuya crossing, it was about 3:05, and we would not meet Mari until 3:50, so, after living my best life by crossing the street a few times, we went into a mall where Shawn could show me the Tokyu (not a misprint) Food Show.

Shawn failed. The "food show" that was there in 2020 seemed not to be there anymore. Near as I can tell, a food show is a (figuratively) elevated food court. However, whatever Shawn had in her long-Covid-ridden brain had vanished, so we ended up just going to the local Daiso so that we could both go to the bathroom.

The bathroom, as I was now getting used to, was accessible only by going through a painfully narrow hallway, which is a good description of how one inserts a catheter. So, after squeezing my way to the urinal and divesting myself of pee, I met up with Shawn and we went back outside to Shibuya crossing to meet up with Mari.

Mari was someone Shawn had met when she toured Japan for the first time, back in 2018. She needed someone who could show her around and, thanks to the reviewing-part of the Internet,[8] she discovered the highly rated Mari. Shawn told me that Mari was the most extraverted person she

---

8. The Internet has three parts: reviewing, judging, and bots. The reviewing-part suffers from negativity bias, meaning that the people likeliest to review an establishment are the ones who had the worst time with it. This makes the proprietors of said establishments miserable, who then turn their misery into judgment of strangers, which makes up the judging-part of the Internet. Finally, some people respond to the reviewing-part's negativity bias and the judgment-part's misery by creating bots to produce endless streams of insipid positivity about people and places, making everyone distrustful of positivity and plunging us all further into negativity. The only way out of this doom-loop is to be as bland as possible. In other words, if you find yourself living in Russia, just pretend like you're from Minnesota.

has ever met, and, keep in mind, Shawn is married to *me*, someone who enjoys asking strangers about their medical histories and old ladies about their past. Shawn returned to Japan in 2019 and 2020 and, rather than fix something that was not broken, she repeatedly made use of Mari's services each year, apparently much to their mutual delight, as Mari continued to allow Shawn to pay her money in exchange for lunacy.

Shawn had told me a lot about Mari, and was hopeful that I would enjoy her, but fearful that I wouldn't. Despite these bulky expectations, I eagerly awaited meeting this tour guide whom I reckoned would reduce me to silence, and not because of her awkwardness. But speaking of waiting, you'll have to wait until the next chapter to hear about her.

# 6

# Staying Married Around Unmarried Mari

When we returned to the statue of Hachiko, it was only 3:40. Shawn texted Mari that we were there, waiting for her, and she replied with something like, "You are early! I will be there in ten minutes!" After ten minutes had passed, still no Mari. But then, out of nowhere, someone grabbed Shawn from behind and screamed at her! Shawn shrieked with surprise, and I looked on with some startlement to see that a 5'5" Japanese woman in a bright, fluffy, green sweater and an orange, ankle-length skirt was the mystery grabber. We quickly realized it was Mari, and I quickly realized that she would be an excellent paid assassin. Much tittering ensued. After I finished tittering, Shawn and Mari stopped staring at me and turned to reliving old times.

It had been three years since Shawn had seen Mari, and, though Shawn would dispute this, neither woman had changed much. Shawn showed her a recent picture of our son Briscoe, and Mari was very pleased to see what a tall, handsome boy he had become. Meanwhile, Mari had suffered a divorce. Me: "Oh, what happened?" Mari: "Covid." That was a bit vague

# THE MOST AWKWARD MAN IN JAPAN

as an explanation, so I pressed her, and she said that her husband had lost his job, so they divorced. That made her appear rather unsympathetic, so I came up with an alternative explanation that made her look more appealing: this is a woman whose preferred job is to take strangers out to get drunk six nights a week; upon having to be cooped up with her husband and see him seven nights a week, she and he both realized that she had a drinking problem.[1]

Mari told us that we had to stay in the area near the Hachiko statue until 4 PM. I didn't know why, but remember, Mari is a tour guide. It's her job to act as a sherpa for us climbers, and to point out the famous dead bodies with green boots we'd see on our way to the top of Tokyo.[2] So I just figured I would do what she recommended. Also, what the hell else was I going to do?

As the clock struck 4 PM, she guided our gaze towards the top of a skyscraper in Shibuya featuring three enormous video monitors. Another nearby skyscraper had a single gigantic monitor. She said, "look at these monitors over here, not that one over there." Shawn asked why the ones over here? Mari: "Cuter." When the clock struck 4:00, the images on

---

[1]. Or maybe they learned that they liked each other only in small doses, I don't know. I will say, though, that Iyer presents some interesting statistics relating to this: "The year after I arrived in Japan [1988], a *Japan Times* survey found that seven in ten Japanese men refused even to consider working for a woman" and "In a survey conducted in 2014, nine in every ten young Japanese women said that remaining single was preferable to what they imagined marriage to be" (Pico Iyer, *A Beginner's Guide to Japan*, pp. 154-55).

[2]. This metaphor ran out of steam half way through, but my internal editor said, "go with it!"

the video monitors changed from the advertisement for—oh, let's say Pocari Sweat—to a huge, and very cute, Akita nosing its way through the mechanisms of a clock to make it read 4:00. The dog proceeded from the first video monitor to the second video monitor to the final video monitor. It was darling! Also, remember that Hachiko is an Akita. It's sweet that they honor the dog who dutifully waited for his master every day at the train station for nine years by having millions of people dutifully wait for images of that dog to appear every day at 4 PM. Makes me cry, actually.

Mari asked if Shawn had shown me the Shibuya scramble. We said yes. "But have you seen it from *Starbucks*?" she pressed. I had not! In fact, most of the things I have seen in my life are things I have *not* seen from Starbucks. As it turns out, though, there are only a few suitable locations to watch the Shibuya scramble if you want both (1) to see the whole affair at once and (2) for free, and one is the Starbucks. So, to the nearest Starbucks we went.

There is little to comment on regarding this Starbucks, except for the fact that it was big (two storeys) and its specials were centered around matcha. I did get a delightful view of the Shibuya scramble, and I have to say, when you can see the whole mass of people from above, you notice that there are a lot of weirdos![3] I saw one guy absolutely book it across the scramble, only to run up to a van, slap one of its windows, and laugh at the person who came out. I presumed either that he knew the driver, or that he was playing, poorly, a very dangerous version of ding dong ditch. I witnessed a man walking across the scramble, occasionally pausing to swing a plastic flail. I guess Japan's weirdos have to congregate somewhere,

---

3. I realize this is self-incriminating.

or the proximity to the Hachiko statue incites men to act like dogs. These are the only two possible theories.

We did one more thing in the Shibuya area, which was to visit Drunkard's Alley. Drunkard's Alley was a small area consisting almost entirely of izakayas. An izakaya, in case you don't know, is a Japanese bar that has food. I suppose the only reason that we visited Drunkard's Alley is that it was famous; famous for drunkards, I'm supposing. I'll tell you this, though: at 4:30 PM, on December 30 (one of Tokyo's least populated days), I didn't see anyone who was visibly drunk.

Japan: nation of liars.

After we visited the highlights of Shibuya—dog statue, crosswalk, commercial with a dog, Starbucks, alley full of Applebee's equivalents—Mari wanted to know what we wanted to do next. Shawn told her that I liked looking at university architecture, so I wanted to see a pretty university. Mari thought we would enjoy Waseda University in Shinjuku. "It's just a train ride, then a quick walk." On to the train we went.

It was not a quick walk. Waseda University was two miles away from our stop. That's forty minutes of walking! Now, I realize that by this point I had met Mari for only seventy minutes, but this was classic Mari. She had a job where she would meet with curious non-Japanese speakers twice a day, six days a week, and then walk with them for about four hours a day. Because of all that walking, a few years ago she developed edemas in her legs. So, to her, a forty-minute walk really was quick; and anyway, what was the alternative? Being alone with your thoughts? As an extravert myself, I know how horrifying that possibility is, because those bozos come unbidden and then make you feel weird things. They're like pets who slap you.[4] No thank you.

---

4. In other words, cats.

The point is, Mari had a way of making this seem like the most natural thing in the world. And, though we were both already tired from walking, and extremely hungry to boot,[5] we went along with it.

Waseda University was significantly bigger and prettier than the other two universities I had seen. Its most famous building was Okuma Auditorium, which was a large clock tower combined with, presumably, an auditorium. Moreover, there was an archive designed in such a way that it appeared as if a gigantic spider-web was branching out from it. Mari knew all about this university. In fact, she knew a lot about a lot of the places she took us to. She was a tour guide, and she liked to talk, and you can't very well do that if you're just making up half of what you're talking about.[6]

Our tour of Waseda at an end, we took another train to Shinjuku's red-light district, despite our grumbling bellies and feet. Among other enticements, this is a place where Tokyo's "hosts" collect.

"Hosts", as I understand the term, are people whose company you pay for. Now, of course, one way to pay for someone's company is to pay them to have sex with you, and it's my understanding that you can pay hosts to do that. But I got the sense that often, people would literally pay hosts just for their company.

At this point, I was going to make a joke about how the Japanese equivalent of a handjob was someone simply holding your hand, but many people in the USA also pay other people just to hang out with them (we don't call them "hosts", though; we call them "therapists"). That said, there were a lot more *advertisements* for hosts than I'm used to seeing in

---

5. This is a pun about walking.

6. I just made that up, but it seems true.

the USA for sex workers. It's not just that there were ads for hosts in the Shinjuku red-light district; there were also trucks driving through Shibuya with pictures of hosts on them.

Two things were noteworthy about these ads for hosts. First, the hosts looked extremely strange in the pictures. When I say "extremely strange", I mean "altered" or "photoshopped." But these hosts' pictures were not photoshopped to have their blemishes removed or to look extra handsome or pretty. No, the photos were changed to make their subjects look inhuman. Eyes and irises were enlarged, lips overplumped, and noses sharpened to a point. They looked like a cross between aliens and plastic surgery victims.

This baffled me. The pictures did not make the hosts look attractive. Quite the opposite: these hosts had fallen, and were now trapped, at the bottom of the uncanny valley. Moreover, I was quite sure that the hosts did not look like this in real life. I'm not saying it's impossible for *any* of them to look like this, but I am saying it's impossible for *all* of them to look like this. There just aren't that many young people who have had extensive plastic surgery and who want to allay the salacious desires of strangers.

Are there?[7]

No, there aren't. Mari informed me that the hosts look like this because it was a way of both advertising what you were going to get while keeping the hosts' identities secret. Anyone who wanted the company of a host knew that what you were going to meet in real life would look significantly different from (and, one hopes, better than) the pictures. The pictures were homages to the humans, not representations of them. I also

---

[7]. Some food for thought: approximately 2 million Americans are content creators for OnlyFans.

suspect, though Mari didn't mention this, that showing mere insinuations of the hosts' faces allowed people to get carried away by their fantasies. "She of course doesn't look like this; she's surely much better looking. I wonder how much? Maybe I should buy some time with her to find out!"

The second noteworthy thing about the pictures of hosts is that perhaps half or even more were pictures of men. Now, I don't know much about sex work, but this went against one of the things I *thought* I knew about it, which is that you can't really make a living by trying to get straight women to pay you to have sex with them. Both female and male sex workers cater to men, not women. So why are so many hosts men?

One possibility, of course, is that women don't pay male hosts for sex, but just for their company. Indeed, that's what I figured was going on. But it was more complicated than that: Mari told me that the largest clientele for male hosts was female sex workers. The idea is that after a long day of having to cater to unpleasant men's unpleasant desires for pleasure, you want to have more control over the situation, or just to vent. It's like how a vole, after it spends all day trying to gather nuts and fruit while being hunted by lynxes and the northern spotted owl, gets home and then just wants to hang out with another vole, or possibly a shrew. It's like that.

Besides the disturbing yet sensible pictures of hosts, the Shinjuku red-light district looked like a busy Tokyo street. Except that rather than a car-filled road running between the buildings, there was a walking path for pedestrians to stand and gawk (and then, presumably, to decide on whom to, um, "hang out with" for the rest of the night). There were also lots of besuited men standing outside of establishments looking tough and unwelcoming. I got the message: stay married.

# 7

# Eat, Drink, and Be Mari

Sensing our weakness, hunger, and sexual frigidity, Mari took us to a place to get some food, deciding on yakitori (skewered meat) at Omoide Yokocho, aka "Piss Alley" (also in Shinjuku). If I recall correctly, Mari said that the alley was given its name because in the 16th century, they were tanning a lot of leather here, and it gave the alley the smell of urine. According to "Genevieve", writer of "The Wanderbug,"[1] Piss Alley got its name because, when it began "as an illegal drinking quarter in the 1940s, there was a lack of bathroom facilities...which led to patrons relieving themselves in the streets." I don't know who's right, but I presume that my own explanation—it's between a milk alley and a fudge factory—is probably wrong.

The first (and her favorite) place that Mari took us to was, on account of the holiday season, closed. She pointed out that she and Shawn had gone there before, and that Shawn liked it a lot. Shawn had no memory of that. The second (and second most favored) place she took us to was also closed, also on account of the holiday season. She pointed out that

---

1. https://thewanderbug.com/golden-gai-piss-alley-tokyo/

she and Shawn had gone there before. Shawn had no memory of that. The third place was also beloved, closed, and forgotten. In fact, there was no place for us to go to in Piss Alley, so we made our way to Kabuki-chō, an entertainment district in Shinjuku that additionally houses a series of small idiosyncratic bars collectively called "Golden Gai."

Although many of Kabukicho's establishments were temporarily shuttered, Mari managed to find three that would have us for the evening. The first one was a yakitori restaurant.

This yakitori restaurant looked quite crowded and cramped; I wasn't sure that we could eat here comfortably. Lucky for us, it had a second floor, and when we ascended the stairs, we saw that there were only two patrons, and all the other tables were empty. The waitress seated us next to the other occupied table, gave us menus, and we started to survey them hungrily.

Before we got very far, though, an employee went up to us and started talking to Mari and the other patrons. They spoke for quite a while—maybe two minutes of continuous dialogue? I realize that doesn't seem like much, but when you're very hungry and thirsty, and people are going back and forth with many raised eyebrows, you start to wonder if one of you is wanted for arson. As it turns out, though, he was just explaining that this entire top floor had to be ready for a group of people by 7 PM, so we had to be out at least a few minutes before then, to give them time to clean up. Would that be ok with us?

Without bothering to ask me and Shawn, Mari said it was fine. Even though it was already 6:10 PM, she was right to do so, as by this point I was hungry enough to eat a big bowl of Circus Peanuts. Luckily, it didn't come to that. Not quite.

Like many Japanese restaurants, this place had pictures of its offerings on the menu. Mari ordered pork and chicken skewers, some gyoza, a beer for me, a concoction for Shawn that consisted of green tea and alcohol, and, as Mari put it, "pork boobs." This was not a mistranslation on her part. Besides having pictures of all their offerings on the menu, this restaurant (whose name, alas, we never got) displayed a drawing of a pig on its menu and had various parts of the animal shaded in, with lines going from the shadings to the dishes. The dish that Mari ordered pointed straight at the boobs. And every time she said "pork boobs", she loosed a deep chuckle, like Butthead, Beavis's famous friend.

The gyoza were the best gyoza Shawn and I ever had, though admittedly, hunger is the best sauce. Still, they tasted almost exactly like the first pot stickers I ever tried, when I was a child in Dayton, Ohio, at a Chinese restaurant called Keeng-Wa. They were crunchy on one side, smooth on the other, unctuous but not too rich, umami-tasting but brightened with herbaceousness—truly glorious. Who would have thought I could find a bit of my Ohio childhood in Tokyo?

Equally marvelous was the beer I had. Remember, by this point, Shawn and I had been wandering for seven hours, and we hadn't eaten since the 7 AM breakfast buffet. Consequently, that cold beer reached a part of my body I didn't know existed. There was apparently a second stomach behind my first stomach, and the beer went straight to this unused stomach, inducing in me a feeling of relief that almost amounted to joy. The beer tasted immaculately crisp and refreshing.

By contrast, Shawn's alcohol and green tea drink tasted, as Shawn put it, "like green tea and alcohol." In its defense, there was a lot of it.

The pork boobs were ... not my thing. Don't get me wrong, I love boobs. But when it comes to *eating* boobs, well, they're very chewy and not particularly flavorful.

Finally, those skewers. Technically, they were pork and chicken, in that they derived from the flesh of pigs and chickens. However, they were not the parts I would have selected.

For one thing, the chicken was not chicken meat, but chicken skin. And it's not like it was roasted or fried chicken skin. It was, I guess, lightly sauteed? So, technically, it was cooked, and, therefore, safe to eat, but it was very chewy, like you were chomping on tape. If it had some divine sauce or something, maybe I would have liked it, but the avian version of chewing gum was not quite my tempo.

The pork meats were pork liver and pork thymus. The liver was pasty, dense, and earthy. It tasted like liver! Nevertheless, I find liver to be most delectable when spread on bread, rather than consumed in large quantities and alone. Plus, it looked like it was charred on its ends, so I expected that nice, charcoal flavor, but I didn't end up tasting anything like that. I guess the liver taste overpowered it, so I felt tricked: tricked by pork.

As for the thymus, it tasted much like the liver, but it had the texture of chewy pork loin. Once more, I anticipated a pork chop-like flavor, but it never materialized.

I ate most of my portion; Shawn had a harder time. None of us could eat more than a piece of the chicken skin (well, maybe Mari could; I didn't pay attention to her eating, because I was trying to determine a way to spit out my food without her or anyone else noticing). Now normally, if I told you that I decided against finishing my pork liver, thymus, and sauteed chicken skin, you'd say, "yeah, man. Me neither." But we were really hungry! The fact that we didn't finish our portion speaks strongly against the possibility that either of us would have *ever* liked these particular yakitori.

After finishing up at the (to me and Shawn) anonymous yakitori restaurant in Kabukicho, we made our way to a bar that Shawn actually remembered having been to before: Bar Drop Kick.

Bar Drop Kick is a bar owned and operated by professional wrestlers; specifically, the professional wrestlers of DDT Pro-Wrestling. Unlike the main wrestling company in Japan, NJPW (New Japan Professional Wrestling)—which focuses on hard-hitting, gritty matches but doesn't spend a lot of time on complicated storylines—DDT (which stands for "Dramatic Dream Team") imitates the WWE style of heightened drama and gimmicky matches, but takes it to eleven. The writeup on Wikipedia gives you a feel for the kind of matches they do:

> DDT is in many ways a parody of American pro wrestling, particularly WWE, using over-the-top gimmicks (most notably Danshoku Dino) as well as unique match types including hardcore matches in a campsite (which featured use of bottle rockets as weapons), an "Office Deathmatch" (where the ring was set up to resemble a section of an office building, complete with cubicle walls and computers), and a "Silence Match" (where wrestlers were forbidden to make loud noises, resulting in slow-motion chops and punches and featuring the commentary team speaking in a faux-whisper).
> https://en.wikipedia.org/wiki/DDT_Pro-Wrestling

Bar Drop Kick can be found at the bottom of a narrow flight of stairs. Once you descend, you'll find yourself in a small room with a few tightly packed tables and a bar that overlooks a tiny kitchen. Posters and signs from previous DDT matches adorned the walls, and fans occupied the tables. At one point, in her very recent adulthood no less, Shawn *really* liked professional wrestling.[2] So she wanted to go to Bar Drop Kick in part because it's a pro-wrestling bar, but also because she liked the food the last time she had been there.

The guy who ushered us to our table didn't look like much, but I could tell he was a professional wrestler, based on the fact that he had substantial cauliflower ear. One of the two guys cooking in the kitchen behind the bar was tall and broad — he looked like a professional wrestler. As for the third guy at work that night, maybe he was just a regular cook? Or maybe he was a wrestler, and his gimmick was that he would try to cook his opponents!

---

2. One day, I was watching WWE on my laptop in bed and Shawn was sitting next to me looking at her tablet. She peeked her head over and took a look at the hairy, muscular man dressed in white with gold trim and asked, "who is *that*?" "Seth Rollins," I said. "Why?" "He's hot!" she gushed, and an interest was born. She quickly mastered the vernacular and history of pro wrestling, adding a few more crushes along the way: besides Rollins, there was Finn Balor, AJ Styles, and Kenny Omega, a stable of wrestlers she dubbed, "The Four Hotmen." Eventually, though, her love of wrestling faded, crowded out by love for K-pop, in particular the group BTS, seven men who are OK at singing, really good at rapping, extraordinarily impressive at dancing, and really super stupendously excellent at looking gorgeously wistful in photoshoots. The hopeful way of predicting the trajectory of Shawn's interests is: she is getting interested in progressively larger groups of athletic men. This would be great, because it would mean that by 2027 she'd finally be ready to cheer for the Cincinnati Bengals with me, and our marriage could unite around our common hatred of Patrick Mahomes and whoever the hell this Taylor Swift person is. The less hopeful way of predicting the trajectory is: in a couple of years she's going to leave me so that she can join the upcoming *Cirque de Soleil* show, "Sex Rooster."

After settling us down at our table, they presented us with regular laminated menus and a separate menu featuring today's specials, which had been handwritten. Today's handwritten specials were also laminated.[3]

At the top of the special menu, I noticed a Japanese word with two exclamation marks after it. I asked Mari, "hey, what's this word?" Mari (focusing on it): "It says, 'recommended.'" Me: "if it just says 'recommended,' how come there are two exclamation marks after it?" Her: "Because it's saying, 'RECOMMENDED!!'" Very amusingly, she screamed that last word, but how else would a pro wrestler recommend something?

Anyway, it pains me to say that I don't remember much of what we got to order. (The perils of writing a book about your life after it's already happened.) That said, I did get an interesting Japanese concoction called "Hoppy", which tasted like a chicory-flavored beer, and was poured over ice. And the food Shawn remembered liking was sauteed pork intestines. Kind of off-brand for Shawn, and not what I thought I would want to eat after just having eaten some of the more lamentable parts of the pig, but as it turns out, the intestines these pro wrestlers delivered were fantastic! This dish, resembling a pork chop in texture, was enhanced by a deliciously salty olive sauce that made us momentarily forget about our previous pig.

While we ate, Mari made conversation. She wanted to know if I had any stereotypes about Japan. I said, "yeah, lots!" She made a "bring it on" gesture with her hand, and I regaled her with my list of stereotypes about Japan:

Me: They work very hard.

---

3. I haven't mentioned this yet, but a lot of stuff is laminated in Japan. I think it's because they not only love *using* paper, but *keeping* it, so they need to recruit lamination to protect their country's most precious resource.

Her: ... true.

Me: They love food.

Her: ... true.

Me: They drink a lot.

Her: ... true.

Me: There are a lot of rules.

Her: ... yes.

Me: They're not very individualistic.

Her: ... yes.

Me: They're conservative.

Her: No!

She didn't explain why they weren't conservative (by which I meant socially conservative), but she was pretty insistent that the Japanese aren't conservative. More on Japan's alleged lack of conservatism in Chapter 20, but I forgot to mention one very important detail about Mari that communicates her difference from other Japanese just as quickly as her fluffy lime-green sweater and ankle-length orange skirt: she didn't wear a mask! In fact, at the Hachiko statue, she told Shawn to stop wearing her mask. Shawn replied, laughingly, "but everyone else is!" To this, Mari looked at her blankly, like she didn't understand the relevance of the point. Apparently she experienced the world with so much Mari-ness that the idea that you should do things merely because other people did them just didn't register with her. No wonder she didn't experience Japan as conservative: she felt no social pressure.

I admired her so much.

Later on in the conversation, she asked me how many Americans went to college. I said, "I don't know ... maybe 30 or 40%?" She said, "only 40%! In Japan, it's 80%!" Me: "uh...no, that's not true." Her: "what?" Me: "well, I mean, you're Japanese, and you know a lot more about Japan than I do, but ... there's no way 80% of the Japanese go to college." Her: "you're mean!" At that point, I felt a hot flush, like I had gone too far. But you can't blame me! I was hungry and thirsty, and that stereotype question primed me to be unusually honest! But then she said, "I like people who are mean!" Oh, ok, crisis averted.[4]

At around that point, a fairly small (5'7" or so) DDT pro wrestler named Tetsuya Endo entered, holding a championship belt; he (and two teammates) had won the KO-D (King of DDT) 6-Man Tag Team Championship the night before! Swinging his belt around, he proudly displayed it to the onlookers, and then raised it triumphantly as they erupted in applause. He then mingled with people in the back of the bar while Shawn, Mari, and I chatted some more. Later, while he was leaving, Mari called out to him and spoke (what I can only guess was) Japanese. He then stopped behind Shawn, playfully putting her in a semi-headlock as I captured the moment in a photo. Fun! It must have been cool for him to be so close to greatness.

During the dinner, Mari pressed Shawn to drink more, on the grounds that "you're cute when you're drunk!" In response, Shawn made the universal kawaii[5] pose. Mari really seemed to want Shawn to get drunk! Joke's on Mari, though: by that point, Shawn was already drunk.

Later, she asked Shawn whether she remembered the time that she, Shawn, got so drunk that she, Shawn, made out with her, Mari. Shawn

---

4. For the record, 35% of adult Americans have earned a 4-year college degree, and 47.5% have earned either a 4-year college degree or 2-year college degree. As for Japan, 53.7% of their adults have earned a college degree. It seems that they don't have associate's degrees over there, so that's 53.7% to 35%. I was very impressed by 53.7%! But it's still not 80%.

5. To anyone of generation X or older: "kawaii" is Japanese for "cute".

did not! I can assure you this is true, because if Shawn had remembered making out with Mari, she would have come home from her trip, told me that she made out with Mari, said, "you're welcome", smashed a glass of wine against the ground, and left with her arms raised in triumph. And I would have remembered if she did that, because my memory is good. Unlike Shawn's.

Now that I think about it, perhaps Mari's divorce from her husband, as well as her constantly pressing Shawn to drink more, as well as her telling Shawn that she was cute, as well as her (heretofore not mentioned) desire to go live among the parts of the United States that have "more advanced thinking" (Mari's words, not mine), all share a common explanation: Mari has a crush on me![6] Alas, I never got to the bottom of this one.

We settled our tab at Bar Drop Kick and then went out to the next place: Bar Asylum. Bar Asylum was, among all the places in Golden Gai that were open, Mari's favorite place; and among all the places in Golden Gai, open or closed, her tenth favorite place.

To get to Bar Asylum, we had to ascend yet another narrow flight of stairs. And I mean narrow. Both of my shoulders literally pressed against the walls as I squeezed my way to the bar. I felt like the Hulk! Usually, I feel like the Hulk because my ass and belly press unflatteringly against

---

6. Think about it: she divorced her husband to have a chance with me; she wanted Shawn to drink more so that she would embarrass herself and make me consider other options; she told Shawn she was cute so as to flatter me for my taste in women; and she was thinking of me in Los Angeles when she was talking about advanced thinking. Like, what's the alternative? That she's gay for Shawn? But why would a lesbian like a short-haired woman with glasses who has lots of traditionally masculine traits?

the tight purple pants-shorts I like to wear every day. But in this case, I felt like the Hulk because I was so broad-shouldered.

The bar itself was also quite small: all told, there were eight stools, a bar, and a single bald, bespectacled Japanese bartender in his approximate mid-fifties.[7] The walls of Bar Asylum were festooned with handwritten white pieces of paper taped to the wall.

When we arrived, there were three American bros boisterously conversing at one end of the bar. One of them recommended the homemade jalapeño tequila. I don't speak bro fluently, but I think he said it was "lit" or "off the hook" or something. I smiled and politely nodded while internally treating his testimony as radioactive garbage that I threw onto the curb while wearing lead-lined mind-gloves. So I didn't order it. Instead, I asked the bartender for a whiskey. He asked me what kind of whiskey I liked. I told him my favorites: Laphroaig, Lagavulin, Kavalan. "Oh, you like the peaty ones!" He only had domestic whiskey to offer (very fortunate, as drinking off-beat, hard-to-find Japanese whiskey was one of the things I most wanted to do in Japan), and I eventually settled on Suntory Whiskey Crest, Aged 12 Years. One of the neat things about it was that it was a whiskey they don't make anymore. You can't get much harder-to-find than gone! One shot of it was only about 1,200 yen ($9). It was good, at least for a whiskey that's gone for good.

While the gentlemen lingered at the bar, Shawn, Mari, and I engaged in whispered conversation, allowing me to immerse myself in the continuous mash-ups of '90s rock and '00s hip-hop playing in the background. I have to admit, I was surprised and impressed. I'm not saying this is the

---

7. Why write "approximate mid-fifties"? Isn't "mid-fifties" approximate enough? No, because he could have been anywhere between forty-five and seventy.

greatest music in the world, but, like the music by GirlTalk, it's the kind of music that pleases me immensely. I don't know why it was playing at Bar Asylum, but I certainly didn't mind.

Not too long after we arrived, the three bros left, and I felt myself more comfortable. I started chatting up the barman, whose English was excellent. I asked him what kind of whiskey he liked, and he said he liked only Japanese whiskey (apparently, the really good American and Scottish whiskey is hard to find in Japan). He asked me what I was going to do in-country, and I mentioned that on January 4 I would watch NJPW's Wrestle Kingdom show at the Tokyo Dome (see chapters 32 to 35). Because this bartender was apparently made in a lab to cater to my tastes, he of course knew all about Japanese professional wrestling, and he pointed out that Shinsuke Nakamura was going to be wrestling The Great Muta on January 1. I had forgotten about that!

After trying the Crest, I decided to experiment a bit. I ordered the homemade tomato liquor from one of the handwritten menus on the wall. I tried it and it was not for me: it tasted like a sweet cherry tomato, but it had a strong chemical taste. You know who liked it, though? Shawn. To her pink-sweetener-lovin' ass, this was God's gift to alcohol. She couldn't get over how much she liked it. And Shawn's loving this alcoholic beverage also thrilled Mari, for what seemed to me to be barely ulterior reasons.

Since I didn't like the tomato liquor, I decided to go back to whiskey. But this time, I asked him for some really good stuff. So he asked me, "do you know Ichiro? Not the baseball player!" Me: "Not Mr. Suzuki?" Him (laughing): "No! Ichiro makes a whiskey." And he showed me Ichiro's Malt: Heavily Peated, from 2013. It was 3,200 yen ($24) for a shot, but hey, you only live once, so I coughed up the bucks.

Of course, it was excellent. I don't have the skill or vocabulary to give voice to a beautifully florid Japanese whiskey, but what differentiated this whiskey from your peaty scotches or sweet bourbons was its subtlety and smoothness. Additionally, it had a great complexity, where the initial flavor was swiftly succeeded by a distinctly different taste. I was very happy to have had it.

At this point, the bros were replaced by brothers, Jewish as it happens (we showed each other our membership cards). One was a graduate student in political science, and the other was the brother of a graduate student. They were very pleasant company, and easy to talk to. We shared a mutual appreciation for Kanye West—the political views, of course, not the music[8] —and the graduate student managed to correct the bartender about whether the trains would be running on New Year's Eve.[9] The bartender assured us that they would be, but the graduate student counter-assured us that the taxi union managed to finally get its way (those bastards!) and that they would not be. Much to the bartender's (and Mari's) amazement, the graduate student was right! You have never seen a bald, bespectacled, middle-aged Japanese bartender look so gobsmacked.

Soon after that, the brothers left and I had my third (don't worry, mom, it was my final) whiskey: The Essence of Suntory Whisky. It was 3,000 yen (about $22.50) for a shot but I went for it. It wasn't nearly as subtle as the Ichiro, but had stronger peatiness, as well as a pronounced hotness going down. The bartender asked me which one I preferred. I knew I was

---

8. In case it wasn't clear, the three of us, being Jewish, did not actually like Kanye West's torrid love affair with Nazism.

9. I bet Kanye would keep the trains running on time!

supposed to say Ichiro, but I genuinely enjoyed the Essence more. I told him, and he gave me a look that communicated, "no, that is wrong", but, like my preference for McDonald's over In-n-Out, sometimes I prefer the worse thing.

It was at this point that I really began to settle into Japan. Up until then, I was enjoying Japan in a detached manner; my priority was to observe and ruminate, in part because I knew I would be writing missives to my friends and family (which of course would become this book), and I wanted to have observations to share. But also, the things I had done so far—fly on a plane, tour a garden, walk for miles on end, look at universities, go into stores—were not exactly intense sensory experiences; instead, they were mostly just views of vistas.[10] By contrast, when I was in this bar, I was checking something off of my bucket list. I felt the kind of elation you feel when you have high expectations for something, and it meets it.

Before we left, the bartender asked Mari if she wanted him to make her a cup of coffee and read her fortune. She enthusiastically assented to 10 PM coffee, because she is psychotic. He made the coffee, she drank it, and then he looked at the grounds at the bottom. He said she needed to drink more, so she did. Then he inspected the grounds very closely. After about a minute of pondering (during which Shawn joked, "he's trying to remember all the things we said about you!"), he started rattling off a lot of things to her, in Japanese of course. She responded. He replied. She said something again. He seemed to agree. There was a moment of silence. I asked her, "So, what did he say?" She paused, presumably translating his words in her head. Then she said, "he said, this year I will sparkle!"

---

10. Except for crossing the street at the Shibuya Scramble. That was quite intense, like riding a roller coaster! But it was also quite brief, like riding a roller coaster.

He then said something else to her, which started another back-and-forth that lasted for about a minute. I said, "and now, what did he say?" She thought for a bit. Then she said, "that I will sparkle."

Guys, if I'm divorced by the end of the year and Shawn is in Japan, you'll know Mari's fortune came true.

We left the bar. Our time with Mari was coming to an end. Before we parted ways, she asked what we would be doing for New Year's Eve tomorrow night. Projecting our current feelings into tomorrow night, we both said, "sleep!" She said, "no, you should go to Shibuya! Tomorrow for New Year's Eve, it will be like Times Square, only more people!" Then she turned to Shawn. "You should be careful, though: a lot of people will try to grab your butt and your boobs."

This is what happens when you get recommendations from an extravert.

Being an introvert with a strong sense of personal space, Shawn declined. And being someone who gets my fill of Shawn's boobs and butt, I also declined. And Mari, too, wouldn't be there. She'd be returning to her home town of Chiba for the new year, to begin her sparkle project.

December 30 was my first full day in Japan: woke up at 3:30 AM; saw a garden, some universities, and a dog statue; crossed the street; ate the dankest part of the pig; drank some delicious whiskey; and did 15.24 miles of walking. Despite her tired, inebriated state, Shawn miraculously managed to guide us back to Shinagawa with nary a hitch.

All the hitches would come tomorrow.

No, I'm kidding, tomorrow went totally fine.

# DECEMBER 31, 2022

# 8

# The Most Absorbing Thing

The day started with a hitch. Two hitches, in fact.

Hitch the first: I didn't mention this in the previous chapter, but while I was at the unnamed organ meat yakitori restaurant, I slashed my right index finger with a splinter from a chopstick. Always rub your cheap wooden chopsticks together before you use them, people! Short story short: it created a cut that secreted a bit of blood. This meant that Shawn had begun to make good on her pre-trip promise that in Japan I would be punished by prosperity: here I was, oozing opulence.

Hitch the second: walking fifteen miles tires you out and exhausts your legs. Unsurprisingly, when I awoke, my legs were sore. That wasn't the hitch, though. The hitch was that when I put on my Rockport "walking" shoes—Rockport's words, not mine—the right shoe really cut into my right heel. I assumed I had scraped my heel. Yet the skin on it, while fairly red, didn't seem to merit the sharp pain I was experiencing.[1] Regardless, that meant that Shawn once again made good on her promise that our whole trip to Japan would begin with a gale force wind of wealth and increase in intensity until I was buffeted by a cyclone of classiness: here I was, rubbed raw by riches.

I was forced to put on my boat shoes, as has happened to me so many times before.[2] I love my boat shoes—they're my favorite shoes, and a small preparation for when the day comes that I am finally shanghaied and forced to work as a criminal whaler—but they're not made for long walks, and the soles were already worn down to the point of developing small holes. Nevertheless, I brought them along with me because I knew that at some point during my travels in Japan, I would have to have shoes that were easy to slip on and off. Now, they would have to do double-duty, as slippers and as walkers. May God have mercy on my soles.

Fully be-shoed, Shawn and I went down to the breakfast buffet. Once again, they had a lovely assortment of options: smoked salmon; cold cuts; marinated avocado; shooters of orange, apple, and grapefruit juice; various pastries; pork buns; shrimp dumplings; and a hot food station where you could not only get delicious sausages, rubbery bacon, roasted salmon, roasted rockfish, congee, and tofu; but where you could also order some

---

1. I tried to wear the shoes again on my last day in Japan. My right heel still hurt! And I tried those same shoes once again on January 19, 2023. They hurt my right heel just as much! The problem, it turned out, was not the heel of the foot, but the heel of the shoe. In wrestling terms, my shoe's heel turned heel on my heel. Weirdly, on November 1, 2023, the shoes felt fine.

2. When you regularly listen to Christopher Cross, you just find yourself donning boat shoes. Don't fight it.

manner of egg dish. Yesterday, I had the eggs benedict, and today I opted for the fried eggs.

I quite enjoyed them. They had the most intensely orange yolks of any eggs I had seen; Shawn told me that the color of the yolk depends on the chicken's diet, so I suppose these chickens ate a lot of Cheetos.

Not Flamin' Hot Cheetos, though! The eggs, like many foods in Japan, had no salt on them. However, this table, like many tables in Japan, had no salt on it. Luckily, necessity is the mother of invention, so I simply put the fried eggs on some buttered milk-bread. Also, my finger was bleeding.

Wait, what? Yes, the wound on my finger had opened up again. This would have been a good thing if my blood had a nice salty taste to it, but my blood, being what you might call "liquid meat", had a strong iron and umami taste. So, it didn't benefit the eggs. It was a hat on a hat.

From this point on, I was rather self-conscious about my chopstick injury. So, after gulping the two ounces of coffee we had been poured, Shawn and I adjourned to our room.

Shawn decided to go to a local department store, Don Quixote. They would have bandages for my finger, not to mention various sundries that Shawn had forgotten to bring with her from the USA: tampons, and a gun. She asked me if I wanted to go with her to DonQi (pronounced, "donkey"), and I confessed to her something that I had just noticed: I was really sleepy!

She said, "OK, why don't you take a nap while I go to DonQi." Being the dutiful person that I am, I obliged her.

Like all naps, my nap was a great deal of fun, full of tosses and turns as I gradually transitioned from "jetlagged" to "asleep." As I came to, Shawn came back. I wrapped the bandage—which was, I was relieved to see, a Band-Aid brand bandage—around my put-upon finger and went to the hotel lounge on the 26th floor.

The Band-Aid betrayed me, though! A short while after I applied it, it started to peel off! Aside from the lack of salt, the smallness of our hotel room, and the extremely limited coffee pours, this was the only time Japan was clearly inferior to America. As comedian-eventually-turned-into-vodka Yakov Smirnoff would say, "In America, Band-Aids stick to you, but in Japan you must stick to Band-Aids!"

The lounge, however, was significantly better than the Japanese Band-Aids. It offered us a gorgeous view of Tokyo, not to mention a magazine called Hotel Secrets and a snack that looked like, but was not, macadamia nuts. I don't know what the snack was—some kind of salty, crunchy thing. Let's just say it was deep-fried flour doused in salt.

While Shawn tried to take a nap herself, I spent an enjoyable hour composing my first and second missives about my trip to Japan. I just knew that my reflections on all the other days would flow from my mind to my kin's and kith's computer screens extremely promptly. There would be no hitches![3]

After returning to my room, Shawn informed me (probably for about the sixth or ninth time) about what we were going to be doing today: go to an immersive art exhibit called TeamLab Planets. I had no sense of what this would be like, which made it more exciting, like *From Dusk Til Dawn*, if I hadn't seen the previews beforehand.[4]

Shawn guided me through the train station to our stop, which was in a part of Tokyo called Toyosu. On the way to the exhibit, we passed another interesting place, the Gas Science Museum. We couldn't go

---

3. It took approximately eighteen months longer than I expected, much like the US government's decision to invade Normandy.

4. I would have never known it was a vampire movie! The victim was the audience's time!

that day, but if we do visit one day, I should get in for free, as I have contributed quite a lot to the earth's supply of gas. On account of my butt.

The TeamLab Planets building was simultaneously tacky and unglamorous. At the front entrance was a forty-foot tall, but only two-foot wide, monitor displaying a long strand of fire. To make use of this electronic fire, you were supposed to download an app called "Distributed Fire". The conceit of the app was that, once you downloaded it, you could hold your phone close to this digital ember, which would "light" your phone. You could then touch your phone to someone else's phone, which would "light" their phone (so long as they also had the app). It was clever and cute, in both the complimentary and pejorative senses of those terms.

Past the Distributed Fire display, a long line snaked around a couple of times. A sign indicated that it was for the 2:30 PM showing, which we had tickets for, so we got in line.

The line moved quickly and, more importantly, the man behind me was even fatter than I am. Unfortunately, he was not Japanese. So, while this shows that I, Tokyo Rob, am not literally the fattest man in Japan, all the evidence I cared to look at suggested that I am still fatter than any Japanese man.

Once we got to the front of the line, we (and many people behind us) entered a dimly-lit, cavernous room akin to the cargo hold of an airplane in any Mission Impossible movie. I think it could hold about eighty people, maybe? Regardless, the organizers divided us into four lines, with about twenty people in each line, and showed us a video. The video captions read:

> In this museum, you will walk barefoot as you experience the artworks with your entire body. Your feet will get wet

in some spaces. Please take off your socks and tights in the locker area. In some areas water depths are knee-deep even for adults. Please roll up your pants. Mirroring materials are used on the floor in some areas. If you are wearing a skirt, your underwear may be visible. Rental shorts are available for free. Please use the changing rooms in the locker area.

There was more, but that was the important bit. Shawn had apparently taken me to a museum run by kooks. You would walk through water! Mirrors might display your underwear! There were free rental shorts! But if the shorts were free, how could you also rent them?!

We dutifully went to the locker area and picked locker 785 to stow our shoes in. We then entered the museum, making our way to the first exhibition space, called "Water Area".

We walked along a cool, barely illuminated corridor. We passed a small waterfall. Apparently, that was the first exhibit! It was called, "Waterfall of Light Particles at the Top of an Incline". So, not a waterfall, but a light-fall. I will tell you, it looked for all the world like a waterfall made of water particles, but based on the description attached to the exhibit, I'm led to believe that there was no waterfall, but just a play on light to make you think you're seeing a waterfall. In fairness to the light, I don't recall hearing the sound of water lightly pummeling a floor, nor did I experience any splash-back.[5]

I guess that was pretty cool, but it was also quite unaffecting. Like, imagine that you're eating a hamburger, and then you're told that actually

---

5. Contrary to my recollection of the exhibit, Shawn's phone's video shows me getting splashed by water. Which just goes to show: even Shawn's *phones* don't remember correctly!

you're eating a bison burger. If you're like me, your first reaction would be "oh." And that would be it. That would be the end of your reaction. Now, if you ate this not-beef-but-actually-bison burger in a museum as a museum exhibit, you might have an additional thought, like, "wait, what was the point of that?" Well, the only answer I could get to that question was the museum's motto, "Immerse your Body, and with Others, Become One with the World". I mean, that sounds pretty grand, but the same thing could be said about a public swimming pool. The only difference is, I don't generally ask what swimming pools are about.

The next part of the museum was called "Soft Black Hole—Your Body Becomes a Space that Influences Another Body". We interacted with the exhibit by traversing a thickly tremulous rubber floor. It was like walking on pillows, which meant that it was difficult to keep your balance, but also fine if you lost it.[6] Many people fell as they crossed this obstacle. I felt proud of my calves that I could surmount it without losing my balance. My wife wasn't so lucky, but then again, if she were a robot, she would be called "Clumsytron 2000", so color me unsurprised.

Again, I was left wondering what the point was. I mean, it was kind of fun. But a fun museum is like a funny professor: just like a funny professor isn't really funny, but is funny compared to the fleet of resentful mannequins that call themselves professors, a fun museum is more fun than, say, being locked in a bathroom stall, but it's not as fun as, say, being locked in a bathroom stall with heroin.

Lucky for me, the curators told us what the point was:

---

6. In this regard, it was like the relationship between Superman and his bank account.

> In modern life we are surrounded by flat hard surfaces, so that in our daily lives we have lost consciousness of our bodies, we have forgotten them. In natural forests flat ground does not exist. This installation is a space to remind us of the body that we have forgotten in everyday life, and to make us more conscious of our body mass.

I would have just called the exhibit "One Weird Trick to Make You Want to Go Back to Leg Day."

We escaped Soft Black Hole into what was a quite striking exhibit called "The Infinite Crystal Universe". Long strings of LED lights dangled from mirrored ceiling to mirrored floor. The lights changed color, apparently depending on the smartphone activity of the visitors in the room. It was quite an arresting arrangement. I would not say it was beautiful, but I would say it was gripping, sort of like watching Big Punisher swim. Many people positioned themselves to take what was undoubtedly one of the best Facebook profile pictures of their lives.

The question, "what is the point?" seemed more churlish in this room. I suppose I thought that if something was as creatively compelling as this exhibit was, it didn't need to justify itself. That said, I couldn't help but notice that almost everyone's instinctive reaction to the surrounding glamor was to momentarily ignore it all in order to capture it with their phones and, in doing so, subtly change the scene. Perhaps the point was to confront us with the fact that whenever we see anything mind-bending, we want to capture it, even though there would undoubtedly be more professional-looking pictures online. Still, not only would those pictures not contain us, they wouldn't really be ours—just some professional's whose work everyone partook of equally. Which seems unsatisfying. Maybe it shouldn't be, but that's how it works.

Our next stop was "Drawing on the Water Surface Created by the Dance of Koi and People—Infinity." Aside from the incline into the museum (which I don't count as an exhibit), this was the first exhibit that wet your feet. You entered a room with perhaps a foot of water in it, and above the water, bulbs cast lights that depicted colorful koi fish (and other water flora) worming their way through their habitat. Somehow, when you tried to touch the koi displayed on the water with your hands or feet, they disappeared into a dazzling explosion. I don't really understand the technology (though when do I ever understand technology), but I suspect that when we bent over to touch the koi, it would trigger some sort of other light to turn on, which in turn produced the koi's disappearing act.

This exhibit impressed me even more than The Infinite Crystal Universe, though partly that's because of how the two interacted. Whereas the attempt to capture The Infinite Crystal Universe produced mere changes in the color of the lights, the attempt to grab the fish led to the destruction of what you were trying to capture. I don't think I had this thought at the time, but on reflection, I see—or at least, project—that relationship between the two exhibits.

The next exhibit had the portentous title, "Expanding Three-Dimensional Existence in Transforming Space—Free Floating, Flattening 3 Colors and 9 Blurred Colors". Based on that title, what would you guess we were about to see? If you guessed, "big beach balls", you win!

OK, there was more to it than that. What we found was a bunch of maybe-twelve-feet diameter beach balls bouncing around the room, and they changed colors when you smacked them. As with a party sponsored by America's Funniest Home Videos for a masochist, you were invited to literally punch balls. And people took up the invitation, including me. Based on my experiences of him running across the couch and occasionally flattening my testicles, I would say that this, more than anything else, was the exhibit for Briscoe.

It wasn't for me, though. Whether it was because I was in Japan, or because I was in a museum, or because I just didn't trust it, I didn't fully tee off against those beach balls, as several small Japanese children around me happily did. Instead, I limply slapped them and loped off, like a humiliated T-Rex.[7]

What *was* for me was the next exhibit, "Floating in the Falling Universe of Flowers". This room had a mirrored floor and a ceiling on which the artists involved with the museum projected flowers floating through outer space. Not only were they floating in space, though, they slowly listed toward you, picking up speed, until a flower expanded to cover the entire ceiling. The multicolored flowers created a spectacular collage. Moreover, because the floor was mirrored, and because the mirrors were so disorienting, it was difficult to tell where the floor ended and the walls began. When I walked into the room, I became dizzy and had to creep carefully across the floor. Eventually, Shawn and I found a place to sit, and then, like many other observers in the room, we lay down.

So lying, we gazed up at the ceiling and saw butterflies appear and interact with the space-plants. If you had the right app on your phone (an app that was drawn to your attention once you entered the room), you could use the app to populate the ceiling projection with butterflies. Each butterfly showed up because someone summoned them. Again, the museum marshaled our love of our devices for the sake of art.

More than any exhibit, this one resonated with me. I felt like Odysseus among the lotus-eaters; I could easily imagine myself passing several hours here before realizing that I had to go home, kill the men interested in

---

7. It won't surprise you to learn that this is my preferred style of loping.

my wife, and then watch my dog die. It was like looking into a fire on a snowy night: constantly changing, but ever the same. Here, the writers of museum-copy didn't exaggerate when they said, "Lie down or sit still in the space and eventually your body floats and you dissolve into the artwork world."

Floating in the Falling Universe of Flowers was the last installation in the water section. But there was, in fact, another section: the Garden Area. The first exhibit we visited here was called "Mass Garden of Resonating Microcosms—Solidified Light Color, Sunrise and Sunset". This appeared to be a mass of large metal Raisinets, planted in moss below a mesh ceiling. The thing about this exhibit is that it's ideally viewed when day turns into night, as the chrome Raisinets would apparently glow in strange ways after dark. As my favorite saying has it, the freaks come out at night. At 3 PM, though, it was merely like looking at a drunken party girl asleep on your roommate's couch: you know that as soon as she stirs, antics will ensue, but she's asleep, so there's nothing for you to do except wait for her to wake up and accidentally set the couch on fire.

Underwhelmed, we moved on to the second and final exhibit in the Garden Area: "Floating Flower Garden: Flowers and I are of the Same Root, the Garden and I are One". This title really felt like a direct transliteration from the Japanese. It was both stilted and evocative, like if you had an accountant, but he was Irish.

However, the exhibit itself had a gratifying structure. We walked from the "Mass Garden of Resonating Microcosms" to the "Floating Flower Garden"; but this time we had to wait in a line before entering—only a certain number of people were allowed in. At the appointed time, we were ushered through a curtain, but not let into the exhibit yet: we huddled along a wall, looking at the heart of the exhibit as other viewers experienced it from a few yards away. Finally, after maybe five minutes, the exhibit staff led the people out who were inside, and allowed us to enter.

The display was gorgeous and transporting. Above us, a mass of orchids hung from a trellis, and a mirrored wall and floor reflected the jungle of flowery vines. Shortly after we entered, the long orchid vines descended slowly from the ceiling to the floor, entombing us. The floral entombment was cozy, like how a vampire feels the first time he rests in his coffin. I assume.

What really amazed was the experience of a setting that was both bucolic and robotic, merging the traditional and the contemporary—pretty much Japan, in a nutshell. That you had only about five minutes to enjoy the exhibit elevated the experience as well. It was a small exhibit, so you didn't need more than five minutes to explore it, but you knew it was going away, so you wanted to drink in every part. The whole time, I felt a sense of polite urgency.[8]

After that, we were done with the museum. We collected our belongings and left.

I have often told my students that the one thing more diverting than anything else that humanity is capable of—more entertaining than a $300 million movie, more absorbing than the traffic around you that threatens

---

[8] It reminded me of a passage from C. S. Lewis's science fiction novel, *Perelandra*. The protagonist, Ransom, drinks from a fruit on a distant planet that tasted unbearably wonderful – "For one draught of this on earth wars would be fought and nations betrayed" – and yet, he decides against having another: "...for whatever cause, it appeared to him better not to taste again. Perhaps the experience had been so complete that repetition would be a vulgarity—like asking to hear the same symphony twice in a day." That's sort of how I felt as I left the Floating Flower Garden: once was great, and once was enough.

your life while you drive a car, more important than your relationship to your friends and family—is looking a video of a gopher falling into a garbage can. Like, literally anything that could happen anywhere in the universe is less arresting than that, as evidenced by the fact that when people go to movies, drive on the road, or play with their kids, they prefer to look at their phones.

A thought that occurs to me now, though it didn't occur to me at the time, is that this museum channeled our chthonic attachment to our phones into the art itself. It said, "You'll look at your phone, but when you do, you'll change the things around you. So, whether you do or don't look at your phone, you'll be taking part in the art, even if you choose not to enjoy it. Either way, something special will happen."

Throughout my time at the museum, I kept on wondering what it was about. I guess that's what it was about.

# 9

# Kapitel 9: Spazieren Gehen und Zweimal Essen

Now that we were out in the bright open air, we had to figure out what to do next. We decided to walk to a nearby mall, LaLaport TOYOSU, to get something to eat. Along the way, though, we visited Toyosu Park, which borders Tokyo Bay, a body of water that I took to be the ocean but which I later learned, from Shawn, was actually a bay. Oh Shawn, bae: I do not know the difference between these two things, and I never will.

Despite my maritime illiteracy, we enjoyed the sounds of adults laughing, dogs barking, and Japanese children engaging in playful violence while screaming "John Cena!!!" It was a small park, but casually beautiful, like many things in Tokyo. There was no noteworthy sight here, but I feel it would have been legendary in most American cities.

We pressed on to LaLaport mall and tried to figure out where to eat. We both were in the mood for something not-Japanese, so we settled on either the Italian or the German restaurant. There was something off-putting about the font and the pictures of the Italian restaurant. The centrally displayed photo was trying to depict fettuccini Alfredo, but instead of covering it with Alfredo sauce, the photographer apparently decided, "ah, fuck it, let's just cover it with turkey gravy." Turned off by the fugazi Italian food, we settled on a German restaurant, "Schmatz."

Schmatz specialized in beer and sausage. That kind of hearty food was just what we needed after our treacherous journey through the water-logged beanbags that composed TeamLabs Planets Tokyo.

The main reason I wanted to try a not-Japanese restaurant in Japan was not that I'd had too much Japanese food—remember, I was only on my second full day in Japan—but rather that I was intensely curious what the Japanese take on other cuisines would be. Now, Schmatz was not exactly a Japanese restaurant; it was the brainchild of two German restaurateurs, Marc Luetten and Christopher Ax, and quickly grew to over thirty locations. However, it started in Japan in 2015, so it's really a union of Germany and Japan, maybe the first such union of all time? I certainly can't think of any other time when Germany and Japan got together to try to change the world.

In classic German-Japanese style, we were both graciously and ruthlessly seated in a corner of the restaurant where we could look at the passersby in the mall as well as the décor on the walls. There were lots of pictures and small signs everywhere, which contributed to an atmosphere of fun (or perhaps, *Gemütlichkeit*), but nothing stood out as flashy or attention-grabbing; it was what would happen if Germans ran TGI Friday's:[1] "eferyone haf fun, but not too much fun, alles klar?"

Despite the muted egalitarianism of the flair, I fixated on one picture. It showed a mountain—perhaps Mt. Fuji, perhaps some famous mountain from the Alps—on a bright and sunny day, and above it read the caption, "Fernweh."

---

1. The "T" would stand for "Teutonic"!

The Germans have a word for homesickness; it's *Heimweh* ("Heim" = "home" and "weh" = "pain"). "Fern", though, means "far". Literally, then, *Fernweh* is "distance-pain". It's a longing for far-off places. Ironically, we do have a word that has pretty much that meaning in English: it's *Wanderlust*.[2]

I experienced Fernweh as I sat in that restaurant. I was trying to take in as much of Japan as one could in a week. But I knew it would be over before I knew it, so the moments in that restaurant, tired as I was, took on a special significance; I thought to myself, "soon, I'm not going to be in Japan anymore. That's too bad." I was preemptively nostalgic, like I get when I've just started my summer vacation.

Also, I was having a lot of beer on an empty stomach. Spoiler alert for the rest of the travelogue, but the beer here was better than the beer I got in any other Japanese restaurant. There were two reasons the beer was so delicious. First, it was a German restaurant. Germans are fantastic at brewing beer! Second, and unlike every other place in Japan, not every beer here was a golden lager. I started with a dunkel beer and Shawn got a banana-flavored weizen beer.[3] It had a satisfying depth and a nice sweetness. Shawn's weizen was refreshing, but had a thickness to it, and a bouquet of classic banana smell, like the kind of smell food chemists would make in a lab if they were told to make a classic banana smell,

---

2. Yes, yes, *Wanderlust* is a German word, but it literally means "desire to hike", and that's how it's used in Germany today (I think; I accidentally make a lot of stuff up). In Germany, you have *Wanderlust* if you want to walk in the woods, whereas in America you have *Wanderlust* if you tell everyone you're hiking the Appalachian Trail but are really leaving your job to spend time in Argentina with your mistress.

3. Yes, it's true that my dunkel beer was *also* a lager, but it wasn't a *golden* lager.

but they were very skilled, so it didn't smell like something food chemists made.[4]

Regardless, Shawn *loved* this beer. She went absolutely nuts for the banana beer. Hoping to delight her when we got back to America, I texted my professor friend Chewy about banana beers. Chewy knows more about beer than any other person I know. Here is our text-chain:

> We're having a delicious banana beer at a German restaurant. Why isn't there more banana beer? Or is there lots of banana beer?

> There's not zero banana beer. You want me to grab a banana stout I know about? Hefeweizen. Plus that weird banana ale.

> Sure. Shawn loves it. And she wants more.

> I'm on it. See, this is why you travel! To learn about things back home!

Don't worry, I appended a "HA HA" tapback to Chewy's last remark. I understand textiquette.

Anyway, while we were drinking our beers, we ordered and, it being a German restaurant in Japan, we immediately received some food. Because Shawn is absolutely bananas for brine, we ordered a jar of pickled vegetables, as well as a pretzel and three sausages. One sausage was cheese-infused, one was herbaceous, and the last one was smoked. The pickled vegetables were as good as pickled vegetables usually are in the states; the pretzel was, in my opinion, a bit below average, but still good,

---

4. I'm going to be honest, I think food chemists had something to do with Shawn's banana beer.

and the sausages were outstanding. I think the pretzel was subpar precisely because of the Japanese style with which it was prepared—easy on the salt and not much dip to go with it, the idea being to let the pretzel speak for itself. Well, in my experience, pretzels are quite inarticulate. They stumble over their words until they imbibe some salt to loosen their tongues. This guy didn't do it, though, so he was tight-lipped.

The sausages, on the other hand, were way above average precisely because of the Japanese style with which they were prepared, which was to let the sausages speak for themselves. Now, sausages in the States are often too salty, which means when you let them talk, they're constantly using slurs and f-bombs. You need to tone those guys down. The Japanese sausages, despite having cheese and smoke, were toned down but had a strong umami flavor that fits my theory of Japanese culture, which I will reveal in chapter 40.

Unlike American cheese-filled sausages, which spurt a vile cheese-whiz all over your face when you cut into them, this cheese-filled Japanese sausage was marbled with a delicate cheese sauce that complimented the sausage rather than making its eater feel like a nasty boy. As for the smoked sausage, it again avoided the fatal flaw of its breed, which is to have the smoke take the lead and leave the rest of the sausage behind. Again, it was a marvelous union, this time of smoke and umami, like the way my clothes smell when I nearly fall into a campfire.[5]

On the other hand, herbed foods in America often have additional flavors that are too subtle to detect, so you'd think that in Japan, the herb sausage would taste like a normal sausage. These herbs, though, seemed flavor-enhanced, like the strong mint flavor you get when you drink a

---

5. This has nearly happened three times. I don't want to shorten my life or anything, but I'd be delicious!

mojito. I'm not saying this sausage tasted like mint; rather, I'm saying you could really taste the fennel, the basil, or whatever the hell herb the chefs infused into it. Since I'm not a herb-identifier, I really couldn't tell you what herb they used. Like, what does thyme even taste like? Does anyone even know? Let's just say it was thyme. Regardless, the sausage had a great, generalized herbaceousness to it, which is just what you have to do for an herb-flavored anything.

This being a vacation where Shawn promised that I would get overwhelmed by opulence, we got second helpings of drinks. I got a Bavaria Jerez and Shawn got a lemon sour. It's been a while since I drank the Bavaria Jerez; all I can tell you is that it was a helles (German for "bright", not "diabolical") and that it was good. As for the lemon sour, I was quite looking forward to trying it. That creature of Japanese myth and legend, Mari, claimed that Shawn had had several lemon sours the last time they hung out. I was also interested in Shawn getting a drink that would encourage her to slut it up, so not only did I want to try it, I wanted Shawn to drink it.

If you told me that Shawn really liked a lemon sour, I would predict it would taste lemony, crisp, mildly sweet, and with an undertone of alcohol. In reality, it tasted like a club soda with a twist of lemon. That's it.

I wondered, "why would my wife enjoy something so boring? You can't even taste the alcohol!" But then I remembered what she does for a living. She works for an agency of the federal government that does financial regulation. She devotes herself to looking at balance sheets and telling people to follow rules, and becomes overjoyed when the government issues more rules for people to follow. She has the permission to go to other people's places of work and do whatever she wants, and she, like all other lawyers in her agency, chooses to look at spreadsheets rather than ask people there who's sleeping with whom.[6] Taking the joy out of booze is basically her brand.

We left Schmatz with Shawn in an extremely good mood and me in an extremely hopeful mood. I guess the lemon sour worked after all![7]

We returned to our hotel by about 5:30 PM and chilled out for a bit. I now know, thanks to the amazing powers of retrospection, that I should have immediately started writing up our experiences, but I didn't realize that when I got back to the USA that a combination of jetlag and EVERYONE IN MY LIFE[8] would conspire to prevent me from writing this book in a timely fashion.

Still, it was New Year's Eve. We needed to do something special, so at 7:30 PM we decided to go to the hotel banquet hall to enjoy their free (to people with Marriott status) New Year's Eve banquet. It's a good thing we left when we did, because the banquet ended at 8![9]

The banquet hall was the dreariest place we visited in Japan. They may as well have hung a banner that read, "Greetings, Members of the Westchester Rotary Club." It was in the hotel basement, so there were no windows, the décor was uninspired/depressing, and the clientele (including us) looked washed out and frazzled.

By and large, the food was nothing to write home about. So I won't be writing about it. However, they had one of those classic American prime

---

6. If it isn't already clear, I have no idea what my wife does for a living.

7. It didn't.

8. Aka, "Briscoe" and "my insatiable desire for hanging out with people/talking to telemarketers".

9. Happy New Year's?

rib carving stations, and I got a few slices. Let me tell you, this was the best prime rib from a carving station I've ever had. It had a rich and oily beef flavor, yet was light. I'm sure I'm wrong about this, but I think it was some kind of wagyu—like, A1 or A2, if that's a thing wagyu can be. I was shocked at how good it was. I got seconds, even though I wasn't hungry; I wanted to force its imprint into my mind.

Besides the carving station, the mixers were also noteworthy. They had lime cordial! And crème de cassis! Shawn had the tender of the bar (though he was no bartender) make her a vodka gimlet and I had a kir royale. The tender of the bar was also Indian, and spoke really good English, so I started talking him up, asking him what he liked to do here. When I got back to the table, Shawn upbraided me for talking to the tender of the bar so much. I defended myself: "he spoke really good English! Maybe he knows things!" Her: "what things?!" Me: "... *secret* things." In fairness to me, in the previous chapter there was that book in the lounge called *Hotel Secrets*. I didn't read it, but maybe that Indian guy was one of the secret-keepers! She pointed out that it's New Year's Eve! The tender probably has better things to do than to talk to a weirdly interested hotel guest about what are the best restaurants he can't afford! Maybe he wants to do other, better things, like: "go away" and "not talk to Rob"![10]

At 8 PM, they took away the food and maybe even the drinks, while I remained baffled that someone would prefer doing something over talking to me. By then, though, Shawn and I were both exhausted. Rather than go to Shibuya to have Mari's idea of a good time (*i.e.*, a 5% chance of getting trampled to death), we decided to skip the fireworks and make

---

10. This was her tone with me! Restrained near-yelling!

our *own* fireworks. You guessed it: we went straight to sleep. Happy New Year!

# JANUARY 1, 2023

# 10

# Welcome to 2023

New Year's Eve was uneventful for us. Presumably fireworks went off somewhere and two people got sexually assaulted in Shibuya, allowing Japan to meet its yearly quota of crimes. Happily, we weren't either of those two people. In the morning, we awoke, got dressed, and took the elevator downstairs to enjoy round three of the breakfast buffet.

Along the way to the buffet, we encountered three members (presumably) of the Marriott staff.[1] They were wearing traditional kimonos and on a table before them were arrayed numerous square, wooden cups of sake. They offered us each a square. Well, who were we to turn down free morning sake? It's not like we're *not* lushes.

We both drank our sake, and, while the sake was passable, drinking fluid from a square vessel is a surprisingly treacherous experience. Once I put the cup to my lips and tipped it into my mouth, I immediately lost confidence in my ability to capture the liquid without minor dribble. Still, it was a modest pour, so Shawn and I managed to down our drinks

---

1. Many years ago, when we lived in New York City, Shawn and I went to a Ruth's Chris Steakhouse near Times Square. We were having a friendly argument about what cut of beef was better: the ribeye (Shawn's preference), or the New York strip (mine). While we were deliberating, an older, bearded, bespectacled man wearing a suit, and with his hair in a ponytail, approached us and asked how we were enjoying ourselves so far. We responded that we were having a good time, but that we were also having a spirited debate about which was better: the New York strip or the ribeye. He gave a knowing, sensible chuckle and said, in a deep, buttery voice, "well, the New York strip here is excellent, but for my money, nothing beats the cowboy ribeye." Shawn was exultant and I pretended to fume, and we ordered our respective steaks. Later on, our server approached us and asked how we were enjoying the meal. I think I said something like, "your manager was right!" She blinked and said, "what do you mean?" I told her that her manager had come over and asked us how we were doing, and had recommended the ribeye, and that he was right. She laughed and said, "oh, that's not the manager. He's actually a regular. He's just a Ruth's Chris fan. I think he writes for Saturday Night Live or something." I resolved two things that day: first, never to assume that just because someone acts like they work at a place that they really work there; and second, to do to someone else what that guy did to us.

rather speedily, given the hindrances. The older gentleman who offered us the drink immediately offered us another, but if we had had seconds, we would have only been drinking it for their *sake*.

You just got Gressised!

As you might have expected, the breakfast buffet was largely the same as the previous two days. Because it was New Year's Day, though, there was a wide variety of new pastries. In addition, and although I didn't see this until it was too late, they now had carafes of coffee available near the buffet table. I think Shawn's and my asking them for seconds on coffee two days in a row basically convinced them that we both had a significant (coffee-) drinking problem, and they were just going to wash their hands of responsibility for whatever caffeine-induced trauma we inflicted upon ourselves.

Oh, and there was also a robot.

Yes, they debuted a rolling, smiling garbage can to cart away trays, deliver room service, or simply serve as a minor Frankenstein's monster. When I saw it, it wasn't doing much. It was just basking near the buffet while a crowd of three waiters huddled around it, trying either to figure out how to use it or invite it out for after-work drinks. Regardless, it wasn't any of my business, and I paid it no mind, any more than I pay mind to your typical human, many of whom are also rolling, smiling garbage cans.

We finished our last buffet breakfast at the Tokyo Marriott. It didn't feel so much like the end of an era, but rather just a place where we were no longer going to have a good breakfast buffet. We then inquired with the hotel staff about using takkaiyubin to send our excess baggage to the airport.

Wait, what's takkaiyubin, you ask? An article from the website "Kanpai!"[2] does a good job of explaining it, but the quick version is this: because the Japanese post office doesn't deliver packages over 6 kg (13.2 lbs.), a company named Yamato sprang up to run a vast delivery network throughout Japan to deliver them. Their promise is "to pick up your package and deliver it the next day to wherever you want, anywhere in Japan, 365 days a year". They'll even deliver items that need refrigeration!

Apparently, the Japanese are mystified that not every country has something like this, because they use it like gangbusters. Here's why it's limited to Japan: the Japanese people, like British gardeners, are both fussy and good at things, meaning that their consumers have high standards and their workers can meet those standards. By contrast, the closest we can come in America to having takkaiyubin is when Amazon locks their workers in a warehouse until they meet their daily quota. Sometimes they can do next-day delivery, but you might get a severed finger or two with your Fire Stick.

Anyway, Shawn tried to communicate with the hotel staff person about using takkaiyubin (their logo is a black cat; once you notice it, you can't un-notice the logo throughout Japan, like spotting a superfluous nipple), but she wasn't having any of it, as she didn't understand English (it was New Year's Day, so they were understaffed). Rather than follow *my* master plan—give up—Shawn waited for the lady to contact another employee who was better at English. The lady found her man, and he handled our takkaiyubin needs.

Wait, how did we already have excess baggage? What did we buy? Did we decide to give up on our excess clothes and just wear one outfit for the whole time in Japan, like Wes Anderson characters? No, actually: we

---

2. https://www.kanpai-japan.com/travel-guide/takkyubin-sending-luggage

had excess baggage from our shopping trip to Akihabara on December 31, right after visiting Schmatz in Chapter 9. I had completely forgotten to write about it!

Of course, you can't blame me for forgetting. It happened right after we drank a lot of beer! Despite alcohol's greatest benefit, which is making you forget things, it also has a side-effect, which is forgetting things. A lot of people forget that.

# OH SHIT I HAVE TO GO BACK TO DECEMBER 31, 2022

# 11

# Imagine if a Shopping District Was Designed by a Stage 5 Hoarder

So, Akihabara. Akihabara is a shopping district in Tokyo that specializes in anime, manga, toys, video games, electronics, and sex paraphernalia. In other words, it was a Mecca for nerds. Despite my being a nerd, I'm more obsessed by philosophy, pro wrestling, and self-loathing.[1] Anyway, I've never been into Japanese nerd-product, whether be it locking yourself in your room for three days and watching tentacle porn, locking yourself in your room for three days and playing with *Attack on Titan* toys, or locking yourself in your room for three days, forgetting how to unlock the door, fiddling with the lock for seventy hours, and then perishing from lock-poisoning.

---

[1]. Unfortunately, they haven't yet invented a place that caters to those three preferences without also involving BDSM.

Thus, but not ergo, Akihabara was not as exciting to me as, say, visiting Goethe's house ("Kant could have walked here!!!" SWOON), but I could totally, and instantly, get how an enthusiast for Japanese nerd-culture would get high from the fumes of this area. There were rows of tall buildings with blaring lights and cute little characters entreating you to enter, gaze upon them, and dispense your money. The area was crowded with hairy, unkempt, young, and, most important, *overweight* Japanese men. *This* was where they were keeping all their fatsos! I could tell that, in another world, all these Japanese men would turn, look at me—the fattest man in Tokyo, remember—, notice my paunch, and nod their heads in quiet acknowledgement, as if to say, "we accept you, sir, as one of us." Unfortunately, they were too busy enjoying the much more interesting sights of Akihabara to indulge me that bit of solidarity.

Lucky for us, it was cold, so I couldn't smell them. But I could hear their resonant, clipped bellowing, and, though I didn't and don't understand any Japanese, I know nerds, having played *Dungeons & Dragons* all my life, and I knew they were loudly fantasizing about having sex with a cartoon bird-woman or criticizing something. In this regard, they are like literally everyone on the Internet.

Anyway, we were going to Akihabara to buy toys for Briscoe, in particular, toys representing the largest characters from the show *One Piece*. Why *One Piece*? Why its largest characters? Because of how Briscoe was handling his childhood.

You see, children generally look for all sorts of role-models to use in order to figure themselves out. (Children: so like us.) Briscoe's most distinctive physical characteristic (he has a personality, he just doesn't know what it is yet) is his height: at 4'9", he is in the top 5% of all eight-year-olds. Consequently, his role-models are: anything that is tall. At first, this manifested in an interest in the tallest human beings in history (Robert Wadlow, at 8 feet, 11 inches, was a particular fascination), but it later grew (pun intended) to an interest in the tallest fictional beings. For whatever reason, Anime has an absolute truckload of gigantic characters, so I came to Akihabara with a mission: buy toys representing a twenty-two-mile high, eyeless elephant named Zunesha.

I should add: besides having an intense interest in giants, Briscoe has an even stronger insecurity and concern about feet. I fear this will end up as a foot-fetish, but right now it's just a crippling disability, thank God. I'm not sure where it came from, but I have two theories.

Theory #1: when he was five, Shawn told Briscoe that he needed to clean his feet, because they were stinky. After that, he would try to wear socks as much as possible: in the house, to bed, and in the shower (we didn't let him do that last one). In other words, one slightly critical remark from his mother has changed his life-trajectory for the last three years. On the other hand, we've been trying to teach him to improve his handwriting for the last four years and no dice. So maybe Shawn and I didn't fuck him up at all. In your face, *Philip Larkin*.

Theory #2 is a theory that relates to me (and remember, Briscoe is part me!). When I was very young–about five–I would draw all the time (we didn't have YouTube back then). Whenever I drew someone, I would start with their feet because, well, that was the part of the adult body that I as a child would first notice. So theory #2 is the theory that, at around age five, and thanks to his mother's remark, Briscoe started noticing everyone's feet, and, like his mother, felt that they were God's greatest mistake (in fairness to Shawn, her feet are definitely a mistake). However, like me, he is both terribly passive-aggressive and conflict-averse. So, because he doesn't have the willfulness to tell other people to cover their disgusting leg-ends, he tries to send them a subtle message by concealing his own hooves and hoping that everyone else in the world will take the hint.

## THE MOST AWKWARD MAN IN JAPAN

OK, back to the narrative. Since Briscoe wanted figures of the largest characters from *One Piece*, the first place we went to—and believe me, I have no idea what it was called, and I'm pretty sure none of these places had names or any identifying information whatever[2] —was a place that specialized in toys from Japanese anime.

I couldn't really make heads or tails of what I was seeing. I mean, I was looking at toys, and they were on shelves, but there seemed to be no rhyme or reason to them. There were big toys, small toys, toys from anime, figures from American horror movies, and figures hailing from fictional locales I've never visited. Some figurines were wrapped in plastic lunch bags, while others stared balefully from professional-looking boxes. The prices of toys ranged absolutely wildly, from, like, $1.25 to over $1,000.

Bewildered and, frankly, threatened by the disorder of it all, Shawn and I went to the next establishment, which appeared to be a vertical strip-mall. It seemed to promise toys on the fifth floor, so that's where we took the elevator to.

The fifth floor had a lot of toy stores. I think they were selling different things. I mean, I know they were, but I couldn't tell the differences among any of the stores. Some sold cards, some sold clothing, some sold figurines, some sold action figures, and they all sold all of what I just said, and placed them just wherever. It was like a shopping center designed by a cobra: there was no apparent human intellect behind this spontaneous disorder, and I sensed something venomous lurking somewhere. Overwhelmed, I left this store too.

Shawn had told me that there was another Japanese store in another area called Nakano Broadway. It specialized in toys, was the size of an aircraft carrier, and was disordered even compared to these places.

---

2. Huh. Perhaps what I quoted from Pico Iyer in Chapter 5 was right after all!

Apparently, its owner had read Jorge Luis Borges's "Library of Babel" and thought it was an instruction manual.

My sanity was quickly slipping away, so I followed Shawn's suggestion to just go to a nearby department store and buy something there.

This department store, Bic Camera, was eight storeys tall and was, I think, designed just for men. On one floor was liquor, on another floor was electronics, and on another was toys. (I assume that the top floor was a combination fight club/pornographer's club.) Since I was looking for toys for Briscoe, I obviously went to the liquor floor first.

I admit, it wasn't *all* liquor. There was other stuff. I just don't remember anything except the liquor, because like any other man from Generation X, I'm simply on the lookout for liquor, toys, and resenting boomers and millennials. I thought long and hard about whether to get some good Japanese whiskey to send to the airport, but I didn't understand what customs would allow me to take with me so, reluctantly, I had to hope that the airport would have a good selection (spoiler alert: it did! But I messed it up. You'll see how in Chapter 37).

On the fifth floor, I found the toys. Since Briscoe's continuing affection for me hinged on how good a job I did of finding him excellent consumer goods, I looked long and hard in this (relative to its competition) extremely intuitively organized business.

Now, the thing I wanted most was big toys from *One Piece*. They had a *One Piece* section, but because I don't watch garbage,[3] I didn't know which of the toys, if any, represented a large creature. In addition, they were pretty expensive. Finally, none of them was articulated—i.e.,

---

3. Two things. First, I've never seen *One Piece*, so for all I know it's actually quite good. Second, I totally watch garbage; I've never seen *The Real Housewives of Orange County*, but I'm fairly confident that it's my favorite show.

none of them seemed to have any moving parts. They were just small, mass-produced statuettes of, let's just say, Japanese goblin spirits. So I had to give up on my *One Piece* search.

Luckily for me, there was a large Mecha-Godzilla figure. It was really big, and it actually wasn't as expensive as I expected based on the size. Maybe it was $50? A Mecha-Godzilla this big, and from Japan, would probably cost $200 in the States. So I purchased it.

I didn't learn this until I got back to the USA, but it turns out that the toy was not really a toy, but a large puzzle. Not a jigsaw puzzle, though. Instead, it was like a very large model airplane, and had about 500 parts to glue together. Moreover, once you glued it together, it couldn't move. It would just stand there, like Mike Pence, but he looks like Mecha-Godzilla. Mecha-Pence!

I never glued it together. It's sitting in a box in my garage.

One day, though, I will fill with determination, put it together, and stand it up in Briscoe's room.

And he won't notice it. Then his friend Hyruss will accidentally destroy it and blame Briscoe's other friend, Tucson.

And that will be the end of the saga of my time in Akihabara.

# JANUARY 1, 2023, MORE FOR REAL

# 12

# Bullet Train: Fine, and Better than Bullet Train

After sending our excess baggage—read: a soon-to-be-disappointing Mecha-Godzilla, and a few other Godzilla-themed kaiju —to the airport, we decided to examine Gotenyama Trust City park in the daylight.

In the morning brightness, it was a glorious welter of autumn colors (even though it was winter!), but it didn't have the inviting eeriness that it had shown a couple of days ago, at 4 AM. No longer did it seem like an uncanny ode to a fey trash can, but more like a typical—albeit beautiful—park, the kind of place an American like me would visit in order to throw rocks at the pigeons. It was still the sort of location I would delight in, but in the brightness, I felt a little vulnerable, as though Japanese people (or worse, other tourists) would pass through, thereby disturbing whatever reverie I had worked myself into.

After about fifteen minutes, we had our fill of the park. Shawn and I bid Tokyo farewell and began our journey to Kyoto. First stop: the Shinagawa train station!

We had tickets awaiting us at the train station, but unfortunately there was a line to pick them up. So, while we waited in line, I browsed the brochures for cities to visit while in Japan. One brochure I examined advertised the Ōita prefecture. Among the many activities you could do in Ōita, one stood out to me: eating chicken. Ōita was proud to announce that its little city, Nakatsu, was home to one of Japan's "top three chickens."

I saw this reference to "top three" maybe a couple of more times in Japan; at least once to "top three eggs", and (perhaps) another time to "top three cats."[1] Now, if someone in the US said something like, "this is a top three regional law school", I would think: it's the third best law school in the region.[2] After all, if you were talking about the second or

---

1. There's a significant chance that I never saw mention of top three cats but instead imagined my terrible cat, Avon Meowsdale, trying to justify his existence by claiming that he was a "top three cat." He is not a top three cat. He might be bottom three. Maybe you think it's unkind for me to rag on my cat like this. But you don't know him. He drools, he scratches the furniture, he pees on our curtains, blankets, and couches, he has really stinky poops, he always tries to stick his face in whatever I'm eating while I'm eating it, he wakes Shawn up at 3 AM to feed him, he won't let anyone pick him up, he vomits on a daily basis, he induces stronger allergic reactions in Shawn and me than any other cat in the world, he's mean to strangers, and he's scared of Briscoe. His only redeeming features are that he's a very handsome cat, and he's always been in incredible health, which is actually not a virtue when you take into account what his health is keeping alive. If you're a cat-lover, don't worry: I don't hate cats. I just hate *him*.

2. I owe this observation to Scott Aukerman, the host of the podcast *Comedy Bang! Bang!* I have never met Mr. Aukerman, but I did once see him milling about in an establishment called Pirates Dinner Adventures.

first best thing, why wouldn't you just say that? But in Japan, it seems to be a way of bragging with plausible deniability. If enough merchants claim their product is a top three product, you realize that they're saying that what they're selling is at least very good, and that perhaps is the best, but they're not putting themselves out there enough for you to be sure. Indeed, I wonder whether they themselves get confused about what they're claiming. If you want to be a tall poppy, but you don't want to be the *tallest* poppy, then maybe use a scale that confuses even *you*: "guys, look at me! I'm 104 inchimeters!"[3]

Anyway, after getting our ticket, I picked up some meals for our two-hour long train ride to Kyoto. I have to say, what they offered at the train station was jaw-dropping. They had more prepared meals than Trader Joe's (or maybe I should say Trader Yosefu's) and they ranged from sashimi to (cold) fried chicken. (I gave that range because I got Shawn some sashimi and myself some cold fried chicken.) That said, they also offered beef meals, extravagant sushi platters, edamame, rice, and so forth. And I should add that everything was elegantly packaged. Shawn's sashimi looked like it was wrapped in a beautiful green leaf, and my fried chicken came in a fetching container that suggested that your Japanese wife prepared it for you without expecting any thanks, and did so simply to help you ease your brain after you had ruthlessly dunked it in an alcohol bath with the boys after you all lost ¥87,330 at the horse races. I may be projecting here.[4]

---

3. This dovetails with an observation Iyer observed: "'The Japanese managed to create a competitive society *sans* competition,' Arthur Koestler concluded in 1959" (*A Beginner's Guide to Japan*, p. 167).

4. Part of me has always wanted to be a horse.

Anyway, the fried chicken came with a pile of rice topped with a sour plum, a side of pickled ginger, and what was probably seasoning. I should have used the seasoning, because that fried chicken was dry and tough. (I didn't use the seasoning because I thought it was desiccant. But why would food come with inedible and poisonous desiccant? I don't know, maybe you want to kill yourself because of how dry that fried chicken was!) As for the sashimi, it was nothing special, even for trainfish, except that the mackerel was delightfully oceanic and vinegary. Mackerel rules.

Before consuming the food, I was feeling a little depleted, so I got myself a hot coffee from the hot rack of a drink stand, and got Shawn a cold coffee from the cold rack of the *same* drink stand. I was amazed that small tornadoes weren't constantly coming into being because of the uninterrupted mingling of hot and cold fronts.

Finally, we boarded the Shinkansen to Kyoto. If you're reading this, chances are you're more familiar with the English rendering of "Shinkansen": *Bullet Train*.[5] Yes, I was finally on a bullet train, ready to be launched at 200 miles per hour into the heart of Kyoto.

I presume the bullet train reaches such high speeds thanks to a gigantic, centrally located coal furnace, as the heat inside our train-car was like being plunged into a fryer. Even though I was sitting next to the window seat, I had to take off my coat and sweater immediately, for fear of melting into a top three puddle. And yes, I considered taking off my T-shirt and wowing the Japanese with my shock of chest hair,[6] but I also knew that

---

5. If you haven't seen the movie, you must drop whatever you're doing and immediately avoid it.

6. My brother once described the pattern my torso hair makes as "a lobster, holding two pepperoni, flying above a Christmas tree." The pepperoni are my nipples.

doing that would lead to my instant and permanent imprisonment, so I sadly yielded to local propriety.7

While I was next to the window, Shawn got the middle seat, and taking his seat next to her was a small child, Briscoe's age or younger, who was sitting near, but not next, to his parents. This was an ill omen, as children, especially little boys, range in behavior from "fidgety" to "war criminal", so Shawn and I got ready for the likelihood of being buttonholed by a yammering Japanese child who wouldn't accept either that we didn't understand Japanese, or that we didn't want to play with him, or that we didn't secretly enjoy having drinks constantly spilled on us.

This being Japan, though, the child was a model of good behavior. His parents gave him his own ornate lunch box, from which he dutifully and competently ate his victuals. Once he was done with that, he took out some paper and drew pictures, and then he read a book. A couple of times, he got up and went over to his parents, but I think this was just to share

---

7. One thing that I've noticed since writing this book is that, throughout my time in Japan, I had an abiding, lowkey fear of being thrown into a Japanese jail. As it turns out, Briscoe is also always scared that the slightest infraction will lead to his and my imprisonment. Example: the other day, I wanted to go to the movie theater, get some movie popcorn, and leave. I was with Briscoe at the time, and, upon hearing of my plans, he begged me not to do it. "Why not?" I asked, genuinely confused. "Because it's against the law, and the police will come, and we'll be put in jail, and we'll die in jail." Here I thought I was often nervous in Japan because there were so many unwritten rules that I feared violating, but I'm relieved to know that it's just hereditary paranoia, and I will forever be scared of my environment, no matter how benign.

his latest patents.[8] It goes without saying that his parents were also quite patient with him. Classic patient patent parents.[9]

As for us, we had four jobs to do: Shawn, of course, was on Tik Tok duty; she needed to be aware of whatever mischief the Chinese Communist Party was up to, and the only way to track them was to watch two hours of make-up tutorials and short videos of BTS members flirting with their audience, in particular the forty-year-old wine-mom segment. I continue to be amazed by her vigilance with regard to the ChiCom menace.

I had to do the other three jobs: first, write some of this Japan travelogue. Check. Second, take a twenty-minute nap. Thanks to the 95 degree room temperature, I didn't so much *do* this job as it *befell* me. My third job was to see Mount Fuji from the bullet train as we left Tokyo. I regret to say that I fell down on the third job. Either I slept through it, or I wrote through it, or Mt. Fuji is like that gorilla in the background of that one psychology video. I was too busy focusing on words to see the famous, gigantic mountain that the train conductor probably screamed about.

Gressis, you had *one* job to do, and you only did two of them!

---

8. "In the 1990s, scientists living in the United States won forty-four Nobel Prizes, while those working in Japan–with a population and funding roughly half as big–received just one. Yet, in the same period, Japan applied for far more patents than any other nation on the planet" (*A Beginner's Guide to Japan*, p. 49).

9. I smile every time I read this. I'm so great.

# 13

# Frankenstein's Monster's Master's Servant's Hotel

It was only when we were arriving in Kyoto that Shawn pointed out the similarities between Kyoto and Tokyo. Not any similarities in the cities themselves, but rather their nominal similarities: both city-names comprise two syllables: "to" and "kyo". You have "To-Kyo" and "Kyo-To". When you put "to" in front of "kyo", you get "eastern city", and when you put "kyo" in front of "to" you get "capital city." Of course, Tokyo is the capital city today, but back when Kyoto was named, it was where the emperor resided, and as I discovered when we explored Kyoto, there was a lot of residual emperordom.

I'll get to that in chapters 19 and 30. In the meantime, we arrived, and we had to figure out the best way to get from the Kyoto train station to our destination, the Kyoto Ritz-Carlton. As we had just spent a long time in a very fast sauna, our brains were misfiring, and we couldn't figure out what to do. Well, Shawn couldn't figure out what to do, because she was suffering from long Covid on top of heat stroke; I didn't even try to figure out what to do, as by this point in our journey I had become fully used to putting my life in Shawn's hands, and just wanted to be told what to do.[1] Psychologists have a name for this phenomenon: it's called "fully embraced helplessness."

Since Shawn couldn't think her way through navigating the bus system, we opted for a taxi. Now, Shawn had told me about the peculiarity of Japanese taxis: the driver was supposed to open the door for you, you were supposed to get into the car, and then he was supposed to close the door after you.

Reader, that's exactly what happened.

Anyway, he dropped us off at the Ritz-Carlton, and I have to tell you: boy, is this a nice hotel!

It's contiguous to the Kamo River, and from the opposing bank,[2] you can take in the whole structure. The building is long and squat, with the first trio of floors protected by beautiful greenery, while the fourth and fifth floors face the world through giant windows. There was something a touch brutalist about it from the outside, as though the hotel quietly muttered, "nothing to see here. There aren't lots of rich people inside, silkily escaping life's privations. Move along."

The hotel entrance, however, was through a quiet side-gate (there's no entrance where you'd expect a front entrance to be), into what I'll call an off-kilter courtyard. Whereas a typical courtyard grandly supports you with a big square of lawn or sweeping porte cochere drawing you toward an impressive double-height door, the Ritz instead presented you with a short, irregular flagstone pathway to a discreet and normal-height sliding door. A rock garden bordered the left and trees bordered the pathway to

---

1. I should note that by "journey" I mean "our twenty-year relationship".

2. "Body of water", not "financial institution".

the right. Does that make any sense? As I've mentioned before, I'm not good at describing layouts.[3]

Anyway, upon entering the hotel, you should see a prominently displayed, out-of-commission rickshaw, a tribute to servitude. Then, upon turning onto the flagstone path, you walk straight ahead for around 100 feet, and then the entrance to the hotel is on your left. By the way, if you continued walking straight ahead and neglected to enter the hotel, you would tumble over a railing into a rivulet about thirty feet below. I should say, none of us entering the hotel actually failed to notice the railing and flipped into a watery hospital bed or, more likely, grave. Instead, we would just, like, glance down and notice two floors of hotel, not to mention the pretty rivulet below us, and then walk into the hotel.

The hotel was instantly luxurious, with a staffer guiding you to the bar and even showing you where to find free hand sanitizer. We were led past a narrow lobby with plush chairs arranged next to windows concealed by dark, slatted blinds. Doors separated this slip of a lobby from the rest of the hotel. Passing through the interior doors, you encounter another lounge, one doubling as a servery for breakfast in the morning and high tea after noon. This spot was considerably brighter than the first lounge and exuded library-vibes. Passing through this tea-brary, we were seated at a high-top next to a bar and given refreshment. Finally, the staff member who initially escorted us handed us off to another staff member, Igor, from Russia.

Igor spoke nearly perfect British English, with nary a tell that he was a non-native English speaker (the only giveaway was that he punched a

---

3. My wife was in and out of that hotel more times than I was, and she assures me that my description bears no relationship to reality. Note that I wrote that description while looking at photographs of the hotel.

nearby Ukrainian). He walked Shawn through the logistics of the hotel room (free breakfast, a luggage valet, what credit card would be on file, etc.) and, most important, put up with my many questions: "Where are you from? Why do you do your hair like that? How long have you lived here? What do you do for fun? Are you familiar with the more famous Igor, from literature?" I'd tell you his answers, but I don't really remember, because for me the point of asking questions is not for the askee to answer them, but for me, the self-absorbed asker, to ask them. I'm a philosopher, remember?

After we finished up with Igor, they assigned us a lady staff member wearing a kimono, and she also walked Shawn through many forgettable formalities, but I was too intimidated to question her in the same way I had interrogated Igor. After several minutes of paperwork, she escorted us to the elevator. As Shawn and I walked into the elevator, she stayed behind, told us to have a nice day in Japanese, and, as the doors closed, entered into a full bow.

I don't think I will ever forget that full bow as long as I live. Probably no one in my life has ever so strongly conveyed, in a single motion, that they were there to serve me, and that I was an honored guest. Like, if an American did that, it would come off as deeply inauthentic. Indeed, it was difficult for me to accept: I felt fraudulent, like I don't deserve such treatment, but also that no one should give such treatment. I felt alienated from the culture, wondering what kind of place would have people who thought of me and themselves in the way that that bow communicated. I felt my cheeks flush, and I felt embarrassed that I was here at all.

I'm probably making much too much of a big deal of this simple motion. I don't know if there is any culture where touching is exclusively reserved for intimates, but if there are such cultures, perhaps members of those cultures would feel the way about handshakes that I felt about bows. Probably for this woman, this bow was just her way of saying, "have a great day!" while she examined her shoes for scuff marks.

I quickly overcame my discomfitedness and followed Shawn to our hotel room. It was a glorious suite. And it had better have been: it cost $1,200 a night, in 2023 dollars! I must add, though, that *we* didn't pay that: instead, we used points earned through Shawn's American Express card to cover the room. Truly, this was the room that hooch and BTS merchandise built!

Though a video–or, to be frank, literally anyone–can do a better job of conveying to you what the room looked like, here's the gist: our chamber was organized into two parallel passageways that both led into the main room. Beyond the bed, in the main room, a serene table sat next to a window that opened onto a Japanese garden tableau visible only to your room. This garden immediately and powerfully impressed calm upon you. The design of the room was compact and elegant: wooden drawers pulled out to tempt with displays of alcohol, tea, and coffee, all paired with glassware and fine china. A walk-in closet lit automatically. The bathroom had a large tub perched on teak slats and smoked glass for privacy. Presumably, the toiletries were also fancy, but I would no more recognize a fancy toiletry than I would a yoga pose, which is to say I would recognize it only if it was made by P90X.

As useful as this description may be for giving a sense of what the room looked like,[4] it couldn't communicate how I *felt* upon arriving in this room: rich. I felt like a rich person. I immediately wanted to find some minor imperfection in the room so that I could punish someone for it. But no imperfection was found, which made me even more furious! Unable

---

4. It's not.

to vent my spleen, I settled for going to the bathroom, where I pooped pomp and micturated majesty.

Rather than explore Kyoto, Shawn and I baptized our habitation of this room in the way that a long-time married couple, very much in love, does: by lying down and looking at our phones.

# 14

# In Which I Really Make a Meal Out of This Dinner

After gorging on our daily dose of curated oblivion, we put our smartphones down and got to exploring Kyoto. We had a 5:30 PM dinner appointment at a highly regarded sushi restaurant, Sushi Gion Matsudaya, and Shawn thought the walk to the restaurant would occasion a pleasant opportunity to see her favorite Japanese city, Kyoto.

As of 2023, Kyoto had a population of 1,459,640 (according to my favorite website, worldpopulationreview.com), making it almost exactly as populous as San Antonio. I've never been to San Antonio, but I imagine it looks like an old-timey western frontier town with tumbleweeds for townsfolk and a cow for a mayor. Kyoto is quite different. Indeed, Shawn told me she thought it the most beautiful city in the world.

I didn't. To me, Kyoto looked unimpressively squat and washed out, its buildings the color of weathered wood. In part, this must have been due to the weather, and my location: my first day in Kyoto saw dark clouds hovering above our hotel, which was perched next to the Kamo River. Rather than having pale walls running alongside, the river was bordered by dry, yellowing grass. And, perhaps because it was New Year's Day, there weren't lots of people walking about. It wasn't deserted, but it felt like we weren't near the action. There also didn't seem to be many colors, nor were the buildings particularly tall or eye-catching. Like the Mos Eisley spaceport, it felt like a place where people went to be inconspicuous.

And yet, there was a subtlety and grace to Kyoto that you had to work to notice. Behind the dark clouds, there was a hint of sunlight, and no threat of rain. The grass around the river gently rolled up to pleasant, well-maintained walkways. The people were uniformly nice to look at—draped in soft colors, with few loud humans or t-shirts doubling as product placement. Despite the limited color palette, the pattern of grays that coated the buildings was thoughtfully done, and seemed designed to exemplify architectural dignity.

I would describe *Florence* as beautiful, not Kyoto. As I use the term, beauty has a certain drama to it—striking colors, unusual symmetry—that Kyoto lacked. But what I would describe Kyoto as is *graceful*.

The walk from our hotel to Sushi Gion Matsudaya (so named because it was a restaurant serving sushi made by Chef Matsudaya, and was located in a part of Kyoto known as Gion), was, of course, pleasant and easy. One thing I learned about cities from my time spent observing Japan is that a city's layout and presentation gradually creates certain moods in its dwellers. This is a commonplace observation, one I've seen others make, but my time in Kyoto was the first time I noticed it happening to me, in slow motion. I felt a lightness dawn on my person.

Eventually, we had to take our leave from the river and stroll into Gion, the historical heart of the city. The small restaurant was at the end of a maze of twisting, narrow streets. The exterior was stylishly sleek and unremarkable—it would have been easy to miss if you didn't know what to look for. As we had arrived five minutes early for our reservation, we had a little bit of time to get ourselves ready.

Sushi is one of my favorite kinds of food, and Los Angeles has an excellent set of offerings. I've been to some extremely high-end sushi restaurants in LA, but I had the feeling that, as good as it was in my homeland, it would be even better in its homeland. Consequently, I was very excited to have fish in the environment in which fish originally evolved: carved into strips by a taciturn Japanese man on a wooden bar in front of six tourists. So, that's how I got ready: by thinking about how good this dinner was going to be.

Shawn and I, along with a pair of women, entered as soon as Sushi Gion opened promptly at 5:30 PM. A couple of minutes afterwards, another couple entered. I remember nothing about them except that they were white Americans, he had a beard and was tall, and she wore a dress and was short. They said maybe six words during the entire meal, two of which were "water, please". I will not refer to them again.

The picture on Sushi Gion Matsudaya's website is highly representative, down to the five bottles and one jug on the left-hand side of the kitchen. It was a small place: the bar seated six people, and the restaurant was run by a husband-and-wife team—he did the food preparation (I was going to say "cooking", but there wasn't much of that) and she spoke most of the English, took our drink orders, delivered us our libations, and no doubt did a lot of important behind-the-scenes things. He was the talent and public face of the operation, and she was the person who kept the venture afloat and prevented him from falling into the gorilla pit at the local zoo.[1]

---

[1]. I may be projecting from my and, to a greater extent, Shawn's marriage.

Chef Matsudaya himself appeared to be in his sixties (which, being Japanese, meant he was probably in his late 180s) and his wife looked a few years younger. He had an expression and demeanor that I can describe only as "disdainful Basset hound". As for his wife, she gave off real Fievel-from-An-American-Tail energy. She was delighted by everything and very short.

We could choose from a small array of beverages on offer: draft beer, shōchū, Hibiki whiskey, Yamazaki whiskey, plum wine, white wine by the glass, various wines by the bottle, Royal Blue Tea,[2] "Nothcold" [sic?] green tea, still water, and sparkling water. The end. However, you had only one option for the food: the chef's tasting menu, aka "omakase."

As you might expect, there were a lot of different sushi and sashimi on that menu. I don't have the vocabulary to reconstruct my gustatory-visual

---

2. I was extremely intrigued by the Royal Blue Tea. The restaurant gave each pair of patrons three sheets of paper: one that I already described to you, listing the general beverages; one listing the wines they had on offer; and one singing a hymn to Royal Blue Tea. At the top of that paper was the profligately capitalized catechism, "Is This Wine? No, It is Tea. A New Standard in Luxury Tea, Royal Blue Tea." After that, much laudatory prose followed (starting with the question, "If this is tea, what was I drinking before?" and ending with the remark, "On a par with the best of wine and champagne, the dream of the perfect tea come true"). I like tea, and I love novelty in dining, but I *love* fancy whisky and sake, so the offer of such fascinating tea, on this occasion, felt to me as though I had received word that I got into my dream graduate school, only to learn moments later that I *also* got into Hogwart's. In other words, despite my strong desire to sample that tea, I just couldn't justify spending my limited beverage space on something that didn't get me, like, really drunk.

experiences in such a way that they don't become repetitive. So, get ready for some repetition!

The meal began with Chef Matsudaya getting six bowls out and heating some tuna soup on a stove behind him. In addition, he took out some unusual implements, the most alarming of which was a yanagiba knife with a two-foot-long, presumably vorpal, blade. He and his wife left the room, leaving you to your building anticipation, but soon returned bearing a plate with two large octopus tentacles next to two glistening flesh-tubes,[3] then plated some filets of tuna, mackerel, salmon, and yellowtail, among other less-famous sea beasts.

While we waited for our tuna soup and its successors, Shawn and I, as well as the two ladies, received the glassware that would hold our drinks, along with the standard hot towel to clean your hands and face. My glass was thick-lipped, sturdy, and smoky, and festooned with five large, red seashells, while Shawn's more squat glass was gold and traced with red veins and dotted asymmetrically with red dollops. Red and white blobs floated weightlessly over the glass interior. The overall effect made the outside glass seem like a snapshot of a forest fire while the inside looked like cherry blossoms adrift in the wind. Shawn cooed over the glassware, as she could tell how well-crafted and expensive it was.

The two women to our left had asked Mrs. Matsudaya for wine recommendations and had received a bottle of white wine over which they delighted with quiet glee, while Shawn and I shared a bottle of Isojiman sake. The two bozos to our right got a glass of wine and a beer, and I swear that's the last time I'll mention them.

---

[3] Sometimes, you have to be really skilled to describe something so that it *doesn't* sound pornographic. I humbly apologize for my lack of skill.

Tangent: I think sake may be my favorite alcoholic beverage, tied with whiskey. More than any other drink I've ever had in my life, it pairs perfectly with food, to where if I'm eating sushi without having sake, I hallucinate sake-tastes as I eat.4 The quality can go through the roof too, and although there's always a sweet riciness to the body of the sake, the bouquet and the aftertaste can vary a lot. When we poured our sake into our fancy glasses, the fluid in my vessel appeared light green, as though it was a gentle tea, whereas Shawn's looked bright red, like fancy Kool-Aid.

Back to the meal: the chef prepared a green paste on a dense cutting board shaped like a tennis racket. Shawn and I quickly realized that he was making us real wasabi, not the green horseradish we get in the USA. This made Shawn very excited, because I guess real wasabi is very good? Spoiler alert: I tried it (obviously!) but I detected little difference between real wasabi and fake wasabi. Then again, I prefer Mrs. Butterworth's to real maple syrup, so I guess my taste in condiments, like my taste in women, sometimes veers to the skanky.5

Unfortunately, I'm not sure whether what I'm about to recount is the exact order of all the dishes. I tried looking online for refreshers, but Chef Matsudaya changes the menu daily, depending on the quality of what's available, so that was a no-go. Instead, I'm relying on my phone's recordings, as well as my fairly expansive experience with sushi, to reconstruct this wonderful meal:

---

4. My doctor has told me this is a rare condition called "pre-delirium tremens", and that my having it means I'm in terrible danger, and that I must stop drinking. I told him, "more like pre-delirium tremendous!"

5. If you think I'm saying *Shawn* is a skank, you'd be wrong. Alas. If she ever decides to get a snake tattoo, though, you'll be the first to know!

"YOU'LL NEVER TAKE ME ALIVE!" Shawn screamed, as the orca whale, now free from the electro-harpoon, barreled toward her through the flooded restaurant. The ChatGPTigershark, which Chef Matsudaya promised us would not try to take over the world, was immediately attempting just that. Now fully a werewolf, I charged the orca, hoping not only to save my wife, but also to avenge the deaths of those two people who never spoke, who had prophesied all this before.

And that's all I remember.

Back to reality: the first real dish featured three kinds of sashimi—seabream, yellowtail, and medium fatty tuna—served with a dipping vessel of sesame oil, and laid across beautiful china. The yellowtail was extremely good, and the medium fatty tuna had a nice sharp taste to it, a great union of the fattiness of fatty tuna and the crispness of lean tuna. I don't generally like seabream, because it's always tough, but this one was not, allowing me to finally focus on seabream taste, which was ... forgettable. I mean, I'm sure there are seabream aficionados out there whose eyes would roll back in their head when they tried this, but I am not one of them, I have never met one, and I hope I never do.

As good as the sashimi was, the best part of the experience was the presentation. Matsudaya-san began by forwarding a slab of yellowtail shaped like a horn. Off the bottom of the horn he sliced a small piece, which he deposited almost disgustedly on a small white plate. Homing in on the yellowtail, he positioned his left hand near the base, and the other hand lined the fiendish knife alongside his fingers. Pressing the knife into the flesh, he pulled it toward himself, and the knife seemed to topple over, like a drunkard tripping over a rock. He did this six times, creating six equal wafers of yellowtail. Each time, I involuntarily held my breath, not because I was fearful he would slice his finger off (whereupon I would feel obliged to eat it, simply out of politeness), but because he somehow conveyed great drama with each motion.

He used a very different technique in preparing the seabream. Though he brought out a long, thick slab of the fish, he cut off a quite modestly sized rectangle. Holding the smaller piece tightly with his left hand, he gingerly sliced through it with the blade held in his right. Finally, crossing his left hand over his right hand, he draped one square of seabream over another that was drooping like a poisoning victim. Again, the whole display was mesmerizing.

So mesmerizing, in fact, that, dummy that I am, I simply enjoyed him preparing the medium fatty tuna instead of recording it for the purposes of sharing it with you. When will I learn: special moments are to be captured, not enjoyed?!

I should say, while writing this entry, I got hungry. So I went to If You Don't Like It, You Can Sushi, a new sushi restaurant near me. It was quite the experience, recollecting my time in a Michelin-starred sushi restaurant in Japan while dining in an all-you-can-eat sushi restaurant in Los Angeles. The main thing they had in common was that in both places, you could only stay for two hours. After that, I'm struggling to locate any similarities. I suppose it's sort of like comparing General Patton to Mr. Beast? Still, the server at You Can Sushi helped me identify some sushis in the video that I did record, so for that I'm thankful.

The next dish was my favorite kind of raw fish: mackerel. I'm the only person I know whose favorite sushi is mackerel because I get how the world works, and no one else does. By that, I mean that if you eat fish, you should eat it because you like how fish tastes. Tuna-lovers are people who like bland protein for their big stupid muscles. Swordfish-lovers are people who wished they had a steak but are settling for fish. Salmon is delicious, and is technically a fish, but is sui generis—what other fish tastes like salmon? Steelhead? Trout? That's only three fish total! No, mackerel is where it's at: it tastes like a fin-fish should taste. When the Divine made mackerel, it's like God said, "what if fish, but more?"

We'll get back to mackerel in a moment. Before I describe it, though, I need to note that this is when Chef Matsudaya finally sliced into the pale, glistening flesh-tube that had otherwise been unobtrusively throbbing to the side, like the penis of a shy creep. He nonchalantly sliced it into six pieces and placed it on a pan below his working surface, hidden from view. "What's that one?" I asked. "Blowfish", he said. It was at this point that the mood of the room turned from quiet to boisterous.

Blowfish liver, as many people know, is deadly poisonous to some people. As I learned on January 2, from our (then future, now past) guide, Helga (you'll hear more about her in chapter 20), some people are allergic to blowfish liver, and some aren't. If you're not allergic, you'll be transported to a paradise of flavor. If you are allergic, you'll just be transported to paradise. I mean, you'll die. And the thing is, the only way to discover whether you're allergic to blowfish liver is to try it.[6]

This was not blowfish liver, though! It's illegal to prepare blowfish liver in Japan, so a swanky joint like this wasn't going to risk its license to sell food just to perhaps murder westerners, as appetizing as that may sound to some xenophobic Japanese. Still, it was blowfish, and *used* to have a

---

6. This is what Guide Helga told me! But it's not true. Well, it's true that blowfish liver is lousy with a neurotoxin called "tetrodotoxin"; it's true that even if you cook it, you don't destroy the poison; and it's also true that you *can* die from it. But what's false is that you *always* die from it. According to the article, "Tetrodotoxin Poisoning Due to Pufferfish Ingestion in the United Arab Emirates" (see https://www.ncbi.nlm.nih.gov/pmc/articles/PMC9911934 ), you can survive tetrodotoxin poisoning, though I didn't read the article, so maybe you can survive it only if you live in the UAE.

blowfish liver, which made it thrilling. It's not like meeting Al Capone, but it is like meeting his lawyer.

We'll get back to the blowfish in a moment. We're still on the mackerel! Taking out the mackerel filet, the chef pulled its skin off like the satisfying peel of the plastic covering off of a new television (don't worry; later, he put it back on). At this point, my recording stopped, though I did see him wiggle his fingers above the mackerel carcass, as though he was involving the somatic components of a necromantic spell. Whatever he did, he ended up with twelve slices of mackerel that he placed on a pan laced with parchment paper. He slid the pan into his small convection oven, and put it on blast.

While the oven got to blasting, he focused on one of the octopus tentacles that had been menacing us this entire meal. His cutting technique was different with the octopus tentacle, because he must know that, even in death, octopuses are cunning adversaries. Instead of slicing through the piece in a swift motion, he sawed through the tentacle with a rocking movement, as though he had to struggle to get his blade through the quick-witted octopus flesh.

When finished with that, it was time to remove the mackerel from the convection oven. By this point, an aroma of piscine[7] crispiness caressed our smell-buds as he presented the cooked mackerel.

Immediately after the pan of mackerel departed the oven, a new pan of blowfish took their place, all thanks to Chef Matsuyada's busy fingers. I could have sworn I heard the two pans say "morning, Sam. Morning, Ralph" to each other, but again, I stupidly forgot to record the exchange.

Matsudaya removed the mackerel from the cooking parchment and gracefully transferred it via chopstick to six ceramic plates. Once expertly

---

7. Pretentiousness is the price of non-repetition, o reader.

positioned together, each pair of mackerel received two brushes of oil. Two thick hunks of octopus nestled next to the mackerel, sesame seeds sprinkled on top. The chef placed a sprig of green seaweed on top of the mackerel, positioned a spot of mustard next to the octopus, and drizzled yuzu sauce on the corner of the plate.

It was, of course, the best mackerel I ever had, making it the best sashimi I've ever had. It merged the fresh, oceanic, oily taste of mackerel with the carbonic flavor of blistered fish-skin. I didn't think I could have those two flavors from the same thing simultaneously, but here they were, together, as bizarre and enjoyable as an employee training video directed by David Lynch.

This, by the way, gets to a theory of mine on fine dining. If you're going to splurge on food and spend $600 on a dinner (which is roughly what we spent), then it's not a successful dinner unless you have at least one of the best somethings—the best ribs, the best fluke, the best cheese—you've ever had in your life. Obviously, then, my meal at Sushi Gion Matsudaya was already a success.

I thought at this point that Chef Matsudaya would just throw us out, his job done. But no, the dinner kept going! It was time for the blowfish. The blowfish underwent a pretty dramatic metamorphosis in the oven: each piece transformed from springy, shiny scallop to fire-roasted marshmallow. Crackling developed around the blowfish chunks, giving each a sturdy appearance, as though it was a dumpling, but upon coming out of the oven they all sighed and collapsed in on themselves, like ruined soufflés.

Matsudaya pinched the skin of each blowfish-piece briefly, lightly lifting the loose casing of each one, and then sawing through the center, producing a divided blowfish unit. He used a thin, metal spatula to slide the pieces onto small blue-and-white platters, holding on to the skin during the precious moments when the pieces hovered in the air between the paper and the plate.

And then, we ate it.

I wish I could say that eating blowfish was as satisfying as David Copperfield's making the Statue of Liberty disappear,[8] and that this meal was all leading up to this moment. But it wasn't like British royalty eating pineapples in the 18th century. That said, it differed from any fish I've ever eaten. It was like eating crab Rangoon, but none of it was cheese or flour—it was just all fired-fish-flesh.

As I said above, when we learned that blowfish was on offer, four out of six of us became boisterous. The two robots to our right didn't seem to give a shit, but, as I said, I will never discuss them again. However, the two women to our left opened up at this point.

"Well, that was different," the larger, tanner, blonde one said in a British accent. The petite brunette nodded yes. "I can't say I'll recommend that to other people, but I'm glad I tried it!" she continued, in an American accent. "How was the wine?" I asked. "Oh, it was amazing," the American said. "Ah. We love wine, but when I'm having sushi, I have to have sake," I said.

I didn't remember either of their names, but the petite American looked like a "Rebecca", while the burly blonde Brit looked like a "Lucy."[9] I sat right next to Rebecca, and when she talked, she would turn to make eye contact with me. She was pretty, had big eyes, patches of acne on her cheeks, and a head shaped like an upside-down pear. Her hair was up in

---

8. All he actually did was sell it back to the French.

9. Though I've described Lucy as "large" and "burly", I don't want you to conclude that she's overweight. She wasn't. She just had the energy of a thick, strong biker chick who'd been in a lot of fistfights.

a bun, while Lucy's hair looked in profile, and from the perspective of someone who knows as little about women's hair as he does about their shoes, like a bouffant.

"Where are you guys from?" Rebecca asked. "We're from Los Angeles." "Oh, where in LA?" "The valley. Have you been to LA?" "Yeah," Rebecca replied. "I lived there for nine years!" "Where do you live now?" I asked. "England," she said. "Why England?" I wondered. "For love," she said, and smiled at Lucy and squeezed her arm.

"Ah," I sagely thought: "Lucy must know Rebecca's boyfriend."

Rebecca and Lucy had what looked like an asymmetrical relationship. I couldn't help thinking of bug-eyed Steve Buscemi and taciturn Peter Stomare, only they're lesbians, and they have sex with each other (as opposed to next to each other, in a Minnesota motel room). Rebecca's gaze flitted among Lucy, me, Shawn, and the restaurant; and she described everything as "beautiful" ("this wine tastes beautiful"; "this salmon looks beautiful"; "this text message is beautiful"), while Lucy only looked forward throughout the entire meal, saying very little, probably thinking of her next kill.

The next stage of the meal involved five kinds of fish: squid, halibut, fluke, lean tuna, and fatty tuna. I never off-loaded my memories of how he prepared the squid and the halibut, so just assume there was a knife involved, but despite two carafes of sake and one blowfish, I found his approach to the fluke noteworthy enough for me to resume my recording duties.

Chef Matsudaya retrieved three butterflied fluke filets from his magical repository and stacked them in a pile. He then placed the three filets flesh-up on his carving station. Next, he cut along the left and right sides of the fluke spines. He had cut the three full filets in half, and he now had six filet halves. I understand what happened, because before our trip, I had been helping Briscoe with his third-grade math homework.

Now, he attended to each filet-half. First, he sliced, at a fifteen-degree angle, a deep impression into the flesh, leaving a flap in the middle of the filet. Turning it over, he scored the back six times. After doing this to two filet-halves, he stacked the pair on a ceramic platter, alongside the six strips of squid and halibut, until he had six sliced-and-scored fluke filets.

The lean tuna looked like a giant fish liver: stone grey on the outside, bright red on the inside. I suspect the outside was lightly seared, but I saw no sear marks. Taking a big block of the tuna, he very deliberately sliced it at a seventy-five degree angle. Once he had a stack of six pieces, he moved them to the ceramic platter.

Finally, Chef Matsudaya started work on the fatty tuna. If you've ever seen wagyu beef, it looked like that: pink flesh streaked with countless white capillaries of fat. He sliced it at a similar angle as the lean tuna, scored the flesh (to punish its gluttony), and stacked it once more. He now had a platter of thirty fish slices, but I forgot to note: his wife had brought us ginger before we got to eat. This wasn't sashimi at all ... this was sushi!

Sure enough, after presenting five kinds of fishy[10] offerings, the chef pressed an agglomeration of sticky rice into the underbelly of the squid, and after going back and forth from hand to hand, offered the first piece to Lucy. Stone cold murderer that she is, Lucy knew her edomae table manners, and gobbled it up before Rebecca got her piece. He proceeded in this manner, going next to me, and then Shawn, and presumably even

---

10. Don't worry, I will never write "piscine" again, even if you claim you can use it in a sentence more naturally than I can. I won't be baited into a piscine contest.

offering pieces to the two marble statues sitting to Shawn's right, though I won't again waste anyone's time by even referring to them in the future.

The squid was more tender than squid sushi usually is, but I don't generally like squid sushi, and though I didn't dislike this, it left no impression. The fluke came next. It had a light taste, but was mildly briny, and benefited from crispy skin. Finally, he took out some live prawns. Cradling one in his palm, with its head at his wrist and its tail at his fingers, he speared it through with a six inch wooden stick. When he impaled the prawn it reacted like nothing had happened, because prawns are extravagantly moronic, but he pushed the stick forward until the prawn's tail retracted. It looked much more like a nervous reflex than a thought-through response, much like when I ask my students whether they did last night's reading:

Me: did you read the article by Joseph Heath?
Student (without missing a beat): yes!
Me: did you understand it, or did you find it confusing?
Student (no pause): oh, I understood it.
Me: oh, good! How would you put his main point?
Student (immediately): I didn't read it.

Again, this is just a nervous reflex, which you can produce in the common California college student (genus: collegium studiosum) by presenting it with almost any question.

Having moved on from sake, I was now enjoying the exquisite Hibiki whiskey. Whiskey makes a man mean, even when he expresses himself one year after he's drunk it. (Hence my previous remarks about my students.)

Anyway, though he prepared five prawns in this manner (I wasn't getting one, being allergic to them),[11] he didn't give them to us yet, because he needed to char them a bit. While the prawns suffered in a lidded cast iron pan, he readied the lean tuna.

Chef Matsudaya smooshed the rice into the undersides of the lean tuna flanks, and then brought out a small container of mustard. He somehow lifted individual globules of mustard from the tin using chopsticks, depositing one on each lean tuna slab. Nothing was done to the fatty tuna, except its receiving its customary smudge of oil. But really, doing any more than that would have just been gilding the lily, like putting a dog in an astronaut suit. Don't get me wrong, that's awesome, but the dog doesn't need any adornment.

The lean tuna and the fatty tuna were excellent. The lean tuna was the best I've ever had of that genre, and the fatty tuna was tied in excellence with many top-end sushi places. However, I was quite curious about the prawns, for three reasons. First, I'm allergic to crustaceans, so I'm always curious about them. Second, they were, mere moments ago, alive, and selected by a great Japanese sushi chef. So, these would be at the very top end of crustacean quality. Third, his preparation of them was quite thorough: he slathered some orange ... stuff(? I really don't know what it was) under the prawns, presumably to get them to stick to the rice. He then slapped and patted them all over their bodies, like he was

---

11. Eagle-eyed readers with the memorial powers of elephants will wonder, "hey, if you're allergic to prawns, you're probably allergic to crustaceans, right? And if you're allergic to crustaceans, then how did you know what crab rangoon tastes like?" Yes, I am allergic to crustaceans. As for knowing how crab rangoon tastes, how do you think I figured out that I'm allergic to crustaceans?

massaging tiny mobsters. This just added to my interest in these little oceanic criminals.

It's not the first time something like this has occurred to me. Shawn is not allergic to crustaceans, and we've been to a lot of fancy restaurants together, so I've had many occasions to ask her how good top-end crustaceans are. And every time, her answer is the same: "you're not missing much."

"This time it'll be different," I thought to myself.

Me (whispering): Shawn, how's the prawn?

Her (whispering): You're not missing much.

It was a relief to know that, after a relationship of twenty years, my wife was still willing to lie to me so brazenly.

This whole prawn-situation raised another question for me: what would I get in lieu of a prawn? Supposedly, my replacement-food was always better. However, my alternative didn't seem as promising as the prawns. Whereas Chef Matsudaya made a great show of murdering shrimp, when it came to my dish, all he seemed to do was fetch a large bowl filled with salmon roe. The roe was then perched like a flock of bats on a half-dome of rice, and I landed the whole company in my gullet. Roe may or may not vary significantly in quality, but if it can, then I guess I'm not astute enough to track it.

The next offering was castle stone clam piled on a paper towel in a bowl. It made them look cheap, like a college student just pulled them from his mini fridge. The chef's procedure was as follows: he would grab one from the pile, dry it, slap it with a dab of wasabi, palpate it into some rice, and then brush a soupçon of yuzu sauce on it. It was good, but not the kind of thing you write home about, unless you're a real completionist about your trip to Japan.

The penultimate dish was uni (*i.e.*, sea urchin). If you like sushi—and not just spicy tuna, salmon, and California rolls, but sushi—then of course you love uni. That said, from my amateur point of view, there's not that much to making uni; you just get really good uni and, like, give it to someone. What was most interesting about the uni here was that it came in a wooden box stuffed with other uni. It was almost kind of gross, seeing all that uni; it was like going to Arby's and having them open a can of cheddar sauce in front of you before they give you your beef n' cheddar. Still, it was uni, pure concentrated ocean-goodness, and the chef gave it a dash of sesame oil before presenting it to us on a big green plate that looked like it was made of dried seaweed (it wasn't). In other words, the meal continued to be much better than Arby's.

The last dish of our evening was eel. The chef prepared the eel in a standard way—hot and with yuzu sauce—but in lieu of rice, he wrapped it in seaweed paper and offered it to us as a handroll, Chef's Matsudaya's equivalent of a handshake for a job well done. Probably also an implicit "thanks for all that money!" as well.

You're welcome, Matsudaya-san!

And with that, we left the meal. I wouldn't say we made new friends that night, but I will never forget that mackerel, or those two people who never said anything, whose empty-headed stoicism I will forever admire.

# 15

# Gates Are Only Fun When They Lead to Somewhere That Is Not Just Gates

After our elaborate and satisfying meal, which ended promptly at 7:30 PM, we left for Fushimi Inari-taisha.

What's "Fushimi Inari-taisha"? Explaining that takes some unpacking.

Let's start with Shinto, the indigenous religion of Japan. Shinto revolves around the worship of spirits, aka "kami." Kami are believed to dwell in certain areas, and where there are kami, the Japanese sometimes make shrines to them (as opposed to temples, which are religious places for Buddhism, Japan's other major religion).

One of the kami is "Inari." Inari is the rice god—pretty important for Japan, which for centuries was deprived of pasta. "Fushimi" is a ward in Kyoto and, though Google translate doesn't render it this way, "taisha" seems to be equivalent to "shrine". So, "Fushimi Inari-taisha" is a shrine to the rice god Inari in the Fushimi ward of Kyoto. Or I'm wrong. But it's definitely one of those two possibilities.

Now, not only is Fushimi Inari-taisha a shrine to the rice god, but it's considered to be the most important such shrine. This may be why it is the way it is.

And what way is it? Well, it's built on a mountain that's 769' high and it's not just a single lonely building, but is instead a few buildings and approximately ninety billion torii gates. A torii gate "mark[s] the approach and entrance to a shrine" (japan-guide.com). To me, a torii gate looks like a very large staple. No, not a stable, where horses live, but a staple, a citizen of a stapler.

I don't know why there are so many torii gates dotting this mountain (aka "Mount Inari"), but my theory is that, in honor of rice itself, the Kyotoans created a rice-like amount of gates. These torii gates are colored vermillion and made of wood, rather than colored white and made of rice, so my theory, unlike these gates, may need more support. But, like rice, I'm sticking to it.

Many of these gates were bought (and installed? It wasn't clear) by families or individuals trying to honor someone (themselves? It wasn't clear), and some (allegedly; it wasn't clear) cost a lot more money than others. Because of this system of gates-for-hire, some of the torii gates had writing on them and others didn't.

Aside from the fact that some gates had script carved into them and some didn't, and some had faded paint and others didn't, it was very hard to notice any differences among any of them. It was like going to an amusement park where every ride was bumper cars. I mean, it's fun pretending to team up with an eight-year-old boy only to double-cross him immediately, but after a while, you get kind of tired of making your son cry. Then again, this was, fundamentally, a religious site rather than an amusement park, so perhaps my grumbling would be like a Japanese dude going to St. Peter's Basilica complaining that there wasn't enough manga in the compartments in front of the pews.

A nice thing about Fushimi Inari-taisha is that, unlike other tourist sites we'd visit, it wasn't a one-way path through the grounds. Instead, as with an ant colony, paths away from the epicenter of the shrine were regularly available. This was good, because it takes between two and three hours to surmount and then descend through all the gates. Still, whenever you're on a gated pathway (pathways range from dozens to hundreds of gates long), you're got gates above and around you, and thick trees or steep mountainside right outside those gates, making each short walkway on the grounds feel like a tunnel. It was like a maze where every path you took led to the exit.

This was a useful feature, for after about half an hour of Fushimi Inari-Taisha, it was dark and cold, so we decided we'd had enough of the chilly monotony and just wanted to go back to our lovely hotel. So, we walked to the subway station and took the Karasuma line to the Karasuma Oike stop and, lo-and-behold, whom did we meet at the station but Igor, the Russian staff member who first welcomed us to the Ritz Carlton!

It was strange to see Igor in his street clothes, him leaving the hotel, us going to it.[1] He seemed embarrassed and caught off-guard to see us, as though part of him wanted to go home and the other part of him wanted to tell us about the subway's amenities. We both paused, looking for something to say, and I asked the searching question, "so, uh, where are you off to?" "Oh, I'm going back home", he told an unsurprised us. "We were just at a place with a bunch of toro [sic] gates", I volunteered. "Fushimi Inari-taisho [sic?]", Shawn elaborated. "Oh. They're very nice," he said.

Pause.

---

[1]. There was an episode of *The Simpsons* where Bart and Milhouse saw Principal Skinner in a convenience store. Principal Skinner was wearing slacks and a polo shirt instead of his usual suit and tie. Naturally enough, Bart and Milhouse thought he had gone crazy. Seeing Igor in this setting was like that.

"See you tomorrow!" I said.

"I won't be there tomorrow. Tomorrow's my day off," he replied.

Pause.

"Well, in that case ... goodbye forever?"

We went back to the hotel, went to sleep, and dreamed of Igor performing various services for us. Not sex things.

# JANUARY 2, 2023

# 16

# In Which I Look My Gift Horse in the Mouth and Enjoy Its Mouth (the Ritz is the Gift Horse)

We started the day off with a western breakfast, which we had scheduled for 7:00. We arrived promptly, and were, as of 7:00 AM, the only people present in the modestly-sized dining room, aka "La Locanda". This being Japan in January 2023, we arrived at our tables masked, and then immediately took off our masks. However, since it was a fancy hotel restaurant, they provided us with stylish mask cases to store our masks. Our mask cases had "MASK CASE" written on the lower left-hand side, as well as an illustration of a three-dimensional trapezoid with what looked like a dark flap coming up.

At the time, I thought the drawing of the trapezoid was appropriate, and gave it no further mind. "There are pictures on things, ignore them, that's life", my mind presumably informed me. But looking at a picture of it now on my smartphone, I'm really struggling to decipher it. I *think* the picture on the mask case is a picture of how to properly fold the mask case once you've put your mask in it. I guess it meant, "close the dark flap over the top of the mask case". But the mask case itself had no dark flaps! Honestly, I'm not sure there were any flaps at all, dark or light. It's quite possible the mask case was aspirational, letting you know merely the kind of thing the mask case would like to be.

Anyway, before we got our menus, they offered us juice. I chose grapefruit and Shawn opted for, eh, let's say also grapefruit, and we each received a shooter—approximately two ounces—of our respective juices. If I were a more conventional thinker, I would take a moment to complain about the small Japanese portion sizes, but I realize that, from a global perspective, we Americans are the odd ones out. So, replace the ritualistic "I can't believe how small Japanese portions are!" with a similarly ritualistic "I can't believe how much my American upbringing has deformed my appetites!"

As for the menu, we didn't actually get much choice. Our choices were: coffee or tea (no choice at all, if you ask me) and either a savory egg dish or a sweet French toast/pancake/waffle dish. Both Shawn and I selected the egg dish; she asked that her eggs be poached while I requested benediction for mine.

Besides the shots of juice we started with, they also offered us American-sized glasses of juice. I found that kind of weird: like, "here's your coffee. Also, here's your more-coffee." I received a healthy pour of thick green fluid and Shawn some freshly squeezed orange juice. Around this time they also presented us with a choice of baked good: French roll, chocolate croissant, almond croissant, regular croissant, or an "isaphan croissant", an invention, apparently, of apparently legendary French baker Pierre Hermé, who, it's apparent, is not a parent. The isaphan croissant was a lychee-raspberry-rose croissant. Of course I chose it over the alternatives. Again, I found this kind of weird: like, "you have a choice of three rental cars: Honda, Buick, or rocket ship." Who wouldn't take the rocket ship?![1]

Because the Japanese are very good at making baked goods, the croissant had a beautifully flaky crust, bands of lychee-raspberry glaze, and a trail of rose petals adorning the top. As for the taste, it was ... fine. I mean, it was good! Really! But it wasn't *great*. This, I think, is also a Japanese thing. Or rather, in my four days of experience with Japan, my American palate noticed that there was often a contrast between a food's appearance and my expectations of its flavor. For sweets, this was welcome, as we Americans generally make our confections cloyingly sugary. Even so, the divergence in Japanese food between appearance and taste was occasionally jarring. It's like the books on the bookshelves in an IKEA—you see lots of books with interesting-looking titles, but when you try to read any of them, all you find are paeans to fyrkantigs or flärdfulls.[2]

Anyway, after the croissant, the Ritz presented us with the next item customary in any western breakfast: a tray with lots of stuff on it. Upon our trays were: a glass of thick European-style yogurt topped with honey and granola; a fruit plate comprising a strawberry, an orange segment, a small slice of honeydew melon, and a single green grape; a helping of smoked salmon sprinkled with pickled onions and chives; a ... bowl of cold, cream-colored fluid? And an ... endive and lettuce salad with ... more rose petals? Looking back on it now, it felt like this breakfast was designed by someone who was getting increasingly drunk.

---

1. Shawn picked the almond croissant. Buicks for Shawn!

2. I've actually never opened a book in an IKEA, I have a phone.

Although the salad and ... fluid[3] made me raise my eyebrows, it didn't make me raise a ruckus. Instead, I simply enjoyed everything (except the fruit plate, which I ghosted), and after I finished my salad, salmon, and soup, they gave me my eggs benedict.

Again, this was *beautiful*, a real knockout. On the left side of the plate was a piece of thick, delicious ham laced with grill marks; a plump duck sausage; a piece of crispy bacon atop those two; and on top of *that* a delicate parmesan tuile. On the right was the most perfect-looking eggs benedict you've ever seen: a globe of poached egg perched on a lightly toasted and buttered English muffin, both of which were coated with almost exactly the right amount of golden hollandaise sauce, such that only a smidge dripped off either the yolk or the muffin. Looked at from above, it was like looking at Saturn and its rings, covered with hollandaise sauce.

Those eggs benedict were not as tasty as they looked, but they were *delicious*. And a cool thing was, when you cut into the poached egg with your spoon, the bright-orange yolk spilled out. As you may recall from Chapter 8, I know yolk color results just from the chicken's diet (as opposed to being a one-to-one farm-to-freshness function), but I couldn't help but feel that the bird that produced this egg was a top three chicken.

Truly, I was getting sand-blasted by splendor.

After we finished our breakfast, we walked around the hotel a bit. It was an exquisitely furnished building, and I wanted to explore. Aside from the bank of suites and hotel rooms (which I didn't want to explore – I

---

3. I'm not going to lie, I'm not entirely sure what it was. It was listed on the menu as "dip". But dip for what? There was *way* too much of it for the salad, which came accompanied by a sweet sesame seed dressing anyway. So I just ate it straight, with a spoon.

felt like running into other patrons would have spoiled the illusion that this whole edifice was erected for my benefit on Shawn's command), there were, from what I could tell,[4] three floors. First was the floor we were on, the ground floor: it had La Locanda (swanky breakfastery by day, Italian restaurant by night), the reception, a Pierre Hermé boutique (so *that's* where the isaphan croissants came from!), and a really baller bonsai tree. It was little, but it looked bright and brimming with life; they may as well have glued googly eyes on it, and then glued sunglasses on the googly eyes, and then called it "Johnny Sap."[5] This was a cool little tree!

As for Pierre Hermé boutique, it's a famous French boulangerie with multiple locations worldwide. One was in Kyoto, here in this hotel! It was very alluring, a thirst trap for diabetics. Brightly colored macarons and darkly tempting pastries lorded over an L-shaped glass counter, behind which stood a uniformed employee, fancy marmalades, expensive oils, and upscale cookies, all of which (save the employee) filled adjoining walls. Though I wanted to splurge at Pierre Hermé, I had just eaten breakfast, so I felt no compulsion to burn through our voucher money yet.

---

4. I am not ruling out the possibility that there was a secret floor full of Batman.

5. Once, my brother was running a Dungeons & Dragons game, and, owing to a variety of happenings, it ended up that our party of adventurers had to protect an intelligent, divinely-favored tree from a band of monsters bent on its destruction. The tree had sunglasses, he talked like Elvis, and his leafy branches made it look like he had a mop of curly hair. Upon learning that his name was Johnny Sap, the entire group of players was more motivated to save him than we have been motivated to save anything in our lives, real or fictional. So desirous were we to defeat those who menaced him that you may as well have called him "Helen of Tree."

The second floor was the floor below us. Let's call it "B1." This had Mizuki, their Michelin-starred Japanese restaurant, as well as some large-scale fine art. Finally, there was the floor below B1, which had a small clutch of conference rooms presumably reserved for one last weekend of decadence before Anton Chigurh discovers you and makes you flip coins.

Famous sociopath Ferris Bueller said of his friend Cameron's house, "The place is like a museum. It's very beautiful and very cold, and you're not allowed to touch anything." I felt that way about the Ritz-Carlton, on account of its beauty and the scarcity of people. It didn't feel lived in. But despite that, I felt welcome; I sensed I was allowed to go wherever I wanted, even though I'm probably worth significantly less than the carpet. Making me feel welcome is actually a difficult feat; I'm pretty self-conscious, even paranoid, a lot of the time. I usually think that the difference between people having fun with me and throwing me onto a garbage scow is one wrong remark or misplaced defecation.

Even though I'm not of the leisure or business class that occupies places like this, it seemed like it was permissible for me to be here. I realize that doesn't sound like the most complimentary Yelp review, but given how beautiful, fancy, and important this place was, I sincerely appreciate the good people at the Ritz-Carlton.

# 17

# Public Displays of Religion

After our post-prandial exploration, it was time to walk to Kiyomizudera, a Buddhist temple dedicated to "Kannon, Goddess of Mercy, Lord of Compassion" (according to japan-experience.com). Apparently, "Kiyomizudera" means "pure water temple" (or so says japan-guide.com), and I'm guessing it was called that because the Hosso sect of Japanese Buddhism founded it (in 780) near Otowa Waterfall.

From my brief researches, the Hosso Buddhists followed a school of Buddhism in the Mahayana Buddhistic tradition that believed that the world as we think of it—as an independently existing thing—is an illusion. Instead, the only thing that is real is consciousness.[1]

Despite its ultimately illusory nature, the complex of buildings that composed Kiyomizudera was real enough for my purposes. The first really

---

1. As it happens, I also endorse (or at least, am quite attracted to) the view that the world as we know it consists fundamentally of mentality rather than matter. This view is called "metaphysical idealism." Part of the reason I endorse it is that when people tell me that my fears are all in my head, I can say, "yes, I know. That's literally my view!"

striking structure you encountered was Nio-Mon (the "Gate of the Deva Kings"), a startlingly bright red pagoda at the top of a steep flight of stairs. You did not have to go through the Gate of the Deva Kings to access the rest of Kiyomizudera, though. You could, instead, go through a different pagoda right next to it, Sai-Mon (the west gate). Or you could just walk in the space between the two pagodas.

If you walked through the Gate of the Deva Kings and then hung left (which means walking east), then you would discover a quite peaceful nook that didn't seem to attract many people's interest. In that nook, you'd find a small chamber called Zuigi-Do (Zuigi hall)[2], a bell tower, a Shinto shrine (called "Kasuga-Sha" for "Kasuga Shrine"), another small building called Chuko-Do ("The Restorer's Hall"), and, most interesting of all, a small temple called Mizugo-Kannon-Do, which translates to "Aborted Fetus Temple Dedicated to the Goddess of Mercy."

It wasn't clear to me whether Mizugo-Kannon-Do was dedicated to miscarriages, fetuses that were intentionally aborted, or both. Whichever, it made me wonder, briefly, how the Japanese thought of abortion. Finding the subject uncomfortable, and not getting any answers from the temple, I focused my attention on a basin full of sacred water next to me.

The basin was made of stone, and rested atop a pile of intentionally organized rocks. A bamboo shoot attached to a pipe dripped water into the basin, and above the bamboo shoot was a sign that read:

Do not drink

<u>The sacred water</u>

Please treat with utmost respect

Although the flow of water was quite weak, it seemed to run all the time, making the water overflow from the basin into the rocks below,

---

[2]. Not to be confused with a similar building nearby, Zario Hall.

and staining one side, as though the basin had been weeping. The overall effect was a sad tranquility.

On the stained side was carved a single Japanese character. There was, alas, no translation, but since this basin was very near Mizugo-Kannon-Do, my guess is that whatever the character meant, it was something rueful, like "PTA Meetings."

We made our way deeper into the complex, past five more pagodas—Sutra Hall, Founder's Hall, the Middle Gate, Asakura Hall, and the Covered Passageway—until we got to Hon-Do, *i.e.*, the Main Hall. The path to the main hall welled upward; as we walked towards it, our elevation increased, until we got to the main hall itself.

Besides housing a fairly large statue of Kannon, the Main Hall is most famous for its wooden stage, which juts out from it like a stone outcropping, and which stands forty-three feet above the ground. Most interesting to me is the fact that the main hall, as well as its stage, were all constructed without the use of nails! Pretty amazing for a building made in 780 A.D., especially given how large the Main Hall and its wooden stage are. IKEA, take note![3]

Although I have some facility with describing food, I have realized, in composing these entries, that I am uninterested in architecture (unless it's part of a university, in which case I'm quite interested, because university architecture makes it easier for me to imagine myself in my dream job,

---

3. This is the second time I've mentioned IKEA in recollecting this day (see the previous chapter). I'm not sure why I had IKEA on the brain, but my guess is that my chain of associations goes something like this: (1) people building things reminds me of (2) me building things which reminds me of (3) IKEA because (4) I have only ever built things by IKEA, which reminds me of (5) meatballs.

as a publicly disgraced university president). I know this for two reasons. First, I have almost no architectural terms in my vocabulary. Whenever I can remember the word "trellis" (see Chapter 8 for proof that I can), I burn with pride. This suggests to me that I've made it to middle age with very little awareness of what I'm walking around in. The second reason I know I'm uninterested in architecture is that I have very little recall of the layout and presentation of Kiyomizudera, thanks mainly to my having taken few photos of it.

What I *do* remember, though, is the people. There were a few tourists and a lot of Japanese people around the temple. This I did find important, because it's the inverse of how sacred spaces function in Western Europe.

In Italy, for example, you can go to Florence and see the amazing Duomo di Firenze cathedral. You, and the other tourists, will be blown away by the attention to detail and the sheer beauty of it all. What you won't see, though, are many people using the facility for the purpose for which it was intended, *i.e.*, worship. Maybe there will be a few old ladies there, not to mention some priests, but whenever I visit religious facilities in Europe, it seems that people enjoy them as art-pieces, not as having any spiritual use.

By contrast, in Japan, it seemed that people actually used their shrines and temples. Not just in Kiyomizudera; everywhere I went in Kyoto and Tokyo, shrines appeared to welcome a stream of presumed locals. That was true here, too: people bought and hung sutras—small wooden planks inscribed with sayings from holy scriptures—on stands, the way that devout Catholics light candles in churches.

Moreover, shrines and temples visibly dotted Tokyo and Kyoto. I suppose this is true of Los Angeles and New York, too—there are churches all over the place—but unlike with Japan, I rarely see people go to them, and I get the feeling that these places of worship are on their last legs.

Once enough people die and the Saturday night bingo game closes up shop, there will be nothing left for the church custodians to do, and the churches will be converted into Popeye's.

Religiosity seemed to be significantly more integrated into Japanese culture than it is in American culture. Don't get me wrong, there are a lot of religious people in America—I count myself as one of them—but our religious life seems more fraught, because cordoned off. Among many Americans, there seems to be an unspoken bargain: I'll keep my religious beliefs private as long as you keep yours private. Given how diverse our country is, this is a useful bargain, as long as it's kept.

But it's a bargain that comes with costs, too; one of the things Japan hit home to me is that there's a lot of value to be found in a public religion. By "public religion", I don't mean a state-funded religion, but rather a set of religious practices that people engage in as unconsciously as they followed other social norms, like how to walk up an escalator or how to ignore the homeless.

As an American, the first question that arose in me once I realized how embedded religiosity was in Japanese culture was: do they actually believe what the rituals imply?[4] I don't really know, but my guess is that they probably believe it at least reactively. For example, even if you (think you) don't believe in ghosts, you may nonetheless get nervous sleeping in a cemetery. Same with many Japanese people, I wager: if they don't carry

---

4. After asking myself this question, I found this nugget from Pico Iyer: "In answer to a poll conducted in 2005 by the country's largest newspaper, the *Yomiuri Shimbun*, barely one in four Japanese answered 'Yes' to the question 'Do you believe in any religion?' More than 96 percent, however, admitted to participating in religious rites of some kind." (Iyer, *A Beginner's Guide to Japan*, p. 93)

out the ritual they're supposed to carry out on New Year's Day, they'll feel some guilt or anxiety. If they do, they'll feel a sense of accomplishment or relief.

Now, I'm not saying that we need to change America so that it's like Japan. The thing can't be done, first of all. And for another thing, I was only in Japan for four days when I realized this! It's not like I actually know what I'm talking about. I can only say that when you don't live in a community where people daily reaffirm their religious sensibilities through small gestures, it becomes more difficult to maintain those sensibilities in the ways in which they were originally developed. So I found myself wanting what the Japanese had, and disappointed that I couldn't get it.

After watching the various pilgrims milling about on the Hon-do's stage, we walked down some steps past the Otowa Falls. From what I read, its waters divide into three separate streams, and visitors can use a cup attached to a long pole to drink from the waters. If you drink from one stream, it will contribute to longevity; if you drink from another, it will contribute to success at school; and if you drink from the third, you're supposed to have a good love-life. You're not supposed to drink from all three, though, because that's greedy. If statistics regarding average lifespan, internationally comparative test scores, total fertility rates, and Mari are to be believed, I would bet that all Japanese people have drunk from the first two streams, and none has ever drunk from the third.

We didn't linger at the Otowa Falls, opting instead to loiter at Koya-su-no-To, which translates to "Easy Childbirth Pagoda". Supposedly, a visit to this pagoda will "bring about an easy and safe childbirth." Now, I wasn't pregnant, but since at this point my sister-in-law was, I considered saying a prayer for her and her unborn child when I arrived at the pagoda. The thought crossed my mind that perhaps I shouldn't utter a Catholic prayer in front of a Buddhist pagoda. I thought it possible that I would end up disrespecting both religions or, worse, cause a nearby bear to refrain from eating fish on Fridays. I learned, though, that Japanese black bears are critically endangered in Kyoto prefecture, so I thought it unlikely that my prayer would cause a bear to lower its caloric intake to dangerous levels—there were just too few bears for this to be likely. Apparently, my prayer worked, as my sister-in-law gave birth to a healthy baby boy with almost no fuss and only a fair bit of muss.

Alas, when checking the *Yomiuri Shimbun* for early January obituaries, I discovered that a beloved Japanese black bear, Burinkī, tragically passed on at the age of sixteen. He was survived by five fish and three crabs.

# 18

# A Walk That Walks the Walk

Now finished with Kiyomizudera, it was time to stroll in the direction of something called Ginkaku-ji, or "the Temple of the Silver Pavilion." This was the main event of the day, as Shawn had told me that it was the most beautiful site or, for that matter, sight, she's ever seen in her life. With a description like that, I prepared myself to pretend to agree with Shawn that some modestly handsome structure—presumably decorated with photographs of BTS members — was the most beautiful thing I've ever seen in my life.

However, we weren't going to do a straight shot from Kiyomizudera to the Silver Pavilion. Instead, we were going to engage in some hardcore meandering.

The first turn in our meander was to stop by the cemetery attached to Kiyomizudera. The cemetery was both orderly and wild, like something out of Terry Gilliam's *Brazil*. Think of it as a series of islands separated by narrow walkways. Each island boasted an explosion of headstones of dramatically varying heights. In fact, each island had so many headstones, crowded into such small spaces, that it was unclear what the (literally) underlying reality was. Were all these people cremated, with their remains interred underneath their respective headstones? Or were the headstones merely final memorials for people's loved ones, stone fingers indicating, "Hideki was once on our plane of existence?" Or (least likely of all), were there mass graves within each plot (no judgment!)?

Now, in the midst of the marble markers, you may have a sensation of being overwhelmed, but not paralyzed—more like navigating through Times Square than trapped in Los Angeles traffic. The pathways are narrow and short, but egress is always visible. When you look down on the mess of memorials from above, though, it looks jam-packed, like a game of Stratego where every square is taken.

American graveyards are comparatively serene. In my experience with them, though there are lots of plots, there is usually a respectful, and thus, respectable, amount of space between them, and the cemeteries are located in grassy, pastoral areas. American graveyards are designed to be peaceful, allowing you to have some time alone with your deceased and your thoughts. By contrast, this Japanese cemetery was so busy that it almost seemed like a party, as though the afterlife was downtown. The American cemetery is designed for the mourner whereas the Japanese one is designed for the mourned.

After finishing up at the Kiyomizudera cemetery, we stopped at a convenience store for refreshment. Though Japanese hotels are fairly light on coffee, the convenience stores are full of it to bursting. The bodega we went to had row after row of hot and cold coffees, with lots of loud characters and a recurring cast of colors (brown, gold, black, and white, mostly), all tightly packed together, like the headstones in a Japanese cemetery.

After a delightful little jaunt past, but not in, another temple ("Jōdo Shū Head Temple CHION-IN," if you must know) and some charming canals, we made our way to "The Philosopher's Path," the next portion of our meander.

I can't deny that I was both professionally nervous and excited about what this path would amount to. Philosophers sometimes fill websites with public commiserations about "the plane ride"—that situation where you find yourself sitting next to a stranger who wants to make conversation, and who asks you what you do for a living. For philosophers, this is a dreadful moment; many have claimed that when they answer this question with "philosopher", they're asked follow-up questions like, "oh, what's your philosophy?" or "oh, what are some of your sayings?" Eminent philosopher Simon Blackburn has even reported that he responds by describing himself as a "conceptual engineer."

Now, I call bullshit. First, unless you're sitting next to my mom, no one talks to strangers on planes anymore.[1] So if you hear anyone grumbling about this in 2024, assume that they're doing this for the likes on Instagram or Twitter, or that they're writing an exaggerated comedic travelogue.

Second, before the Covid lockdowns turned us all into hateful introverts, I also used to be asked by my seatmates on planes what I did for a living. I would answer truthfully and unhesitatingly, "I'm a philosophy professor." No one ever asked me what my sayings were, or what my philosophy was. The closest I ever got to a question like that was, "oh,

---

[1]. Without fail, whenever my mom travels from Dayton, Ohio to Los Angeles, California, she will say one of two things. Thing one: "the man who was sitting next to me on the plane was a real sourpuss. All he did was look at his computer. He wouldn't say *anything* to me." Thing two: "the woman I traveled with would not shut up. We talked for five hours!"

who is your favorite philosopher?",[2] which is a totally fine question! But usually they would just go, "oh, wow! Philosophy is hard." And then that would be that.

Third, if I answered the "what do you do?" question with "conceptual engineer", I hope I would get back the response, "well, fuck you too."[3]

Anyway, one reason I was nervous about The Philosopher's Path was that I feared, like the mythical plane ride experience I just described, it would be some layperson's imagined version of what a philosopher's path should look like—like, a bunch of statues of Socrates or Plato, with occasional stops where you could smoke a pipe, drink some scotch, and scratch your chin.[4] On the other hand, living with my fear was the hope that it would, somehow, be a path that was genuinely philosophical. And if it could be philosophical in a Japanese way—which was a philosophical tradition I knew almost nothing about, except that there's a famous Japanese philosopher named Keiji Nishitani—then all's the better.

Well, as it turns out, all's the better, for the Philosopher's Path was named for Kitarō Nishida, Nishitani's teacher! Japan-guide.com: "The

---

2. "Kant."

3. Here is the quote from Blackburn: "The word "philosophy" carries unfortunate connotations: impractical, unworldly, weird. I suspect that all philosophers and philosophy students share that moment of silent embarrassment when someone innocently asks us what we do. I would prefer to introduce myself as doing conceptual engineering." (*Think: A Compelling Introduction to Philosophy*, pp. 1-2) In fairness to Blackburn, he doesn't say that he *actually* introduces himself as a conceptual engineer, only that he would "prefer" to. Nevertheless, I want to punch him in his face.

4. Now that I think about it, that sounds rad and I should make it.

path got its name due to Nishida Kitaro,[5] one of Japan's most famous philosophers, who was said to practice meditation while walking this route on his daily commute to Kyoto University." The Stanford Encyclopedia of Philosophy—the gold standard for general philosophy references, at least in the English-speaking world—describes Nishida as "the most significant and influential Japanese philosopher of the twentieth-century." So, walking this path was like walking the ground where Wittgenstein[6] trod! At the time I walked the path, I didn't know he was the Japanese Wittgenstein, but in retrospect that makes me both envious of my past self for having walked those steps, as well as disappointed for having not appreciated that more at the time.

The path itself struck me as well-organized and unassuming. The place where we started resembled a bike path, but it was soon divided by a canal (part of the Lake Biwa Canal). Small bridges spanned the canal. The walkway was occasionally caressed by trim, sedate grass. I felt myself relax and become thoughtful as I walked along the path. Also a bit nostalgic—it reminded me of when I frolicked in my backyard in Ohio as a young boy.

I found it somewhat interesting that this path, despite its lofty provenance, was still being used as a path. It wasn't extremely busy with foot traffic or anything, but there were a fair number of people walking around—schoolchildren, cyclists, and old Japanese ladies complimenting each other's hunchbacks. The path was lined with shops like glassware stores and restaurants.

---

5. Wikipedia has it as Kitarō Nishida, whereas Japan-guide.com has it as Nishida Kitaro. I don't know what to do. I thought about just jumbling all the letters together to write, "Hi, Dan, I is art, OK?" But then, who's Dan?

6. Ludwig Wittgenstein, arguably the most influential European philosopher of the twentieth century.

Although I wasn't around when the path was first inaugurated, I had the feeling that the path, in its present condition, was still true to its original purpose.[7] It was neither neglected nor converted into tract housing.

I enjoyed the whole experience. Not in a visceral way, like drinking a mug of gravy, and not even in an intellectual way, like appreciating a well-crafted Mitch Hedberg joke, but in what I can only describe as a wistful way. As with Japan's noticeable, suffusing religiosity, walking this path offered an experience that I don't seem to get in the USA. It made me want to have this around me, despite knowing that I could never get it. It reminded me of when I frolicked in my basement in Ohio as a teenage boy and wanted to frolic in my backyard with Sandra Bullock.[8]

Of course, the question naturally occurred to me: "am I making myself feel this way because I think it's *supposed* to make me feel this way, or do I feel this way because this is just what this path does to people?" I strongly suspect it was the former; I was, indeed, trying to enjoy the path as I walked it, out of a kind of occupational solidarity. But: I *did* feel that way. The thing worked. I can't always do that, you know. For example, when I teach my students, I want to feel as important and life-changing to them as Robin Williams is to his students in *Dead Poets Society*; but despite that want, I often end up letting everyone down, like Robin Williams in *Hook*. Or *Mrs. Doubtfire*. Or *Jumanji*. Or *The Birdcage*. Or *Death to Smoochy*.

---

7. Given that I had only seen this path in its present state, there is no reason to trust this feeling. But for all that, the feeling might be right!

8. I also wanted to be friends with Matthew Perry. This is all true!

# 19

# A Palace Fit for a King

Having finished the Philosopher's Path, we were now close enough to the Silver Pavilion. According to Wikipedia, its official name is "Jishō-ji" ("Temple of Shining Mercy"), though whenever we mentioned to anyone that we were going to visit the Silver Pavilion, no one ever corrected us or looked confused.

There's an interesting story behind the Silver Pavilion, which, when known, makes for a provocative contrast with its appearance. The story is this: there was a shogun, Ashikaga Yoshimasa (1436-1490 CE), who didn't have an heir. His not having an heir caused the Ōnin War (1467-1477), a civil war in Japan over who would be the next shogun. According to most historians, the Ōnin war precipitated the end of the Japanese feudal system, which in turn incited the Sengoku Period (or Warring States Period), "a long, drawn-out struggle for domination by individual daimyo [local lords], resulting in a mass power-struggle between [sic] the various houses to dominate the whole of Japan."[1] The Warring States Period lasted between 1467 and at least 1568. Heckuva job, Yoshi!

Because of the turmoil of the Ōnin War, Yoshimasa had his underlings build a "pleasure villa for the shoguns to rest from their administrative

---

[1.] https://en.wikipedia.org/wiki/Ōnin_War

duties."[2] I don't know what pleasures he indulged in, but I guess he had enough by 1485, for that's the year that Yoshimasa became a Zen Buddhist monk. He asked people to convert the pagoda into a Zen Buddhist temple after his death. And they did! Very selfless of them.[3]

It's called the Silver Pavilion because Yoshimasa asked his builders to cover it with a silver foil, which would not only look blindingly resplendent in the sunlight, but would prevent its inhabitants from being mind-controlled by the CIA. The builders managed to drape it in silver foil, but they didn't manage to do it in time for Yoshimasa to live to see it. Moreover, the silver foil, owing to earthquakes, fires, and, presumably, the ravages of time, eventually peeled away entirely, living on in name alone.

Though the Silver Pavilion was massively restored in 2008, the restorers decided not to include its silver lacquer, meaning not only that "[t]he present appearance of the structure is understood to be the same as when Yoshimasa himself last saw it"[4] but also that it (supposedly) appears unfinished, thereby allowing people to classify it as an instance of "wabi-sabi" aesthetics, which is an "aesthetic [that] is sometimes described as one of appreciating beauty that is 'imperfect, impermanent, and incomplete' in nature."[5]

I just now learned the concept of wabi-sabi in writing this entry, but: I can't imagine anything less wabi-sabi than the Silver Pavilion, for

---

2. https://en.wikipedia.org/wiki/Ginkaku-ji

3. That was the only Buddhist joke I could think of.

4. https://en.wikipedia.org/wiki/Ginkaku-ji

5. https://en.wikipedia.org/wiki/Wabi-sabi

the grounds of the Pavilion were the most manicured, thoughtful, and controlled bit of nature and artifice I've ever seen.[6]

Our visit started out on a stone path toward a small archway, built in the Japanese style (this part of the complex was called "Somon"). Through the archway stood a three-and-a-half-foot tall wall made of moss-covered stones, on top of which was a three-and-a-half-foot high bamboo fence. Finally, behind all of them were some tall, beautiful trees, which you couldn't see past. You had no choice but to walk down a 200 foot long path, which turned sharply to the left once you got to the end. I couldn't help but to feel that I was about to see something secluded and amazing.[7]

What I found was the reception area. Secluded, but not amazing. But it's fine. Pavilions gotta make a living too. We bought our tickets and walked under the archway into the main grounds.

OK, now we were starting to get somewhere, because the next area was a nicely-sized, grand building ("Kuri" ["that"] and "Daigenkan" ["main entrance"] were the words the website used to designate it). Given that I knew these were grounds designed for a shogun, and that a large, thick, white wall separated this area from the rest of the complex, I figured

---

6. Don't worry; although I just now learned the concept of wabi-sabi, on January 3 I would encounter the Platonic form of wabi-sabi in chapter 23 (and it rocks! That's a pun, as you'll see), so I know what I'm talking about. And also: don't worry if you don't know what a Platonic form is. I'll tell you in Chapter 21!

7. Apparently, this was the wrong reaction. The website for the pavilion informs you that "[i]t is thought that this area was meant to act as a division from the unprotected outside world, but the solemn and artificial atmosphere is actually meant to purify one's idle and worldly thoughts." I can't believe something on the Internet "well, actually"'d me!

that this was the servants' quarters. Before the grand building stood the three largest ornamental pine trees I've ever seen. They not only looked magnificent, but also magnanimous, like they were gracefully doing you a favor by being there. Around the base of those trees was a sand garden in which monks (I assume) drew figures, which looked like a long, flat fence separating you from the trees. Also dotting the grounds were smaller sculpted pine trees, each of which was a work of art in its own right.

They were striking trees, but not so striking that I felt that now was the time to start lying to Shawn about how gorgeous this all was, and how all buildings I've seen until now were third-rate pieces of detritus, and how we Americans should all be servants of violent, whimsical shoguns, and that I, in particular, should do a better job of serving Shawn, my personal violent, whimsical warlady. Even I knew that we still hadn't arrived at what Shawn, following *The Simpsons*, called "the fireworks factory." *That* was behind the doors taking you out of this area (called "Hosyokan", which Google translates as "Hosyokan") and, finally, onto the main grounds of the Silver Pavilion.

In *The Principles of Psychology*, the philosopher-psychologist William James described a baby's experience of the world, unstructured by organizing concepts, as a "blooming and buzzing confusion." It sees colors and shapes but, lacking concepts, can't make sense of them or separate them into distinct objects.

I felt a kind of kinship with James's baby, for when I first turned the corner, I couldn't immediately make sense of the vision before me. There was so much sculpted impressiveness, both natural and artificial, and of so many varying sorts, that my optical system was paralyzed.

Another way of putting it: imagine you're in a gorgeous restaurant, with a grand buffet full of the best-looking food you've ever seen, and you're in the mood for *everything*. What would you do first? How would you decide? I think that if it hadn't been for the path-markers telling me where to go next, I would have died, frozen in place, like Buridan's ass.[8]

At this point, I will start describing the individual pieces that stood out to me, but I want to emphasize that every single part of this place had a deliberate design or organization. There was not one inch that was ignored. *Everything* was combed over and crafted, and it was a surreal feeling. It was beautiful, but it was also, as my favorite philosopher Immanuel Kant would have put it, "sublime." It's worth quoting him at length:

> The beautiful in nature concerns the form of the object, which consists in limitation; the sublime, by contrast, is to be found in a formless object insofar as **limitlessness** is represented in it ... the former (the beautiful) directly brings with it a feeling of the promotion of life, and hence is compatible with charms and an imagination at play, while the latter (the feeling of the sublime) is a pleasure that arises only indirectly, being generated, namely, by the feeling of a momentary inhibition of the vital powers and the immediately following and all the more powerful outpouring of them ... the satisfaction in the sublime does not so much

---

8. Imagine a donkey is extremely hungry for hay, and stands at an equal distance from two equally tempting piles of hay. Because the piles of hay are exactly as tempting as each other, the donkey has no grounds to opt for hay-pile 1 over hay-pile 2. As a result, he will eventually starve to death due to inaction. If only he, like I, had had a sign pointing him to the left pile of hay!

contain positive pleasure as it does admiration or respect, i.e., it deserves to be called negative pleasure.

> Immanuel Kant, Critique of the Power of Judgment, translated by Paul Guyer and Eric Matthews (Cambridge: Cambridge University Press, 2000 [original publication date: 1790]), pages 128-29.

Kant is not the clearest writer, so let me put this in my own words. Each part of the garden that I studied was beautiful, and created a sensual pleasure in me because of its harmony, as well as an intellectual pleasure because of my awareness of its craftsmanship. Yet, the realization that the entire garden had been cultivated, right down to the tiniest molecule, filled me with fear and then awe. People can do *this*? How? What have *I* been doing with my life? Or, for that matter, anyone I know?

Anyway: the first sight that caught my fancy was "Kogetsudai", a ... sand sculpture, I suppose, that resembled a very large anthill resting on a sandy plot, with concentric circles traced around the base. As striking as it was, I honestly had no idea what it was supposed to be doing. It just stood there, like a shy kid at a birthday party.

The next stop was a two-parter. First, there was a dignified building, "Hojo" ("the abbot's chamber"). I confess, the abbot's chamber didn't move me, but I did later learn that the placard hanging over the doorway read "Tozan Suijo Ko", which means "The eastern mountains move over the water." I always suspected as much about the eastern mountains, though I don't know why this remark would adorn the abbot's chamber.

In front of Hojo was a splendid sand garden called "Ginsyadan". It appeared as though a group of monks had painstakingly dragged rakes through the sand, creating a pattern of stripes that resembled a giant, striped shirt. It was the biggest sand garden I ever saw. It didn't induce any thoughtfulness in me, but it did incite a stillness born of awe.

The best analogy I can draw to it comes from when I was very young, about eight, exploring my backyard. There was a big rock around which several pill bugs would congregate. I was used to pill bugs (we Ohioans called them "rollie pollies"), but one day I lifted the rock, and underneath it I saw not only dozens of pill bugs, but one very large pill bug, the queen. She didn't look any different from the other bugs, but she was just so much larger. The bare fact of her largeness both repelled and entranced me. While this sand garden didn't repel me, it did mesmerize me, simply owing to its scope.

Once you leave Hojo and Ginsyadan, the sights change from buildings and sand to pathways and bridges. Trees surround the pathways, some of which seem to be ornamental, and some of which seem to shoot their branches willy-nilly, but their interaction is beguiling. Surely most of the trees are not, in fact, crafted, but, because there are so many meticulously pruned trees, and because every bit of nature seems like a human contribution, you feel a powerful sensation of design, perhaps like the seventeenth-century natural scientists did when they invented the microscope and saw that nature teemed with incredibly small lifeforms; or when eighteenth-century scientists discovered how the eye worked; or when nineteenth-century scientists found striking correlations between the bumps on a person's skull and his character.[9] To some extent, this sense of ubiquitous could be accidental—if you craft enough trees,

---

9. I realize some people have tried to discredit phrenology as inaccurate, but any quick search of the backs of those people's heads, right behind their ears, reveals that they have swollen combativeness and destructiveness organs, and shrunken amativeness ones.

you end up making all the trees seem carefully sculpted—but I bet it's deliberate.

There is a single large bridge that crosses a small lake. With bamboo rails, the bridge is narrow but still sturdy. The lake shimmers. Moss-covered rocks look like something from a movie-set, not because they look unrealistic, but because they look too good to be true.

Indeed, much about this place seemed too good to be true. Not only was everything enchantingly harmonious with its environment, but every time your gaze turned from the grounds of the silver pavilion to the mountains and city beyond its enclosure, you were met with a gorgeous view of the big, surrounding world.

When you cross the bridge, you'll find a path that leads you into a forest, through it, and then away. The trail alternated between a walkway covered in gravel and short stairs made of stone. Stanchions and barriers on the path warned against touching the mossy stone or venturing into the forest.

The last sight on the path was the building that has come to be known as the silver pavilion (but which the Japanese website calls "Kannonden Ginkaku"). In the midst of all this finely cultivated nature, the fine features of the building disappeared from my concern as completely and abruptly as my thirst for tea after I no longer have a cold. That said, its location, adjacent to the lake, and separated from the rest of the building, transported me into a fantasy.

As I left, I found myself wanting this whole place for myself, and I wanted to eject all these tourists. I wanted to live in this building, with no Internet, with my family and friends whom I would occasionally invite over so that they could praise me and bask in the glory of my property, a property that reflected my greatness like silver lacquer. I would think and I would write great books and I would have no stress or anxiety. I would hike in the forest when I wanted to get away from the stillness and beauty into a different kind of stillness and beauty. I would know that there were great and terrible things happening outside of where I lived, but I would be like a god on Mount Olympus, totally indifferent to it at all. But as I left, the reverie—my horrible, inspiring, revealing reverie—broke, and I was at the gift shop.

My shogunate was over. It was time to return to the hotel.

# 20

# Tasting the Sights

We had been pulverized by the potlatch for our peepers. Shawn continued to keep her promise that she would murder me through magnificence, and I could feel my vital forces leave my body, my blood cells' hemoglobin gradually being replaced by small chambers of luxury. When we got to the hotel, at 1:40 PM, we wanted to take a nap. But we were also hungry.

Unfortunately we had a food tour of Gion set for 5:30. So we faced a dilemma: order too much, be unable to appreciate the food tour; order too little, starve to death from mild hunger. The first horn of the dilemma seemed less sharp than the second. Also, we had a voucher. So we ordered room service.

Figuring that any Japanese portion would be smaller than its American counterpart, and also wanting to eat every part of the voucher-buffalo, I ordered truffle French fries, onion gratin soup, a margherita pizza, a(n allegedly) Kuroge wagyu beef burger, a crème brûlée, and two high-quality Japanese beers.

Now, you're probably thinking that we may have ordered too much, given that we were going to dine at a variety of Kyoto eateries in just three hours. But here's the thing, something you probably didn't consider: no.

And here's another thing you didn't consider: bang-bang dinner.

My professor friend Chewy, a scholar who specializes in Mark Twain, Hannah Arendt, and figuring out the application of tax law to polyamorous communes, was the person who turned me on to bang-bang. Bang bang is when you have dinner at one place and then, right away, have dinner at another. If you eat pizza at one place and hamburger at another, then that's just bang bang dinner. But if you have pizza at one place and then pizza at another, that's bang bang pizza. (Yes, I am not surprised that someone interested in polyamory is also interested in seconds.)[1]

Anyway, I have enjoyed bang bang dinner a few times. Like many of us, I experimented with it in college. And one thing I noticed from my ... uh ... researches is that you can eat way more than you think you can, if you just have the will to do so. And I am about nothing if not willpower.

The food arrived at 2:27, and, though I tried mightily, I couldn't help but to eat everything. It was delicious! The Japanese lagers were crisp and refreshing, and, though I didn't have any,[2] Shawn told me that the hamburger was surprisingly good (I assume the surprise was that the hotel

---

[1]. After writing this, I learned that it was the comedian Louis CK who popularized the concept of bang bang dinner. Wanting to credit the right person, I asked Chewy whether he got the idea from Louis CK or from growing up in Philadelphia, where (I assumed) it was called bang bang because it inevitably ended in gun violence. He said he didn't; he got it from our mutual friend Scotty. I asked Scotty whether he got the idea from Louis CK or from growing up in Boston, where (I assumed) it was called bang bang because the Yankees suck or Jeter has AIDS or whatever. He said no, he got it from Louis CK. I have unoriginal friends.

[2]. Well, I did try to sneak a little bite, but Shawn snapped at my fingers in her typically chelonian fashion.

did a good job on a quintessentially American dish whose quality is often dismissed by Europeans, the spirit animals of the Japanese). The crème brûlée was adequate, but the truffle fries were irresistible. Truffle oil is a subtle and expensive flavoring, and the Japanese are excellent at subtlety laced with judgment, so they pulled it off exquisitely.

We had a lovely time eating room service in the Ritz Carlton. The experience of eating a margherita pizza, a wagyu hamburger, truffle fries, and crème brûlée while staring at a bonsai tree through tempered glass was beyond words, but if I had to choose one, it would be: primal. It was like that feeling you get when you look into a campfire, the realization that you were the product of countless generations of evolution that created this deep harmony between your desires and your experiences. There could be no more authentic way to commune with my hunter-gatherer ancestors.

After finishing our food, we gradually descended into languor. It was time to try to nap.

I managed to take a nice one-hour nap, because I'm actually quite good at sleep. Shawn, because she suffers from a variety of sleep-disorders, and, Captain-Ahab-like, has destroyed her hypothalamus in pursuit of killing them, shambled around the room like a tranquilized bear and then, eventually, collapsed to the ground, caressing her phone. It works for her.[3]

Recovered, it was now time to amble over to the agreed-upon starting point of our food tour: Yasaka Shrine.

I have little to say about Yasaka shrine; our guides, Gourmand Tours, wanted us to begin at Yasaka Shrine, not because we were learning about Shinto culinary customs or, even less, to eat an ancestral ghost, but rather

---

3. It does not.

because it was a very visible, findable location near the Pontocho area of the Gion district, which was what we were going to tour.

Now, our tour guide had given Shawn a very particular location at which to meet her, and Shawn had put it as a pin on her phone's GPS-guided map. Good thinking, and certainly nothing would go wrong.

We were told in the email from Gourmand Tours that we needed to meet our guide promptly at 5:30 PM. Why promptly? Because if we didn't show up on time for the tour, the tour would start without us, and they wouldn't even allow us to meet them at one of the locations. The way they phrased things made it seem like starting late would be like trying to board The Challenger mid-flight: impractical and inadvisable.

This wouldn't be a problem, though, because we made sure to start walking so that we would arrive fifteen minutes early. Again, nothing would go wrong.

Unfortunately for us, although nothing *went* wrong, something had *been* wrong all along: it had been January 2 this whole time! This matters, because this was the day that Kyotans were using for Hatsumōde, the tradition of visiting a Buddhist temple or Shinto shrine to celebrate the new year. The Japanese take this seriously, so the area around Yasaka shrine was quite crowded, not to mention thick with booths selling food, drink, and knick-knacks. And each of these booths had a large, colorful banner flying above it.

The thing is, we were looking for an individual holding a flag reading "Gourmand Tours." And this festival was swarming with individuals, many of whom were under colorful banners. So, we kept on walking through the Yasaka shrine area, repeatedly optimistic that we saw what might be our guide, only to discover that it was yet another Japanese vendor offering fried octopus balls. It was like looking for a particular needle in a very small haystack full of needles: bustling with repeated, sharp disappointment.

As we continued to search for our guide, the clock ticked closer and closer to 5:30 PM. We, especially the Shawn part of "we," were getting ever more manic. Although Shawn was the one starting to panic, I'm a lifelong paranoiac, so I casually indulged in catastrophic fantasies, like getting to the agreed-upon location one minute late, only to see our tour guide and a parade of attendees huffily ignore us as we pleaded to them to allow us to follow. And then, armed guards, hauling us to the highlight of the tour: Japanese prison.

Finally, the clock reached 5:30. "TICK TOCK!" went nothing. Shawn sent our tour guide a desperate email, explaining to her the situation, begging her not to leave without us, and trying to get clarity on where on earth we were supposed to meet. Given my catastrophization, the tour guide was surprisingly understanding, and wrote back an email telling us her location, which was different from what we were told earlier. We desperately looked and, contrary to Murphy's Law, found her instead of, say, another woman interested in taking us on a restaurant-destruction tour. It was 5:45, we were not particularly close to the Yasaka Shrine, and she carried a flag much smaller than the proud crest I envisioned. Think "elementary school nametag" rather than "size 6XL Everquest t-shirt."[4]

---

4. My friend Scotty told me that he once won an Everquest t-shirt (it's an old video game) and that they gave him the option to pick whatever size he wanted. Given that he wasn't going to wear an Everquest t-shirt in public (Scotty is a good Catholic, and therefore ashamed of his preferences), he selected the XXXXXXL shirt, just to see how big it would be. He told me it was the size of a tent. Unfortunately, it now molders in a storage container in Altadena, like the Ark of the Covenant.

## THE MOST AWKWARD MAN IN JAPAN

We were so pleased that the tour guide waited for us that we didn't even think of complaining to her. But after finding her, it was clear why she indulged us: like anything having to do with Morrissey, no one else was going on tour. Part of me wanted her to have started the proceedings without us anyway, waving her banner in the air while holding forth before no one, ignoring our entreaties for entry, pretending to not notice us in favor of imaginary customers.

But no, she wasn't a crazy person, so she happily welcomed us to the tour, and told us that we were the only people to join. She was a blonde Swedish woman whose name was (not actually) Helga, who was about 5'5" and looked like what you would imagine a Swedish woman named Helga would look like, which is to say Pippi Longstocking, sans the pigtails. I was very curious about what her face looked like, as a mask covered the lower part of it, but not so curious that I demanded her to lower her mask.

You may question why I would even entertain such a demand, even to reject it internally. The answer was that I was starved of my very favorite kind of communication: asking incessant questions in English to someone who I think may have answers. As fascinating as I found Japan, I nonetheless was filling up with confusion, like a hot air balloon gliding over a public reading of *Finnegans Wake*. I needed to let some air out by having my questions answered, like: what do the Japanese people think of me so far? How do Japanese airports work? Am I in trouble?

Now, Shawn knew this about me, and she welcomed my perpetual mouthy machine. I mean, before and after Mari, I had no one to talk to about Japan besides Shawn. Shawn is an introvert, so she doesn't care for talking even on the best of days. She makes a special exception for me, on account of our being married (from what I gather, introverts are fans of close relationships, and no other relationships). But she has her limits, so, like a lady considering an open marriage, she was open to the possibility of offloading my constant ejaculations onto some other woman.

The idea of the tour was to walk through Pontocho and Gion Shirakawa, "two of Kyoto's most charming and historical areas." We met Helga in the Gion Shirakawa area, and our first stop was approximately five feet away from our starting point. It was a bakery, and it had a local Kyoto specialty: yatsuhashi.

Yatsuhashi are glutinous dumplings, sometimes filled with sweet paste (when they're filled, they're dubbed aniri-nama-yatsuhashi, which Google Translate tells me means nothing at all). They have a spongy texture and are translucent enough to allow you a glimpse of the filling – red bean, strawberry, plum, sweet potato, etc. The rice-flour-based pastry is sometimes cooked, but Helga told us she preferred them uncooked. Having had a baked, matcha-flavored yatsuhashi at the Ritz-Carlton and a raw one from the bakery she brought us to, I must say that I agree with Helga.

She told us that we needn't buy any yatsuhashi now, for we would be returning to this bakery at the very end of our tour. To get any small amount of drama out of the way—did he buy the yatsuhashi?!—, I did buy some for my brother and his wife, and I never heard about them again. The yatsuahshi, not the family members. They're doing great. The family members, not the yatsuhashi. I assume they were eaten.[5]

We walked from here to a small shrine deeper in the Gion Shirakawa area, which apparently had some connection to geishas. I peppered Helga with all sorts of questions about geishas, but unfortunately, I don't

---

5. The yatsuhashi, not the family members.

remember much about her answers.⁶ All I can tell you is this: I was under the impression that geishas were an elevated form of Japanese sex worker. Being Japanese, I assumed they studied other cultures and then just did a much better job. But apparently, this was not correct; think of geishas more like sorority sisters from Ole Miss, but professionals. Ultimately, many of them become geishas because they want a rich husband, but, fundamentally, being a geisha is about spending a lot of money to become extremely well-informed about a variety of things, not to mention learning about dance and music.

The next location of interest was, once again, not a restaurant, but rather a Japanese opera house, Minami-za. It reminded me of the Magic Castle in Los Angeles (though not so much on a hill, and not as full of wizards), as it was a flashy, gold theater that looked like it could house a couple thousand people. And it was located in the heart of a busy Kyoto downtown, standing out like Spuds MacKenzie at an Indigo Girls concert (RIP, Indigo Girls).⁷

I've never seen kabuki, but I gather that its musical approach differs vastly from that of western opera. Helga didn't elaborate upon kabuki from a musicological approach, but from a historical one. She informed us that kabuki was actually founded in 1603 by a woman in Kyoto, Izumo no Okuni. Indeed, in the beginning, kabuki was performed exclusively by women, and was therefore too ribald. Female kabuki was banned in 1629, leading to it being performed just by boys and, then, just by men. The

---

6. For most of my trip to Japan, I was very much in observe-and-ponder rather than disturb-and-jabber mode (these are my two modes). Ironically enough, my asking lots of questions meant that I didn't collect as much information as if I had just said nothing and stared intently.

7. I assume they're dead?

men-only approach to kabuki lasted about 350 years, and today it's now legally permitted for women to do kabuki too, which I assume happened because people lost interest in it.

Helga told us all this on the bank of the Kama river, next to a statue of Izumo no Okuni. I didn't ogle her statue—not realistic enough—but she was holding a fan in her right hand and a sword in her left one. Pretty baller!

After gleaning some things about geishas and divas, we offed to the Pontocho area, to visit the second eatery on our tour. The second word that came to mind when I explored Pontocho was: narrow (the first word was "Pontocho"). The area comprised thirty-foot tall buildings separated from each other by alleys the width of hallways. Most of the dark-colored buildings had sleek-looking signs with black writing on white backgrounds. Paper globes suspended from facades emitted a soft glow. I found myself wanting to visit each of these places, which in turn made me feel overwhelmed. I was glad that we had a guide, because although Pontocho was easy to navigate, the number of attractive options made it feel labyrinthine.

The first sit-down restaurant Helga took us to was Yuzugen Pontocho. Its claim to fame was that it specialized in preparing dishes flavored with yuzu. Yuzu, in case you don't know, is a lemony citrus fruit originating from China or Korea, but is a staple of Japanese cuisine. The American equivalent would be a restaurant specializing in preparing dishes flavored with hot dogs.

Specializing in a flavor is really cool. I've never been to a restaurant that has done that before (unless you consider Baskin Robbins a restaurant, and "sweet" a flavor), so it's novel to me. And yet, focusing on just one particular flavor seems like low-hanging fruit; why hadn't I run into any place that did this before?

If reality wrote jokes more reliably, I would now say, "well, this restaurant explains why no one's ever done this before: it stinks!" But no, the restaurant was fine.

First, its appearance. The two-story restaurant was, like Pontocho itself, extremely narrow. At the side entrance, a bar faced you on the left (with seated patrons) and three or four two-top tables lined the wall to the right. At the back of the restaurant was a bathroom, as well as stairs to the second floor. A pile of shoes crowded around the base of the stairs, because the tables upstairs were traditional low tables set on tatami mats. Also of note is the fact that the pile of shoes at the base of the stairs was right next to the bathroom. So, if you had to go to the bathroom, you wouldn't have to put your unprotected feet directly in the muck.[8] Instead, you could find your shoes and put them back on or, more conveniently, simply shoe yourself with one of the many pairs of large slippers available for free.

The stairway up wasn't quite as narrow as the stairway up to Bar Asylum (the whiskey bar in Golden Gai; see Chapter 7), but it was narrow enough that if it existed in a bar in the USA, it would become a tourist attraction.[9] The room the stairway opened onto was a living-room-sized dining area with a few tables, completely opaque windows, wood-paneled and cream-colored walls, and coat hangers above each table. A hibachi grill was set into the table, but since we weren't hungry, we didn't have

---

8. I'm sure this says something deplorable about me, but I wouldn't have a problem walking into a public bathroom in socked feet, unless there was visible filth. I realize that it's covered by *in*visible filth, but I figure all surfaces are. And by the way, if you use Twitter (the site never known as X), you have no right to complain about voluntarily engaging with invisible filth.

9. For three weeks. Then the ADA complaints would come rolling in, figuratively and literally.

grilled meat. Instead, Helga chose some yuzu chicken ramen for us, and noted that the menu offered many yuzu-flavored drinks. I opted for a yuzu highball, whereas Shawn got a yuzu sidecar.

I grew up watching professional wrestling (stay with me; I'm going somewhere with this) in the 1980s. In the 1980s, "African" wrestlers like Kamala (he was from Mississippi) would come to the ring with the ring announcer intoning, "from deepest, darkest Africa," while Japanese wrestlers would be described as coming "from the mysterious east!"[10] I think I kept a bit of association of "mystery" and "Japanese," because until this drink I thought of a highball as a unique Japanese cocktail.

Aided perhaps by its (eventually-to-be-dispelled) sense of mystery, the yuzu-from-the-mysterious-east highball tasted excellent. A crisp, citrusy, refreshing slug of booze and sparkling water, it both stimulated and relaxed me, like seeing a student cry. The yuzu ramen was tasty, but lacked depth. You could detect the yuzu in the salty broth, but there wasn't much more to it than that. We also ordered a plate of yuzu-dappled chicken atop a bed of bean sprouts. I ate up, but half out of a sense of politeness, and the other half out of a desire to provide the symmetry needed to finish this sentence.

I also got to see Helga take her mask off! I don't know what I was expecting, but: she was a Swedish lady.

We talked to Helga and got her story. She wanted to learn Japanese because she was interested in getting a master's degree in International Relations, and learning Japanese would help that. So she just up and moved to Japan. Being Swedish, it didn't take her very long to learn the language well, and, being Swedish, she was perfectly happy to denigrate the Japanese for their difficulty in learning how to pronounce English.

---

10. I grew up in Dayton, Ohio, so I assumed they meant Pittsburgh.

She wondered why on earth people who study for as long as they do are as bad at English pronunciation as they are.

I honestly don't know why the Swedish are so good at learning languages, but since we're on the subject of enunciating national characters only to deprecate them, I would guess that when you come from a country of 10,500,000 people, what else are you going to do besides learn a language? Stay in Sweden? Look, I get that the healthcare is great, and quite needful as a respite from the never-ending darkness, but "enjoying healthcare" leaves a little something to be desired as a vocation. If I were Swedish, vacation would be my vocation too.

Anyway, Shawn idly asked Helga something she'd always found a bit baffling: why does she think Japanese people so rarely wear sunglasses? She had asked this same question to Mari, and Mari told her that the Japanese people's eyes were simply less sensitive to the sun.

When we offered this up as an explanation to Helga, she slightly frowned and, after a pause, drawled: "the Japanese have a lot of ... theories." She elaborated upon this to mean that there is a lot of folk wisdom in Japan that is probably baseless, but also not really questioned. (*E.g.*, if you fall asleep with a fan blowing on your face, you may die!) By contrast, we Westerners are more empirical and willing to revise our understanding of the world. To put it in more Western terms: the Japanese are Sagittariuses and we're Virgos!

The Japanese weren't the only people having their theories exploded that evening. After we got our food, I picked up a pair of wooden chopsticks, unbundled them, and started rubbing them together. Helga knowingly informed me, "you don't need to do that. In fact, I don't know why people do that. It's not like you can accidentally injure yourself with chopsticks."

Ever eager to use my incompetence to prove someone wrong, I lifted a bandaged finger and said, "uh, yes you can." I then proudly explained to her the provenance of my injury (see chapter 8), to which she verbally responded with an "oh" and then mentally wrote a note that read, "he stupid."

After finishing our yuzu delicacies, we left the restaurant through the side-door, finding ourselves in a nondescript alley. The sights and sounds of revelry we enjoyed just one second prior immediately dissolved into silence, making me feel like I walked through a door with a Korean goblin and ended up in Quebec City, instantly lost.

Male confidence swiftly replaced the disorientation, as Shawn fearlessly led us back to the main street. We joined up with Helga (she had stayed behind a moment to pay the bill) and made our way to the next restaurant.

This next place was a post-1945 Shōwa-era restaurant. The post-1945 Shōwa-era lasted from 1945 until the death of Emperor Shōwa, in 1989. However, the décor made me feel like I was in an American diner from the 1950s; only, instead of greasers and hipsters, it was full of Japanese businessmen and tourists looking at Japanese businessmen.

Everything was wood-paneled. Chintzy-looking ceiling fans lazily circled above. The walls were covered with old menus and posters loudly advertising who-knows-what. Unsmiling servers, with a stiff determination born of a desperation to get away from or back to their drunken clientele, handed us laminated menus with big pictures of all the food and ushered us past patrons yelling happily.

We ordered three things: fried tofu, a breaded and fried root vegetable, and yellowtail sashimi. The fried tofu was a monument to adequacy, the root vegetable tasted like firmer parsnips, and biting into the yellowtails was like chewing through a roll of tape.

I loved the place.

At the time, I didn't indicate that I loved it. I'm not even sure I realized it myself. But when I reflect on it, I feel a sense of belonging. The food was relentlessly average, and the atmosphere uninviting but accepting. It was like an indigenously Japanese Denny's, a spot where I imagined regular people went to have passable vittles at an affordable price. It felt like a scene where one blew off steam, so I think that I subconsciously relaxed a bit, and wasn't worried (as I usually was, both in Japan and in the US) of accidentally breaking the rules and offending someone.

Appropriately, it was here that I learned (from Helga) that a highball is just a scotch and soda. I had one. It was nothing special. Perfectly so.

# JANUARY 3, 2023

# 21

# The Platonic Form of Averagosity

Our tour with Helga over, we returned to our gorgeous hotel, read books (me) or looked at our phones (Shawn; also me) and turned in. We had breakfast scheduled for 7:00 AM, and we wanted to wake up in time to get to it without having to rush.

In Japanese hotels, you're often offered a choice between "western" and "Japanese" breakfast. I have always found the idea of Japanese breakfast intriguing—I've never been to a restaurant in the USA that specializes in or even offers Japanese breakfast, and thanks to Shawn, I knew that Japan had a distinct approach to breakfast. By this point, I had developed a great deal of respect for how the Japanese do things, so I eagerly anticipated learning about Japanese breakfast.[1] However, Shawn told me that she found the mild nature of Japanese breakfast underwhelming, so I didn't pull the trigger and order one at any time between December 30 and January 2. But today, January 3, I finally took the plunge.

Why today? Why not trust Shawn, skip Japanese breakfast, and enjoy the Ritz-Carlton's take on Western breakfast, which I knew to be really good? I mean, I could have had beautiful-looking and ok-tasting French toast. Why skip that in favor of something I was warned about? Why go into the forest when the signs say "dangerous raccoons?"

Because of Plato, that's why.

Plato, as you probably know, was the second great philosopher in the western tradition (the first was his teacher, Socrates). Plato is to

---

[1]. This may be surprising, but for the longest time, I was not a fan of breakfast (pancakes, waffles, and French toast excepted because, fundamentally, they're just pastries). I didn't like eating eggs or breakfast meats until my mid-thirties, and as a kid and young man, I was never hungry for *anything* first thing in the morning. To quote a college acquaintance, "trying to eat in the morning is like trying to swallow stun grenades." When I got to my twenties, I did start to hunger early in the morning, but not for breakfast food; instead, I would eat anything I had a mouth for: hamburgers, roast chicken, clam chowder, whatever. I found the idea of time-based cuisines to be puzzling, like claiming that this coat looks good on me, but only on Tuesdays. Obviously enough, things changed. Just the other day, my wife told me that she was going to go to a fancy breakfast buffet at 10 at night, and to a square like me, this struck me as a glorious transgression, akin to swimming in a tuxedo.

western philosophy what eggs are to western breakfast.[2] This captures the spirit of the 20th century philosopher Alfred North Whitehead's remark that "[t]he safest general characterization of the European philosophical tradition is that it consists of a series of footnotes to Plato."

One of Plato's many theories is the theory of the forms. To understand that theory, start by thinking of something you have a lot of experience with. Say, an egg in a western breakfast. If I'm eating an egg, and you're eating an egg, then you can look at my egg and your egg and recognize them both to be eggs. But how do you know that the thing you're eating and the thing I'm eating are both the same kind of thing? After all, yours is different: a little bigger, a little saltier, a little more orange than my egg. So, given all these differences, in virtue of what can you discern that I'm eating an egg and you're also eating an egg?

Plato's answer is that both your egg and my egg "participate" in what he called the form of egg. That is, there is this thing, "eggness," and what makes both your egg and my egg into, well, *eggs* is the fact that both of them participate in eggness, the form of all eggs. That is, it is *eggness itself* that explains *why* all eggs are eggs.

Back to material reality: I was at the fanciest Japanese hotel I've ever been to. The closest I would get to glimpsing the form of Japanese breakfast itself would be here. After this, I would be able to appreciate all other Japanese breakfasts by seeing the extent to which they participated

---

2. Socrates is the toast, I guess? And that must make his greatest student, Aristotle, the bacon. If I had to continue, I'd make Epicurus the butter, just because of the common association of Epicureanism with vulgar hedonism. And Diogenes the Cynic, being bitter and cosmopolitan, is obviously the coffee. I'd go on, but the tray has already gotten cluttered. No, wait! Zeno of Citium is the napkin

in Japanese-breakfastness. I would truly understand Japanese breakfast. *That*'s why I ordered it.

It was meh.

To understand the reasons motivating my judgment, let me start, as I always do, by setting the scene. We were dining at the Ritz's Japanese restaurant, Mizuki. Dressed in a kimono, the hostess showed us to a spare, sleek four-top table made (to my untutored eyes) out of two kinds of wood. The dining space was primarily composed of stand-alone tables, with a long bar table and booths near the entrance. However, the focal point was a towering glass panel that showcased a serene garden view. If seated at the bar, you could look straight ahead through this window onto walled-in plants.

Perhaps because of the restaurant's appearance, or maybe because of the novelty of eating Japanese breakfast, I felt guarded at first. It seemed that great propriety was needed, which called to mind the first time I went to a fancy restaurant: there are lots of tripwires here, and if you trigger one, everyone will know that you don't belong. So: be on your best behavior, say nothing, and for God's sake, don't enjoy yourself!

That sense quickly dissipated as I took in my surroundings, because there were other people eating here. First, there was a solo Asian man wearing nice clothing, a baseball hat, and talking in English about some private school in Los Angeles that I had never heard of (but Shawn had, because she's a SoCal social climber); and behind us, in one booth, was a Japanese family of four whose children, despite being Japanese, behaved and ate as American children do.

That made me remember something my mom told me, long ago: if you want to fit in at a fancy restaurant, act normal. Don't allow your ballsack to climb back up into your pelvis, because at the end of the day the staff is there to make sure you have a good time. You don't have to impress them;

they have to impress you. (She never gave this advice to my dad, because if she had, he would have started clipping his nails, which is something he did while seated in movie theaters. Really.)

Thanks to the other patrons, who were, I guess, used to this, I eased up a bit and waited for my meal. It started with hot soup: a dram of miso broth poured over a large square of tofu, on top of which were set scallions and bonito flakes. They served it in a beautiful handmade bowl on top of a ringed steel plate. Smoked green tea accompanied it, which was very nice.

The main event was a large, exquisite bento box with a pattern of (what looked like) black snowflakes painted atop. The whole thing was quite elegant, and confirmed my fantasies of what this breakfast would be like: subtle, pretty, artisanal. Next to it was a large bowl of congee covered by a wooden octagonal lid. But I wasn't interested in congee, which is basically just Asian grits. No, like my slightly uglier doppelganger, Brad Pitt, I wanted to know: what's in the box?!

Unlike Brad Pitt's box, which had only one kind of thing, this one had six, each separated into its own compartment. I will describe them in the order I ate them.

First, in the lower left cubicle was a skosh of Chilean sea bass with a pickled lotus root on it; second, in the lower middle chamber was a fish cake next to a slice of beef, with radish, carrot, and a peapod as their side pieces; in the lower right chamber were two slices of red snapper sashimi, pinning some discreetly placed lettuce leaves. Above them, in the upper right area, were sliced octopus, bell peppers, and mushrooms in a golden curry sauce. The middle right section was itself portioned into four tiny boxes, each of which held pickled vegetables. Finally, in the upper left part of the box was the dessert—two small pieces of melon (cantaloupe and honeydew, respectively), a piece of mango, and an orange segment, accompanied by a toothpick that you could pretend was a harpoon, in honor of the Japanese hatred of whales.

In retrospect, I can't help but to feel I somehow messed up in the way I ate this, but the whole affair made very little impact on me. I mean, it was fine. It was all fine. But, unlike someone whose comments I read on the Internet, I did not find this anywhere close to being "without a doubt the greatest breakfast I've ever eaten." Was I supposed to eat differently? Was I expected to mix the six offerings together in all sorts of different ways? If I was, why were all the foods put into their own areas? It really gave the impression that mixing them was to sully them.

The same person who said that this breakfast was the greatest they've ever eaten added that eating the meal made them "feel like an emperor." I don't know what that feels like! Or do I (see the end of Chapter 19)? Is that what emperors feel like—constantly disappointed by luxury? No wonder those guys kept on going to war.

# 22

# A Staggering Work of Hirsute Genius

I didn't want to go to war after that, so I guess I didn't feel like an emperor. Maybe that's why Shawn and I went straight from breakfast to the Golden Pavilion, "the retirement villa of the shogun Ashikaga Yoshimitsu" (Japan-guide.com).

For fairly obvious reasons, one naturally contrasts the golden pavilion (which is called "Kinkaku-ji" in Japan), with the silver pavilion. Both were built by shoguns as places to take a load off, both were converted to Zen Buddhist temples after the deaths of the shoguns, both were covered by a thin foil to give each the appearance of a precious metal, and both were partially or entirely destroyed by natural disaster or war. Indeed, before seeing the golden pavilion, I recall asking a Japanese employee at the Ritz, "which do you prefer—the golden pavilion or the silver one?" "Golden", he immediately replied, like he'd gotten the question a million times. Because he had. Because the question occurred to everyone.

To allow you to appreciate my (retrospective) reaction to his saying "golden," I need to tell you about beards. Sometimes I wear a beard, and sometimes I don't. Here's the thing about me growing a beard, though: it takes me about a month to develop a solid beard, and once I have it, I parade it around town like it's a picture of me high-fiving ball lightning while sporting a gigantic erection: I think it's obviously glorious, and I assume you will want to ask me questions about it.

Though it takes me a while to grow it, once I decide to shave it off, it disappears in a matter of minutes, falling victim, like so many of history's greatest heroes, to the blade. Given how up my own beard I am, my shaving of it is always an ambivalent occasion, like when Queen Tamora learned what was in that delicious pie that Titus Andronicus was serving her. I mean, the good news is that it's delicious. The bad news ...

Now, you might think the prose in the previous two paragraphs was overwrought, but I really do think like this about my beard. I obsess over it. I ask people questions about it, like, "hey, were you guys thinking of my beard last night?", and I'm always astonished when they say "no, of course not, why would we?" For some reason only God and my therapist know, I appear to think that my beard should be watercooler talk.[1]

I want you to have this background in mind so that you can appreciate the contrast between how I think of my beard and how my wife thinks of my beard. On days where I shed my beard, she comes home, looks at me, and asks how my day was. I look at her intently: "fiiiine", I drawl. She looks back, right at my face, unblinking, and, after a moment, says, "good. I'm going to the bedroom to change."

---

1. The closest I've gotten to people thinking about my beard is when my friend Jonda once told me he was surprised that I was surprised when I learned that he didn't think about my beard in his down time. Still, this was *partially* comforting; he didn't think about my beard, but he thought about my thinking that he thought about my beard. And if he ever reads this footnote, he will think about the fact that I thought about him thinking about my thinking that he thought about my beard. Food for thought. Also, I don't have a therapist.

After she changes, she comes back out, sees my newly emerged face, and continues to say nothing. She just goes about her evening like nothing gigantic has just happened.

In fact, she would never notice at all if I didn't eventually buckle and scream, "MY BEARD!!" at which point she goes, "oh yeah! You shaved it, huh?"

See, Shawn suffers from what I call "beard blindness." She does not see beards—she only sees faces. And she's not the only one: both my mother and Willow, a female colleague, also suffer from beard blindness. It's permanent, it's not treatable, and it's a fucking insult.

I went through all this rigamarole to let you know that anyone who prefers the Golden Pavilion to the Silver Pavilion is lying, insane, literally blind, or, most likely, "beauty blind," because at the end of the day, the Golden Pavilion is just a forty-foot high gold building surrounded by a lake and pretty forest, and you can't go inside. You just walk around, take pictures, and leave, like the detectives at a crime scene.

I mean, there's more to it than that. You walk towards it from hundreds of feet away, and at first, you see a natural backdrop: a forest, the mountains, and the effulgent blue skies above. As you get closer, your eyes focus in on the Golden Pavilion itself, a large, golden building hugged by the surrounding forest and separated from you by the water.

If I try to put on my bad judgment hat, I can, perhaps, see the relative attractions of the Golden over the Silver Pavilion. You could think of the Silver Pavilion as indulgent, whereas the Golden Pavilion is restrained. There is, indeed, a kind of magic in seeing a beautiful, golden, unreachable building lord it over you from the woods. I can see thinking that any notable who lives there must be important, or, once it became a Zen temple, concluding that it houses only the holiest of thoughts.

And though I have described it simply as a large golden building, it has a quite distinct appearance. It has three floors, all made in different architectural styles. In the process of writing this book, I have learned a thing or two about describing physicality, but articulating the contrasts of these old architectural styles is still beyond my powers, so I'll leave it to the snobs at japan-guide.com:

> The first floor is built in the Shinden style used for palace buildings during the Heian Period, and with its natural wood pillars and white plaster walls contrasts yet complements the gilded upper stories of the pavilion. ... The second floor is built in the Bukke style used in samurai residences, and has its exterior completely covered in gold leaf. ... Finally, the third and uppermost floor is built in the style of a Chinese Zen Hall, is gilded inside and out, and is capped with a golden phoenix.

But honestly, regardless of how the Golden Pavilion may be more intriguing and impressive than any single structure of the Silver Pavilion, there's just so much less to do there. Really, it just is: you walk up to the building, you take a picture, you leave. The more I think about it, the more astonished I am at this Japanese guy's preferences. Dollars to donuts says that he didn't even notice that I had a beard.

# 23

# The Constant Garden

Something I didn't tell you in the last chapter is that after we finished our Japanese breakfast, we informed the good people at the Ritz-Carlton Kyoto that we were checking out, and would like our luggage transferred to our next hotel, Suiran, on the other side of Kyoto. They happily obliged, and I tell you this because it just now occurred to me how freeing that is. Rather than having to drag luggage from hotel A to hotel B, stow it at hotel B, and then go about our day, we could just leave hotel A, do things near hotel A, and then go to hotel B. Really, more people should do stuff for me.

One strength of my style of travel is complete ignorance. Once, I went to Hong Kong for a philosophy conference/chin-scratching contest. I thought it was neat to be able to present a paper in China; I had never been to China before, so going to Hong Kong, which I thought of as the Wall Street of China, was mildly exciting for me, but entirely just so I could tell people that I'd been to Hong Kong. Imagine my surprise when I got to the conference and many of the other philosophers there asked me what sites I was going to visit.

Me: "Sites? What are you talking about?"

Philosopher: "Well, aren't you going to look around?"

Me: "Why would I do that when there are philosophers to talk to?"

I'm being completely honest when I tell you that the idea of touring Hong Kong after—or, God forbid, during—the conference didn't cross my mind for a second. I was genuinely excited to talk to a bunch of philosophers about Kant, and to see how Chinese philosophers made use of him, but the entirety of my plan was: arrive in Hong Kong; go to conference; leave Hong Kong. I did no reading about the place beforehand, or afterwards, and I had no interest in doing anything but talk philosophy and network.

I took a similar approach to this trip; Shawn had been to Japan several times before, and she was a Japan-enthusiast, so I put the entire trip in her hands. She asked me if I wanted to know anything about any of our stops before we went, and I told her: nope. I did bring with me a couple of books about Japan, the one by Pico Iyer (which I've quoted repeatedly in this travelogue) and another about the history of post-war Japan, but while I managed to read into them a bit, I ended up spending my downtime reading Terry Godlove's *Kant and the Meaning of Religion*, which is a real corker of a book.

And I'm quite glad that I did, because not knowing anything about any of the places I visited allowed me to experience them with remarkably few preconceptions. I was extremely moved by Gotenyama Trust City, even though it will show up on no list of Tokyo sites to see, and the thing I found most affecting turned out to be a garbage can. I thought the Golden Pavilion was nothing special, even though it's the eighty-fifth holiest site in the world.[1] If I had known more, maybe I would have forced myself to inauthentically like the first less and the second more.[2]

I tell you all this, because I really want to bring home to you that I did not know anything about the next stop on our tour of Kyoto, the Zen temple, Ryōan-ji. Short of knowing a few things about Zen Buddhism in general—such as that it is a kind of Buddhism, and that it makes use of short, gnomic sayings called "koans," which (I think) are meant to induce bafflement, so as to get you into a state of mind of acceptance of contradictions—I didn't know anything about this temple.

I make use of a lot of mystery in my writing, and maybe it's getting tiresome, but I really want you to see Ryōan-ji through my eyes. So I'll first describe for you my visit, and then I'll go back and be a serious historian by telling you what Wikipedia says about it.

Although Ryōan-ji has fairly large grounds, the path a visitor naturally takes is simply to walk into the Abbot's Quarters, which is the most prominent building. When you enter the quarters, the entrance is level with the outside, proceeding to wood flooring elevated above the entrance. Upon entering, you take off your shoes, leave them in the depressed part of the chamber, and put on some one-size-fits-all slippers, which are available for the borrowing in a big bucket. Slippers on, you may now walk about the cabin.

---

1. According to a website called Patheos (https://www.patheos.com/sacred-spaces/kinkaku-ji), though I protest that ranking sites by holiness levels seems at odds with holiness itself.

2. Although as I write this, the philosopher in me wonders, "wait a second ... what makes a liking authentic or inauthentic in the first place? If knowing more about a place leads you to enjoy it more (or less), even if only because you're supposed to, what's wrong with that?" Good questions, me!

Nearest to the area where you first put on your foot-mittens (I don't want to keep writing "slippers") were bathrooms and the gift shop, where you could buy sutras, as well as commemorative art. We also passed a massive black-and-white photograph of a Japanese rock garden. The photo looked a bit aged, like it had been taken in the 1950s. Other than its size, it didn't seem important, so I ventured further in.

Past the gift shop we found the rock garden pictured in the old photograph. However long ago the photograph was taken, nothing seemed to have changed about the rocks. Apparently, and as I should have figured out from the existence of the gigantic photograph inside, this rock garden was the reason people came here. Indeed, there were lots of people sitting down, their feet dangling off the ledge overlooking the garden. Some of the people were talking, a few were laughing, and many were quiet.

I didn't look too closely at the rock garden at first, which was to my left. Instead, I focused on the view to the right, a large room separated from the tourists by columns and cordons preventing ingress. You weren't supposed to go inside this chamber, but were instead supposed to sneak your head indoors and peer at the art.

The art, a set of panel-paintings, was quite pleasing. Each door-sized panel was contiguous with at least one, and no more than two, other panels. The set of eight panels that I could see from the central entrance depicted a Japanese dragon clutching a white circle (a pearl, as it turned out) in one of its clawed hands, while the other opened up over what looked like a snow drift (clouds, as it turned out). Only the dragon's upper body was visible. The dragon sported a protracted, thin mustache, a mess of hair that looked like a toupee, and two long horns. Its tongue stuck out, its eyes bulged, and it appeared to be a smug jerk, looking like it was issuing mocking laughter. The description of the art read, in part:

> Commemoration of the 550th anniversary of the death of founder Katsumoto Hosokawa
> **Special exhibition of votive fusuma paper sliding door paintings of Morihiro Hosokawa**
>
> **Cloud Dragon painting**
>
> **8 Panels**

The dragons depicted on the eight specially exhibited works are known as jade dragons. According to Mr. Hosokawa, the dragons are depicted as having grasped pearls of wisdom amidst raging clouds and smoke, with an expression of being fully satisfied. Seven dragons are depicted in the 32 panels of this 'Cloud Dragon' exhibition. Another eight panels with two dragons are scheduled to be released during spring of 2023, making a total of 40 panels and nine dragons.

When it comes to art, I adore drawings. Part of this must be the fact that when I was younger, I was quite good at drawing. If you ask me to explain what appeals to me about drawing, though, here's the story I'll invent for you: I think it's the visibility of the lines of demarcation, the bounded versatility of the effects that you can use pencils to produce, their intuitiveness as an artistic instrument, and finally—and this is the hardest quality to communicate—the permanent distance between what you're representing and how close your representation is to it. That is, there's no way to draw photorealistic drawings—when you draw a picture of someone or something, that picture's status as an artistic product is inescapable; there is a delightful cartoonishness to drawings that isn't as often found in paintings.

Now, the artist behind these cloud dragons, Morihiro Hosokawa, is kind of a big deal. Not only was he the prime minister of Japan from 1993 to 1994, he was the first prime minister since 1955 who was not a member of Japan's ruling Liberal Democratic Party (LDP). According to Wikipedia, he has been "head of the Kumamoto-Hosokawa clan, one of the former noble families of Japan" since 2005. He's also dapper and handsome. In other words, he is charismatic enough to successfully buck deeply entrenched Japanese power structures, but savvy enough to remain on the ins with those same power structures after upending the apple cart. Finally, he appears to me to be a very gifted artist. So what's he going to do with all that talent?

He's going to go full Led Zeppelin.

Just like how Led Zeppelin at the height of their celebrity decided to pivot from disgusting sex acts involving mudsharks to ballads expressing their moralistic disapproval of Gollum, Morihiro Hosokawa, after making a deep mark on Japan, figured that now was the time to nerd out on cloud dragon fanfic. I admire his trashy authenticity.

Anyway, after having got my fill of Hosokawa's work, I determined I would take a seat on the ledge and take a closer look at this rock garden.

The first thing to note about it was its uniqueness as a tourist attraction. The garden's setup resembles a small amphitheater, with people sitting on a ledge functioning like an audience and rocks acting as the performers, presenting a very still show.

There are fifteen large rocks of varied sizes placed in groupings on white sand. Besides the Abbot's Quarters, which enclosed one side of the garden, a hardened loam wall made up the other three sides. Behind the loam loomed tall, thin trees. The rocks were placed without any apparent principles of symmetry, and there were no obvious reasons for the shape of each pile.

I sat down and looked at the rocks. And then, the weirdest thing happened. I felt extremely unconcerned about everything, but I also needed to keep on looking at these rocks.

I realize those two descriptions are contradictory; anyone who is unconcerned about everything doesn't need to do anything. And yet, that's what it was: I didn't care, and I needed to look at the rocks. It was a need I knew I had, and I indulged it, but I also felt that if something prevented me from satisfying the need, that that wouldn't matter either.

The closest analogy I can think of is being caught in a stare. When I'm caught in a stare, I don't want to stop staring, but neither do I want to continue staring. It's a state where I find myself becoming passive. "I'll just wait and see what happens" is the caught-stare's motto.

Anyway, I wanted to keep looking at the rocks. It's not like looking at the rocks gave me any deep insights. But doing so was immensely fulfilling, in a way I've never experienced before. The best way I can describe it is that it immediately induced a meditative state in me.

Now, I've tried meditation before, namely breathing meditation and mindfulness meditation. I can do breathing meditation—whenever I follow the advice of whomever is leading me, I end up feeling light-headed and relaxed, as though I enjoyed a head rush while lying down, or like I just did a really high-class whippet. But every time I have tried mindfulness meditation, it's never worked. I have never succeeded at intentionally stilling my mind. Whenever I tried to empty my thoughts, really stupid thoughts would pour in, like "how does my cat know what to meow to me?"

But looking at these rocks somehow–miraculously–stilled my mind, and without any effort on my part. I could be wrong, but I think I spent at least fifteen minutes quietly looking at them. And weirdly, other people talking or laughing didn't bother me. Sometimes, I would stop looking at the rocks to say something to Shawn, but then I could dip right back into the meditative state.

This experience allowed me to solve a puzzlement I always felt about Buddhism. According to Buddhism, the reason we suffer is that we have desire; so, to stop suffering, you have to stop desiring. But if you become a convinced Buddhist, won't you develop an overweening desire to stop desiring? And if you have that desire, then it seems like you're back at square one, no?

These rocks told a different story. They said, "after a while, you can get to a point where you stop desiring to stop desiring. And that's actually the way to stop all your other desires too. Not that it matters!"

Eventually, we decided it was time to move on. Interestingly, Shawn had a similarly moving experience with the rocks, as it was also her first visit to Ryōan-ji. We were both amazed that we found it so fulfilling to look at these rocks! Walking away from them, I felt dazed. What had just happened? It kind of upended a lot of my ideas of desire. Like, usually when something is really fulfilling, I want more of it, until it stops being fulfilling. Right? But apparently, you can have your fill of fulfillment, without being full—I had room for more, but it would have felt gluttonous to indulge.

OK, so ends my description of the rock garden given my knowledge base at the time. In writing this entry, though, I learned a little more.

The first thing I'll say is that I didn't want to learn any more. I approached the online sources with trepidation: I feared that learning anything about the garden would undermine my experiences of it. That said, I was still curious to see what would happen when I learned more about the garden. To be honest, not much did happen, except that my respect for its creators increased.

Speaking of its creators takes me to the second thing I'll say, which is the first thing I learned during my 'research': there is a fair bit of controversy about when and who made the original rock garden; some say Zen monks made it, some say untouchable (in the caste sense) gardeners known as "kawaramono" made it, and some say both. However, the editors of Wikipedia claim that there is a "conclusive history ... based on documentary sources" according to which it was designed by Hosokawa Katsumoto and built (by other people) in 1450. Then it got burned down. Then it got rebuilt. The first written description of it, given some time between 1680 and 1682, is that it had nine rocks. However, it seems to have been destroyed (again!) in 1779 and rebuilt in its current form, with fifteen rocks, before 1799 under the designing guidance of Akisato Rito, who is described as a "[g]arden writer and specialist."[3]

The third thing I'll say—and here's one reason that my respect for the creators increased—is that the fifteen rocks in the rock garden are placed in such a way that you can't see all fifteen of them from any position: "The fifteen rocks are carefully arranged so that there is always at least one rock that cannot be seen, regardless of the angle" (discoverkyoto.com). I find that intriguing. You can't ever take all of it in at any one moment. This must be intentional, but I'm not sure what the intention is.

And that takes me to the fourth thing: there is dispute about what the rock garden was intended to mean. The most popular theory is that the rocks are meant to represent a family of tigers crossing a river, which is definitely what it was intended to represent when there were only nine

---

3. https://en.wikipedia.org/wiki/Ryōan-ji

rocks, and which also dovetails nicely with Morihiro Hosokawa's dragon fixation.

As cool as that is, if I learned that's what it solely meant, it would have diminished the experience of the garden for me, like when the Dude desperately retraced Jackie Treehorn's sketch in *The Big Lebowski*, only to discover a bawdy drawing of a well-hung gentleman. The interpretation I would prefer to be true is the one given by the historian of gardens, Gunter Nitschke: "The garden at Ryōan-ji does not symbolize anything, or more precisely, to avoid any misunderstanding, the garden of Ryōan-ji does not symbolize, nor does it have the value of reproducing a natural beauty that one can find in the real or mythical world. I consider it to be an abstract composition of 'natural' objects in space, a composition whose function is to incite meditation." (Quoted in Wikipedia.) I find the idea of designing something quite deliberately so that it can't symbolize at all to complement what I was saying earlier: the garden is trying to get past symbolization like we're supposed to be trying to get past desiring. And since this interpretation coincides with my independently experienced realization about the Buddhist take on desire, over 224 years after the garden was designed, it must be correct.

The final thing I want to say may be the neatest. There was an article, "Visual structure of a Japanese Zen garden", published in *Nature* back in 2002, by Gert J. Van Tonder, Michael J. Lyons, and Yoshimichi Ejima. Using some hoity-toity computer processing, the authors discovered that the combination of the temple and the rock garden, when seen from above, resembles a tree with branches coming out of it, and that the rocks' position represents where the branches would go. Moreover, if you use a computer simulation to move the rocks just a little, it's impossible for it to convey this tree structure, and our visual processing systems can unconsciously sense that the newly positioned rocks no longer convey anything, and all of a sudden the whole production loses its intrigue. They conclude from the rock garden's fine-tuning that its design must be intentional.

I don't know whether that's true—just because something is published in *Nature* and uses computers doesn't mean it's true!—but it is, as they say, big if true. It would be another of history's mysteries, like how the predecessor nut to almonds was teeming with cyanide, and yet people somehow bred almonds to the point where they were no longer deadly poisonous, but were instead just mildly disappointing. You wonder, "how did anyone figure that out?"

Back to the rocks. As I wrote earlier, Shawn and I had moved on. We turned away from the rock garden and walked along the perimeter of the Abbot's quarters. Just a short distance away from the perimeter, there was another building, partially obscured by trees, that was linked to the Abbot's quarters by a covered walkway. Since this new building seemed to hold worlds all its own within, we weren't ready to venture over; we still hadn't finished walking the perimeter.

That took us to the next noteworthy feature: a water basin (tsukubai). This was a small, round stone basin with a square carved into its middle. Over the square, water trickled in from a bamboo spigot. And four large kanji were inscribed next to each side of the square. I didn't know this at the time, but the characters, when read to include the square, read "ware tada taru wo shiru", which means "I am content with what I am." Something to aspire to. In fact, now that I think about it, I know I'll never be happy until I do this!

Again, this basin managed to induce a great stillness in me. It wasn't quite up to the level of the rock garden, but the gentle trickling of the water over the stone, along with the sunlight reflected off the water, was peaceful and calming. But I was still recovering from the dazzlement caused by the rock garden. I don't know about you, but when I wake up from a deep, satisfying nap, my first instinct is not, "let's do the damn thing again, brother." Instead, it's "that was nice. Time to wake up." So too here.

I changed my focus. Instead of scrutinizing the basin, I looked at the sign next to it. The sign read, "This water is not for drinking." Remembering that we were at a Zen temple, I realized that this was probably a Zen koan. I set about figuring it out. Water, of course, is usually for drinking, but it has other uses: bathing, cooking food, and powering hydropower facilities to make electricity. This water was, at the least, not for drinking. Was it also not for those other things?

Resisting the urge to throw the raw chicken I carry everywhere into the basin in the hopes that it would boil into a delicious juiciness, and not noticing any nearby hydropower facilities, I enjoyed the epiphany that maybe the water wasn't for anything. Maybe it was just for itself, and not for us. This was, I imagined, a Zen thought: think about things from their own perspectives.

Continuing along the perimeter took us back to the foyer of the Abbot's quarters. We still hadn't crossed the bridge to the mysterious building, but we figured out that going that direction would take us off the grounds altogether, so now it was time to peruse the gift shop.

That lofty black-and-white photograph hanging over the gift shop took on greater significance now that I had realized what it was they were trying to commemorate. The photograph was not to scale, but it was gigantic enough to convey the importance of the rock garden: bigtime photo for bigtime rocks.

I obviously couldn't buy that photo—I don't recall it being for sale, but if it were, it would have been thousands of dollars. Instead, I looked around for a more workaday reminiscence of the garden. Though there were a few options, what caught my eye was a small, stylized drawing of the rock garden with (what looked like) five monks discussing the garden. One was pointing at something in the garden while the other four looked at what he was pointing out. The drawing was on a cardboard backing that folded in half so that you could stand it upright on a piece of furniture.

I knew this was what I wanted to buy. The plan immediately unfolded itself before me: I would buy this, place it on my desk, and whenever I found myself anxious about work, I would open up the drawing, look at it, and remember the blissful indifference I felt back in Kyoto.

But then, I thought further: back home, I had a friend, Lon, who suffered from a severe anxiety disorder. The real rock garden incited powerful peacefulness in me and Shawn when we confronted it. Perhaps when Lon was feeling stressed, he could open up the drawing, look at it, and feel his stress melt away?

Nah, I wanted it.

But maybe I could buy two, one for me and one for Lon?

Nah, it was $40. Lon can solve his own problems.

And reader, guess what? He did! He started taking drugs. And he says they really worked! Meanwhile, I'm right now looking at a sketch of that rock garden on my desk, smiling in delight. And anyway, I ended up buying Lon a samurai bobblehead.

Commemoration in hand, Shawn and I began our long, lingering departure from Ryōan-ji. We hadn't visited the mysterious building yet, so it was time to cross the bridge and pierce its mysteries!

Well, there was no penetration after all.[4] We weren't allowed inside, so the mysterious building remained mysterious. Moreover, I didn't discover

---

4. Story of my life.

anything about its contents in my brief forays into 'research'. It turns out, though, that the building isn't what's important about this part of the Ryōan-ji grounds, anyway. Instead, the Kyōyōchi pond was the highlight.

Now, the Kyōyōchi pond wasn't immediately visible. It's not like it abuts the mysterious building (the more I call it "mysterious," the more I think it's probably, like, an abandoned pigeon coop). Instead, it emerges after you stroll down a gravel path with some charming trees standing alongside it. Indeed, the entire area leading up to and surrounding the pond is called a "strolling garden" (discoverkyoto.com).

Shawn traipsed through and I loped over the path, which, I'm pretty sure, amounted to a collective strolling. The temple workers had planted a sign on the path. It read:

DO NOT TOUCH
TREES PLEASE

Someone more foolish than I would assume the sign was prescriptive, telling tourists to keep their oily fingers off the nearby bark. I realized, though, that it was another koan. Most likely, it was telling us not to touch the sign itself (after all, the "DO NOT TOUCH" was written on the sign, not on each one of the trees, which would have been far clearer); moreover, it was reminding us that trees please the senses. So, stop touching that sign, and start letting those trees please you! Putting it like that, though, makes it more into a humorous piece of doggerel than a Zen koan. That said, I'm nowhere near enlightened; it's not surprising that I don't grasp the deeper meanings.

After passing a few more copses, the pond emerged. It was a nice way to recover my senses after the sensory-deprivation-tank-like effect of the Zen temple. I saw a small island in the pond (it could have been a peninsula, actually), and ducks were flapping their wings coquettishly, tempting me with their delicious flesh. The nerve. As we left, we passed one last koan, staked at the outskirts of the lake. This one read:

```
               Caution
    This area is dangerous. please do
      not play or come close to the
             edge of the lake.
```

Now, this was a puzzler. First, the area was manifestly not dangerous. Second, the sign was itself close to the edge of the lake, meaning that to even read the sign, you had to go close to the edge of the lake. Third, I get why they were telling us not to come close to the edge of the lake, but why were they telling us not to play? What if kids were around??

It was at this point that I realized that these were not koans at all, but were, instead, pranks. Some enterprising chucklehead decided he'd have a good time at tourists' expense by writing confusing messages. Disgusted, I looked away.

The troublesome japery I suffered as I left Ryōan-ji fills me with dismay every time I think about it. Lucky for me, the drawing of the world's #1 rock garden stands on my desk, reminding me of one of the few times I've had a powerful religious experience.

I don't have the Zen drawing in an honored place on my desk. It's not framed. It's vulnerable to my regular spills, though amazingly I haven't yet doused it in pink lemonade flavored Spindrift or smeared it with banana particles. Instead, it stands, awkwardly, atop a pile of Briscoe's old school work and some journal articles I've read and dismissed. It bends towards me a bit, as though it's bowing or, more likely, about to fall over.

I can't say it dispels my anxiety whenever I look at it. Indeed, I often move it when I periodically clean my desk, and then forget about it, only to remember it and reinstall it weeks later. I can say, though, that when I've been trying assiduously to reconstruct my experiences of the rock garden, it has been quite helpful. Strangely, it doesn't make me calm. It makes me cry. Truly. I'm so happy that the place exists, and so sad that I can't go back there whenever I want.

I think the garden would tell me that it doesn't matter that I can't go back there. I disagree with the garden. I'm not a Zen Buddhist. I think it matters.

We'll have to agree to disagree.

# 24

# Checking on Checking in

Done with Ryōan-ji (though hopefully not forever), it was now time to head to our next hotel, Suiran. Shawn had told me that Suiran, along with the Ritz-Carlton Kyoto, would be one of the two most luxurious hotels we would stay at during our trip. It felt like tempting fate to move from luxurious fullness to Zen emptiness, and then back to luxurious fullness, the travel equivalent of the bends. But although I wasn't a seasoned diver, I figured I could deal.

Whereas the Ritz-Carlton was in central Kyoto, Suiran was located in Arashiyama, a district on the western outskirts of Kyoto. As overwrought as this seems, moving from the Gion area to Arashiyama was like going from one city to another. The area near the Ritz felt like a college town with a certain amount of hustle and bustle to it, whereas Arashiyama felt like Vail, Colorado. When we got out of the subway, there was a long drag of cute (read: pretty but short) high-end shops and restaurants that stretched from the Arashiyama subway station to the Katsura River. This being the Japanese new year, we saw some people walking around wearing kimonos, and this being Japanese Vail, we also saw some rickshaws trundling down the road. There were cars, too, of course, but they moved quite slowly, as though being transported on a ski lift, and people crisscrossed the road in front of them, like so many out-of-control skiers.[1]

Although we couldn't yet visit our room in Suiran, we still wanted to check ourselves in. Heading to the bridge over the Katsura River, we made our way alongside the river down a bright, open path towards the mountains.

It was a glorious stroll. The sun blazed onto the river to our left, the mountains ahead of us were covered by an impenetrable treescape, the sky was bright blue and sparsely clouded, the road we walked upon was perfectly maintained, and a small stone wall blocking off encroaching forest accompanied us as we sauntered towards the hotel. We passed a bank of rickshaws, whose drivers waited outside of their wagons for lazy customers who wanted to slowly see Kyoto while enjoying someone else's visible labor.

Finally, we arrived at the entrance to Suiran. The asphalt road gave way to a large parking lot, with a trio of expensive cars conspicuously parked out front. Perhaps the top three cars in Japan? A stone wall prevented prying eyes from plastering themselves onto Suiran's facilities, and a white-masked, black-coated worker under a shaded arbor guarded a lectern possessing a book of valuable information about future and current guests. Sumptuous trees in all manner of undress proudly peacocked behind the walls, alternately inviting and intimidating.

We marched up to the gate like polite Mongols and gave our names to the lady womaning the lectern. She checked her information, and I was relieved to learn that, yes, this was indeed the place where we were supposed to be.

---

[1]. I've actually never been to Vail. Is it like that?

In writing that, I just now realized that, every time I check into a hotel, I worry that something will have gone wrong, and that as a consequence, I will not, in fact, be allowed to stay there. Because of this abiding fear, when I wait in line, I always prepare myself for a battle that never joins. I pull up the email proving that I did, in fact, make the reservation; I place in hand my driver's license, in case there are any shenanigans involving mistaken identity; and I mentally rehearse the discussion that I fear will ensue, ending with me passively-aggressively asking, "well, can I at least pay for the room I'm not allowed to stay in? I have wasted your time, after all."

I think this all emerges from a childhood incident that has traumatized me: my parents and I tried to check into a Greek hotel in the 1980s but, this being Greece in the 1980s, and this being my Greek dad in the 1980s, someone, probably both parties, failed to do what they were supposed to, and I and my family were turned away, and had to go to another hotel. Now, this really shouldn't be a traumatizing event, for two reasons. First, it's not that big a deal; there are a lot of hotels in the world, especially on the Greek islands, so we didn't find ourselves spending the night trading war stories with sirens in the Adriatic Sea. Second, I'm pretty sure the tale I spun in the first sentence of this paragraph never actually happened. I think it was something I as a child worried would happen and then, thanks to the mists of time and my genetically inherited paranoia, it ended up functioning as a in my decision-making process.

They say that trauma can be genetically inherited; what they fail to add is that if you and your mom are both paranoid, then made-up trauma also can move from one set of genes to another. I haven't researched this, but if my eight-year-old son's exaggerated wailing when he skins his knee is any indication, then it appears that fake trauma is not only heritable, but it's the worst trauma of all!

As I said, though, the employee at the gate confirmed we were where we were supposed to be. Then, she showed us a piece of paper asking us to sign and date our public assent to the following four propositions:

I am in good health with no cough or fever.
I will surely ask the hotel if I get a cough or fever.
I agree to the hotel calling the public health center if I get a cough or fever.
I will check out the hotel in case of hotel close due to the government's call, such as a lockdown.

If my paranoia dissipated after being told that we were allowed to be here, it returned as I looked over these possibilities, as they escalated from fine ("I'm fine?") to bad ("I have a fever.") to terrible ("The public authorities have been alerted!") to catastrophic ("They're closing down Japan!!"). I mean, I'm glad that they had a plan in place, and that they were willing to share it with all potential guests, but it unfortunately carried my mind from the Katsura River to *The Bridge on the River Kwai*.

Psychology tested, we passed the first checkpoint on our way to Suiran. I could now focus, guilt-free, on the rest of what Suiran offered. A path led us past a tea house to our left, and then wound to the right into a rather bigger building containing the hotel restaurant, the reception, a courtyard, and then a couple of floors that amounted to thirty-nine rooms.

We ended in the reception, of course, and it was here that Shawn was hoping to meet Hiromi, the hotel concierge who had been in email contact with her. Unfortunately, Hiromi had not arrived yet, so we were handled by someone else who was quite competent, but whose name I didn't catch. She moved us from the reception, which had a nice, but unglamorous, table with a couple of chairs in front of it, to the waiting room, which felt less glamorous still, consisting as it did of a couple of tables, couches, and carpeted folding screens that looked like they came from the 1970s. A family of four Germans sat nearby: a father and a mother, both somewhere in their mid-sixties to early-seventies, and a son and daughter, both somewhere in their thirties. I wish I could remember what they were talking about, but though my German is pretty good, it's not good enough to make out a quiet conversation.

I eyed those Germans speaking in hushed tones while they were in Japan, ever watchful for the emergence of new Axis powers. Fortunately, they were just tourists.

For now.

The lady and Shawn discussed the amenities and splendors that we, as privileged guests, were entitled to, as well as the cost of the room and the card it would be charged to. At the beginning of the conversation, though, she gave us each a glass of champagne to dull the part of our brains that worries about money, and then told us we could go to what I earlier described as a "tea house", but which is actually called "Café Hassui."

I will go into more detail regarding Café Hassui later. All you need to know now is that as I walked into the cafe, I immediately cracked the top of my head into an overhanging wooden beam before I stumbled into my seat at the two-top they had set up for me and Shawn. Normally, I feel embarrassed about such clumsiness, but in these circumstances it just made me feel proud of my immense height, and less self-conscious about my immense weight.

After horking down another glass of alcohol—this time, simple white wine (pinot grigio, if I recall correctly)—it was time to embark on the next part of the adventure Shawn had planned for us: Iwatayama Monkey Park, a park atop a steep hill sheltering a troop of about 120 Japanese monkeys. I looked forward to this, as I've always wanted to get into a fistfight with a macaque.

That may have been the booze talking.

# 25

# Making a Mountain Out of a Monkey Hill

Off we walked to Iwatayama Monkey Park. To get there, we merely had to go back to the bridge over the Katsura River and cross it. After crossing it, it was a quite short walk to the entrance to the monkey park, up a very steep flight of stone stairs carved into the mini-mountain we would end up climbing.

There was a small fee to enter the park grounds, but since Shawn was paying that, I let my focus wander to a bright yellow sign next to the vending machine. The sign was divided into two halves. The top half showed drawings of a plastic coffee cup and a hamburger, and they were both crossed out. Above the crossed out food and drink read the caption, "Don't throw away coffee cups and leftovers!" The bottom half explained why: at the top of the bottom half were the words, "It is dangerous! Wild boar comes out!" And then there was a picture of a frankly very cute boar with the words "Boo! OINK!" attributed to it.

In one sense, the meaning of this sign was very clear, and it confused only if you paid stupidly close attention, which is my wont as a philosopher. Obviously, you're not supposed to litter with food or drink, because your leavings may attract dangerous wild boars. But why was the boar portrayed cutely? Why not show a snarling, rabid animal that means your death? And why is the boar saying "Boo! OINK!"? My theory is that the boo is coming from whomever sees the boar, and the oink is the boar's oink of protest upon being deprecated by its audience. Or maybe it's just saying "oink" because it's an animal, and that's the sound it makes whenever it makes a sound. But why "boo!"? Why not "run!" or "kill it!"

Regardless of the sign's ultimate meaning, it was something of a useless warning. Essentially, it was a reminder not to litter, but who would even do that in Japan? I guess people usually don't litter out of a sense of propriety or shame rather than a fear of a violent pig barreling towards them, so perhaps it wasn't so useless; you want to do the right thing for the right reason, after all. Much more useful, though, was the multitude of signs counseling you not to touch or stare at the monkeys. Who knew that macaques were as prickly and violent as Ellen DeGeneres?

It was somewhat amazing walking to what I will call "monkey hill." Even though we were in Kyoto, a city with over a million people, to walk to monkey hill you trod a path through a dense forest, making you forget entirely that you were in or near any kind of city. The path gradually sloped upwards, and while you were walking it, you could look far below you (maybe 100 feet?) and see the forest floor. At one point, I looked down and saw a monkey, engaging in some kind of business. I knew we weren't supposed to stare at them, but I figured this only counted when they could see you seeing them. Plus, this little dude was about 100 feet away, so what could go wrong?

I was right! Nothing went wrong. All that happened was that we saw him digging in dirt. What he did was sort of sweep his hand across the ground such that a tiny spray of loose dirt flew in the direction he pulled it. While I was recording him, he did this three times and almost looked up at us. But he didn't!

# THE MOST AWKWARD MAN IN JAPAN

I have to say, his digging technique didn't look great to me. I suppose that millions of years of evolution, plus a few years of monkey school, probably moved him to dig in a fitness-optimizing way. Maybe he needed to sweep instead of really go for it because he was looking for cicadas or grasshoppers that emerged only when gently pulled rather than muscularly pummeled. But from my point of view, I felt superior to him, and almost wrote up a flier to drop on him explaining how to dig.

Still, this was thrilling: I got to see a monkey! In his habitat! And I stared right at him, and even recorded his boring doings with my phone! I'm not saying I was in any danger, but the fact that there were no bars or invisible electric fences preventing him from getting his paws on me made me feel brave, which is not the saddest thing anyone has ever written, but is in the running.

We ascended the slope. I had been doing a lot of walking up to this point, but I have to say, this was a draining climb! By the time we got out of the heavily forested part of the ... well, I was going to say "hill," but I was starting to feel like it was a mountain. Anyway, by the time we left the heavily forested part of the super-hill/nigh-mountain, and we emerged into a more sparsely vegetated part of the climb, we saw not just one, but two monkeys. And, best of all, this monkey-couple was play-fighting.

Detour: when I was young—about nine or ten—I went over to my brother's friend Paul's house. Paul's family had three cats, and while I was there, two of the cats got into a scrap. Not a real one, with screaming, drawn blood, and flying fur, but a play fight where one cat gets on top of the other and presses down while the other lies on its back and scrabbles upwards. I was mesmerized. My family owned a cat, but just one cat, so I had never seen a cat go into this mode. It was like I had owned a toaster all my life, only to discover three years later that it also had a "make standing rib roast" button. At this early point in my life, it was the greatest thing I'd ever seen a cat do.[1]

I tell you this because seeing monkeys play-fight, with their more sophisticated styles of attack and defense, similarly mesmerized me, such that I forgot to record it. Again, I fell for the greatest tourist blunder of all, which is to allow yourself to be immersed in the moment rather than distancing yourself for the sake of showing cool videos to your friends, thereby heightening your status and (hopefully) lowering theirs. Still, I recorded the macaques after they separated, and if you ever listened to the recording—you won't, I won't let you—the panting hope reverberating through each syllable I sputter is palpable.

And the hope was rewarded! Sort of. The monkeys began play-fighting again (if my son and his friend are reliable guides, there must have been a disagreement over when it's permissible to shout "Uno"), but unfortunately, they did it in a location with an obstructed view. So all I saw was heaving monkey-backs, which began to make me feel uncomfortably voyeuristic.

Finally, after a couple more steep climbs, we made it to the summit of monkey hill. A weathered building stood in the center with thick wire screens covering each window. At the edge of the summit were innumerable, beautiful views of Kyoto, and, of course, monkeys. Lots of monkeys.

There weren't just monkeys; there were also people. But most everyone was on their best behavior. So, although monkeys raced right next to the tourists and locals who visited just to enjoy their antics, even the children (mostly) didn't stare at the monkeys. Everyone (except, I assume, for the Australians, who are unable to hide their jubilation on any occasion) sort

---

[1]. And it still is!

of acted like this was just an everyday thing, the way that one dog just sits there smiling when everything around it is on fire. But if you didn't stare at the monkeys, but instead stared at the people, you realized that almost no one was a good actor. Everyone behaved like you do when a celebrity walks into the restaurant you are also dining in. You mutter to your lunchmate under your breath, "hey, that's Gwyneth Paltrow", and your companion says, "where?!" and you say, "eleven o'clock. NO, DON'T STARE!" And then you both pretend not to notice her. But if anyone were to watch the two of you rather than look for Gwyneth, what they'd see would be two people sitting across from each other at a table, studiously gazing in different directions, saying nothing. It is ... not convincing.

That's how everyone moved around outside the building. Inside, though, was a completely different story. When you walked in the building, you found an employee sitting behind a bench. She was the vendor who could sell you drinks or monkey food, aka peanuts, which helpfully doubled as human food. To the left was a big room, full of benches, and lots of windows (covered, as I mentioned earlier, by wire). The room was packed with people, and the atmosphere was boisterous. But the place was not clean. I mean, it wasn't filthy, there weren't piles of scum on the ground, but the vibe for me was "research station in Antarctica." It wasn't spotless, but does it matter? What, are you expecting guests?

Anyway, no one cared about cleanliness. What everyone wanted to do was drop the façade and finally stare their hearts out at monkeys. And, since people could feed the monkeys peanuts, what the monkeys most wanted to do was climb right up to those windows and get their treats. It was the epitome of a win-win situation.

An amusing change is that instead of seeing signs that read, "don't stare at the monkeys," you instead saw signs that read, "do not put your **face** on the fence." This was a perfectly useful sign, right up there with first ballot sign-hall-of-famers "cuidado: piso mojado" and "STOP," because after maintaining decorum for so long, under such tempting circumstances, I, like everyone else, wanted to stick my face right in a monkey's face, as though we were recreating the movie poster for *Enemy Mine*.

We also got to enjoy some good old-fashioned monkey buffoonery, as little toddler monkeys demonstrated acrobatic fence-climbing or pole-sitting, only to lose their footing and roll down a hill. Kawaii, thy name is monkey hill.

This was a straightforwardly great time. Basically, it was a petting zoo, but with monkeys instead of goats, and you weren't allowed to pet them, because if you tried to, they might rip the skin off your face and kill you and yours in a swarm of monkey brutality. Honestly, I think having a lowkey threat of violence hanging around makes petting zoos better; apparently, the perfect petting zoo would consist of goats whom you can pet, but one of them has a gun.

# 26

# Bamboo Forest, But Boo, Not For Us

Bodies fully intact, we left monkey hill and ambled to another of Arashiyama's highlights, the bamboo forest. The bamboo forest is a forest full of very tall bamboo trees, with walkways hewn throughout.

It turns out that bamboo trees reach very high into the sky, such that even in the late afternoon on a sunny day, they partly occlude the sun, casting long shadows over your path. Not only do they form a shadowy ceiling, they grow very close together, making it difficult to see what lies past the first layer.

Two groups would particularly love the bamboo forest: bandits, because they could hide, unseeable, within the trees, only to slowly and noisily emerge with threatening demands on your belongings; and pandas, for obvious reasons.

Eagle-eyed readers will notice that neither Shawn nor I fall into either of those groups. Not only is Shawn not a bandit, but she battles with financial bandits! And not only am I not a panda, but I strongly disapprove of them!

I have given this speech to my students many a time,[1] but here's the short of why I disapprove of pandas: pandas are overrated. To understand the long of why I'm not a panda man, let me take you through the mists of the past, way back to 2009, when my wife and I were on our honeymoon in Thailand. Our favorite city in Thailand was Chiang Mai, which, because of its charm, excellence, and mid-sizedness, reminded us of Ann Arbor, Michigan, the city where we met.

One of the sites we visited was the Chiang Mai zoo, which had a panda exhibit. The exhibit charged an additional fee (about three dollars) beyond the entrance fee, and we also had to wait in a long line to enter. While we were in line, we were warned not to take photos with a flash. Why? Because the pandas blink so slowly that the flash of a camera blinds them. Perhaps this is true of a wide variety of animals, but I'm skeptical, because I have never seen this warning in any other zoo, aquarium, or college campus.

This is of a piece with two other facts about pandas: first, it is extremely difficult to get them to have sex in captivity, to the point that zookeepers have had to show them videos of pandas having sex with each other. I

---

1. This is not storyteller's license (a.k.a., lying): it is, in fact, true that I have, on at least two occasions, explained to my students why pandas are no great shakes. Thinking about it now, though, this confuses me. How did my problems with pandas emerge in my discussions of philosophy? Why did I think it appropriate to rag on pandas, even if the subject did come up? It's not clear to me, and this is both why I study philosophy and why I am a poor teacher of it.

mean, how does an animal not just *know* that? Did they have to show pandas videos of pandas breathing, too?[2]

Second, pandas appear to like only one kind of food: bamboo. The problem is, bamboo is extremely sharp, and is barely caloric.[3, 4] Eating bamboo is like eating gravy off a knife, but there's no way to get the gravy without eating the knife, so the pandas were like, "to hell with it." Consequently, they had to develop extremely thick throats, to deal with the splinters.[5] But those throats were so thick that they could only eat a little at a time. Moreover, bamboo is essentially a plant-rock, so pandas spend between ten and sixteen hours a day eating it, just to make it to day two, at which point the process starts over.[6] I don't know how pandas' evolutionary forebears settled on bamboo as their food of choice, but it seems like they could have picked literally anything else and it would have been an improvement.[7] Like, have you seen American bears? These guys

---

2. Here I'm being unfair to pandas: as it turns out, there are tons of animals that lose the desire to procreate when in captivity. I suppose what's weird is why imprisoned human females get so horny, as evidenced by *Caged Heat*, *Caged Heat II: Stripped of Freedom*, and *Caged Heat 3000*.

3. Did you catch the bear pun?

4. Here's support for my claim that bamboo is not nutritious: https://www.pandasinternational.org/bamboo-the-giant-diet-of-the-giant-panda/ .

5. Here's support for my claim that they have thick throats: https://www.bioexpedition.com/giant-panda-bear/ .

6. https://www.wwf.org.uk/learn/fascinating-facts/pandas. See fact 6 on that link for evidence that they spend so much of their day eating.

7. Did you catch the bear pun?

knock over your garbage, jump in your pool, and fight your dog. They exhibit the spirit of America, which is, in a word, "yeehaw."[8] Why can't pandas be like them? Why are they instead a bunch of slow-blinking, fat-ass incels?

What's really mysterious is why so many people love these idiots. I mean, I get it, they're cute. But lots of animals are cute; the pandas were the only animals in the Chiang Mai zoo that had a line you had to wait in for forty-five minutes so that you could spend five minutes gawking at them. And here's the really strange part: on the same day when people (including us) were waiting to see nature's equivalent of Baron Harkonnen, the zoo also had tiger cubs.[9] Not tiger cubs behind bars, like some common criminals; but tiger cubs, in a box, right out in the open, that you could go over to and pet. With your hands! And there was no line. And there was a line for the pandas. The whole situation was an outrage, and it sickens me to think about it any further.

One thing I can say in favor of pandas is this: they poop about forty times a day.[10] There, I can relate.

Back to the bamboo forest. In my life, I have seen a fair number of movies that include bamboo forests, most notably among them the martial arts gem, Super Ninjas.[11] So again, I have pre-existing associations with bamboo forests. But weirdly, in my imagination, bamboo forests

---

8. My friend Chewy pointed this out to me. He's a professor, so take his slogan seriously.

9. Did you catch the bear pun?

10. See fact 10 of https://www.wwf.org.uk/learn/fascinating-facts/pandas .

11. Sometimes called *Five Elements Ninjas*. Seek it out if you haven't already seen it! I promise you that you may or may not be disappointed!

are populated with European magical creatures, like pixies or sprites, not Japanese magical creatures, like ... uh ... that kid from *The Grudge*. I think what happened is that bamboo forests just look magical, but ninjas don't seem magical (they just seem like murderers who wear disguises), so I guess I ported over creatures from old-school Dungeons & Dragons into this bamboo forest.

Perhaps I unconsciously sensed the disconnect between my two sets of associations, or (more likely) I was probably just exhausted from all the cool things I had seen in Kyoto, so after about half an hour of wandering through the forest, Shawn and I both felt that we'd had enough. It was time to go back to Suiran and finally see our hotel room.

# 27

# The Reward at the End of the Quest

When I was a kid, I played a bunch of fantasy role-playing video games where you would start out in a castle. You would explore the castle, but there would be a bunch of doors you could never open, and so at some point you left to go on your various quests. Eventually, you would get the doom-sword or whatever, and then you would have to go back to the castle and fight some demonic evil that was lurking within. Finally, you could open those doors, and inevitably, there would be all these great treasures and powerful enemies that at the beginning you had been five feet away from but could never access.

That's how things unfolded for me with Suiran.

When we first checked in, we could only go as far as the vestibule. But after surmounting Monkey Hill and surviving the Bamboo Forest, we could now go past the reception and walk into the actual hotel. We had the doom-sword![1] We walked up to our room and approached the door. Anticipation built: we would finally be able to explore the rest of the castle!

---

1. *I.e.*, it was 3 P.M.

Upon opening the door, the first thing we noticed was a lovely painting of Mount Fuji about six feet ahead. The second thing we noticed was that, after about two feet, the floor's material changed from tile to wood. Straddling the wood and tile parts of the floor was a bench, and under the bench were some fluffy white slippers. We were supposed to sit on the bench, take off our unhygienic outdoor shoes, and put on our clean slippers. I am nothing if not a rule-follower, so I did what I sensed I was supposed to do and reshoed myself.

Entering the rest of the suite, a sliding door to the right revealed a bedroom. The bedroom contained its own television.

When I was a youth—say, from boyhood to my early twenties—the first thing I would do when I entered a hotel room would be to turn on the TV. I don't know for sure why I would do that. I suppose I did it because vacation was out of my hands, so I almost never visited a place because I wanted to go there. Instead, travel was merely something that happened to me. Turning on the TV either gave me some measure of control, some reassuring familiarity, or just seemed comparatively more entertaining than whatever I was there to do.

When I started visiting hotels by myself, in my twenties, I would turn on the TV because I wanted to hear some comforting noise while I situated myself in my new environment. This was before podcasts got big. Nowadays, when I'm in a hotel, I'm either there to present a paper at a conference, or I'm there on vacation. In neither case do I want to watch TV anymore. It's a dead appendage to me—I have just as much use for it as I do for the travel brochures you find in hotel lobbies suggesting day-trips to Yosemite, Knott's Berry Farm, or Target. Even Briscoe, when we travel with him, doesn't really make use of the TV. He has YouTube on an iPad or my laptop. I wouldn't be surprised if, in a few years, television sets in the hotel went the way of the business center: shuffled off to the basement, showing nature documentaries, watched only by business raccoons and the mutant woman from *Barbarian*.

Back to the room tour: pretend I hadn't entered the bedroom, but had instead continued down the hall. Oh look! There's a door to my right, just past the bedroom, but unlike the panel door, which slid open, this door had a handle, so you could pull the handle down, push in, and voila!, you'd find yourself in a room hosting a toilet. There was nothing noteworthy about the water closet, other than that there were no windows or frosted glass in it, giving the feeling of sitting in a sumptuous, marble-tiled prison cell, complete with a bidet, a sink, and no bars.

As we continued, the hallway led us into a spacious living room, furnished with a couch, a bar, and another pointless TV set. But the last part of the room was the best of all. Tucked in front of a large window was a little nook, defined by an open bookshelf. Nestled beside a comfortable maroon armchair, a small, round table completed the cozy setup. In addition to offering an alternative view of the courtyard, the chair had a ledge next to it that seemed to be perfect for resting your hygienically beshoed feet.

Also in this open living room was a shower surrounded by clear glass doors. The shower had curtains that you could leave open or closed, depending on the amount of shame you have about your body.

The curtains remained closed.

The second component of the bathroom was the *pièce de résistance*, in fact, the main reason we were staying here. It had an *onsen*— a rotenburo, to be exact.

What's a rotenburo? A rotenburo, an outdoor hot spring bath, is a glorified hot tub. I write "glorified" not because I want to sarcastically diminish it, but because I want to give it its due daps. It really is what happens when a hot tub achieves its full glory. A rotenburo is to a hot tub what great sex is to having your trachea slowly crushed by a shoe.[2]

Let me paint the picture a bit more acutely. A wooden cover was used to enclose the rotenburo. Dark, steaming water appeared underneath a hand-sized hole in the cover. A bamboo faucet poured hot water into the hole at the pull of a rope. When you're ready, simply fold the wooden cover like an accordion and remove it from the top. Cover off, you can get in!

Where does this hot water come from? A hot spring! Apparently, there are about 3,000 hot springs all over Japan. Because the water comes from a hot spring, it has a lot of minerals in it, and back then, I chose to believe that the minerals had healing properties. I still choose to believe it, on the grounds that I am still alive and don't have a pegleg (knock on wood).

After showering we got into the rotenburo then and there. It was great! The air outside was fairly cold, so bathing in the red hot, mineral-infused waters of the onsen felt like how an ice cube must feel when it's dunked into fancy tea. The only things that stopped me from pouring about sixty ounces of honey and lemon juice into the onsen was the fact that we didn't have any, and I didn't want to.

One bit I had neglected to mention earlier is that the lady who checked us in at the beginning apologized to Shawn for being unable to upgrade our room. If what we had was a *regular* room, I imagine that the *suite* had not only an onsen, but a pipe from *Super Mario Brothers* that sucked you underwater and offered you your pick of giant gold coins.

Satisfied, healed, and revivified by the onsen, it was time to have dinner. On the menu? Wagyu beef.

---

2. At least for me, those two activities are distinct. TMI?

# 28

# The Very Definition of Romantic

After our dip in the onsen, Shawn and I had to get ready to go to our dinner. To figure out which restaurant to patronize, Shawn had, stateside, researched the eateries within walking distance of Suiran, and the place she had the best feeling about was a steakhouse called Boruta. She inquired over email of the concierge, Hiromi, about helping to secure a restaurant reservation for us, and whether Boruta was a place we should, maybe, check out. Hiromi was delighted by Shawn's suggestion, for she was going to suggest Boruta herself.

This, by the way, is a life hack I've learned. My previously mentioned friend Lon has strong opinions about things. I told him I was reading a great new book, *The Status Game*, by Will Storr. He asked me what's so great about it. I told him it's great because it agrees with everything Lon already believed, only it added a bunch of endnotes. Lon agreed with me that this was the highest compliment someone could give any book.

So here's the lifehack: all you need to know in order to figure out whether something is good is to answer the question, "does it agree with me?" If yes, it's great! If not, it is at least mildly sus. I call this the confirmation bias theory of excellence, and everything I've looked up supports it.

We left our room at 5:15 PM, even though our reservation at Boruta was for 7 PM. Why so squirrelly? Well, Shawn had been informed that Café Hassui had a happy hour from 5-7 PM, and Shawn was as likely to pass up free booze as an alcoholic was likely to pass up free booze.

On the way from our room to Café Hassui, we passed by a member of the staff, who asked whether the lady in our party was Shawn. Shawn confirmed the staffer's suspicion, upon which she revealed herself to be none other than Hiromi! She was thrilled to finally get to meet Shawn, as though they had learned months ago that they're actually sisters who were separated at birth. Her smile was big and genuine, even under the mask. I was touched and confused by her enthusiasm. I mean, I get it, I'm a big Shawn-enthusiast myself, but Hiromi's excitement was supererogatory. Imagine if, every time you made an appointment with your mechanic, the person taking your car in treated you like their long-lost child and gave you a lamb dinner.

Gosh, now that I think about it, that would be great.

Well, it *was* great. I guess Hiromi probably really likes her job! After about three minutes of pleasantries, we parted ways with Hiromi, never to see her again. I assume Hiromi cried fat, rueful tears, at least until she met literally anyone else.

We made it to Café Hassui at about 5:30. As much as my earlier bump to the head pumped my ego up to Goliathian proportions, it also really hurt, like when David epically bonked Goliath with a sling-bullet. So, I was significantly more careful entering the café on my second visit: Davids could be lurking above every corner!

The place was bustling; apparently, a lot of the hotel's rooms were occupied by people who were rich enough to afford a room at Suiran, but cheap enough to jump on any free stuff that was on offer. I guess that's how they got rich!

It was a cold night, and most of the patrons were sitting indoors. Indeed, if we wanted to sit inside, we would have to wait for a party to vacate its table. We were going to walk from Café Hassui to Boruta, so we were already aptly clothed for the weather. Consequently, we were happy to sit outside.

The terrace overlooked the river with about six tables lodged against the wall separating Café Hassui from the riverbank below, and the river beyond. Even bundled up as we were, it was still too cold for us. I cursed my uncharacteristic overconfidence. It's one thing to wear enough clothing to ward off the cold during a walk—that's fun! It's quite another thing to sit there in the forty-five degree weather, motionless, having no choice but to wait for a St. Bernard to bring you its barrel of warming brandy.

Lucky for us, the St. Bernard came! Only instead of brandy, it carried cava. And instead of being a dog, it was a human. And instead of letting us snuggle up to its warm fur, it—uh, the human—brought us a heat lamp.

Seated at dusk, our balcony table allowed us to gaze upon the river and the forested mountain as the sun set. A few kayaks streamed down the gently flowing river, and joggers traversed alongside. It was a languid and splendid scene, inspiring reflection.

Shawn and I both agreed that it was one of the most romantic nights of our lives. And it was! But, in recollecting it, I'm not sure what the best explanation for that was. The night was definitely romantic, but what was it about that night that was so romantic?

This is one of the two occasions where the dictionary definition of a word is actually helpful.[1] The *Oxford English Dictionary*—at least, the search results allegedly coming from it via Google—defines "romance" as "a feeling of excitement and mystery associated with love" or "a quality or feeling of mystery, excitement, and remoteness from everyday life."

The combination of those definitions captures the romance of the night. It didn't have to do with eroticism, because, quite frankly, I always want to jump Shawn's bones. Instead, it had to do with fulfillment, love, and distance from prosaic concerns. Here we were, in Kyoto, Japan. We were now each on our second glass of delicious wine. The sun had set. Lights from bicycles on a distant road navigating the mountain commanded our attention as they whizzed past. The luminescence of the moon shimmered grandly on the surface of the river. The whole scene was what I assume Norman Rockwell would have painted if the *Saturday Evening Post* had ever commissioned him to paint a picture of FDR's little-known fifth freedom: freedom from taking care of your kid on a Tuesday night.

We had had a good trip, and we were very happy with each other. I was thankful to Shawn for planning it, and I think she was thankful to me for enjoying it, not to mention proud of herself for organizing such a violently opulent vacation.

---

1. The other occasion? Starting a speech!

I realize that this is a bourgeois imagining of a perfect evening. But I am bourgeois![2] And trying to run from what you are is what the *children* of the bourgeoisie are supposed to do, not the bourgeoisie themselves. So I look forward to Briscoe torching our house when he's twenty-two, although knowing him, it will probably be an accident that he later tries to disguise as principled arson.

---

2. I put the point this way in homage to a remark by the philosopher Peter Strawson, one of the most eminent analytic philosophers of the twentieth century. In 1977 Strawson gave a lecture in Sarajevo. Here's how he described his experience of professing philosophy in a Soviet satellite country: "In Sarajevo, where I was only allowed to give one of my two scheduled lectures and had minimal contact with my fellow academics, one perhaps time-serving young man in my audience suggested that my lecture revealed an essentially bourgeois outlook. I replied "But I *am* bourgeois – an elitist liberal bourgeois.' My interpreter commented, *sotto voce*, 'They envy you'" (quoted in Timothy Williamson, *The Philosophy of Philosophy, Second Edition* (John Wiley & Sons Ltd., 2022), p. 350). I may not be eminent, or elitist, or in the twentieth century, but I am like Strawson in this regard: when people criticize me, I tell myself they're just jealous.

# 29

# Beef over Fish

Drunk on happiness, but only tipsy from wine, we shambled over to Boruta. At night, suburban Arashiyama mostly emptied out, and few other people were seen on this January night. The walk took fifteen minutes, and we passed by many buildings that, veiled as they were by darkness, looked to my anxious eyes like they should be swarming with criminals. If I had seen those buildings in America, I would have felt my spine tingle and my hackles raise, prepared for the danger of a drug addict emerging and asking me for $10, and then getting mad at me when I gave him $20.[1] But in Japan, I felt extraordinarily safe, and I realized, for the first time, that there are no bad parts of Japan.

I mean, I'm sure that's false. There probably are bad parts of Japan, but I doubt you'd accidentally run into a den of yakuza in, say, a pug café.

---

[1] "I don't want your charity!!" he'd scream at me.

Regardless of whether it's true or false, it certainly *felt* true.[2] I had the freedom to go anywhere, at any time of night, by myself or in a group, razzlessly. It felt immensely freeing. It made me realize how much I constrict my own movements in the USA. There are all sorts of places I avoid, for fear of getting injured, hearing really disturbing commentary loudly yelled near me, or feeling pressured to give money to someone whom I suspect will spend it all either on booze or crypto.

I think you know the kinds of places I mean.

Don't make me describe the demographic characteristics of the people in these places!

Ok, fine.

I'm talking about amusement parks.

Teenagers still pick on me. And when they're in packs, rambunctious from Pepsi, and armed with slang I've never heard of? Forget it. I'm not going nowhere near there.

In Japan, though, there was none of that, save perhaps at Disney Tokyo. Of course, the language barrier might have helped; maybe there had been many people hooting at me to take my top off or to smile more, and I just didn't understand. But I strongly suspect that that wasn't happening either, as people pretty much pretended like I didn't exist and refused to make eye-contact with me.

---

2. My feeling wasn't *completely* off-base: According to *EastAsiaForum* (https://www.eastasiaforum.org/2023/03/08/crime-in-japan-is-back-to-normal/ ), you're 18.5 times likelier to be seriously assaulted in the USA than Japan, 26.5 times likelier to be murdered in the USA, and 67.9 times likelier to be robbed in the USA. Presumably, Japan's rate of serious assaults (low relative to the USA, but high relative to its murder and robbery rates) is due to rampant sumo-ism.

Back to the narrative: it seemed that our whole trip to Boruta was through back alleys and along unpopulated streets, as though our final destination was the trunk of an arms dealer's car. But I wasn't nervous because, as I mentioned somewhat recently: no bad parts of Japan. Eventually Boruta popped up, seemingly out of nowhere. It looked like it was located in a reclaimed parking garage. Besides the wooden door and two small slits for windows, everything was pale stone. It seemed like it wanted to be easy to miss.

It was not a large restaurant. Inside, there was one table with eight seats, and one counter with seven seats. And that's all the seating there was!

When we arrived, a close-knit group occupied the table. Probably a family, for it included children. Based on their relaxed, irreverent behavior, the patrons who were already there treated the place like a local haunt, the kind of place you go to once a week after a long day at work.

Besides the family, no other customers were present. We told a middle-aged woman who we were and when our reservation was for, and she happily seated us at the unoccupied counter.[3]

There is so much about Boruta that is, from my point of view, quirky. First is its limited operating hours. It's open for lunch from noon to 1 PM, and then again for dinner from 5:00 to 8:00 PM. That's not much time!

I suspect the reason for the limited time budget has to do with the fact that it's a family operation. There is a chef who cooks the steaks (the dad), the server who brings out the food and takes the orders (his daughter), and the person who works the kitchen and handles the miscellany (her mom). Add to this the fact that the daughter is in her forties or fifties, and the parents are in their seventies to eighties, and you have the makings of a sleepy steakhouse.

---

[3]. Don't worry, she worked there.

The second thing to note was that, although it was a top-quality restaurant, it was not that expensive. It was about $100 for the three-and-a-half ounce A5 wagyu filet mignon, and $70 for the similarly sized A5 wagyu sirloin. In Los Angeles, these dishes would cost between two and four times that price. And that price included side-dishes, appetizers, dessert, and coffee. At these prices, this could be my local haunt, the kind of place I visited once a week after a long day at work!

In keeping with the surprising affordability was the fact that, although the interior was clean and spiffy, it did not seem luxurious or expensively-lit like an American steakhouse. Rather than modish, it appeared Boruta was just trying to get the job done. Nothing was gussied up; the brightly lit interior felt to me antiseptically clean and utilitarian, as much chemistry lab as fine dining. As for art, there was one large painting that looked like a big, square portion of mashed potatoes. I should say, I was famished, so Shawn looked like a healthy serving of coq au vin and the counter looked like a breadstick.

While we got seated, the father, resembling liverwurst poured into a chef's uniform, was cooking steaks for the table behind us. We showed up at the tail end of the process, but I could see ramekins of butter, garlic chips, lemon juice, and some kind of pink seasoning next to the range. The daughter, whose open face and trim musculature made her appear for all the world like a friendly lambchop, took our order: Shawn ordered the sirloin, and I the filet. She also took our initial drink order, holding up for us the magnum of sake from which she would pour us our libations, as though it was courtroom evidence that the defendant did indeed intoxicate the plaintiff (verdict: guilty).

Drinks were nice, but it was imperative that we started getting served food, lest I eat the whole staff. They started us off with a small bowl containing a single, large broccoli floret. The bowl was quite attractive and unusual, having sixteen holes running around the perimeter, just under the rim. It was the bowl's way of saying: no soup! Just broccoli!

The broccoli was ... good? I mean, it tasted like good broccoli. Is that better? The point is, it wasn't anything divine. I'm not sure broccoli can be divinized. God came to earth in the form of a man, not a vegetable. Though now that I think about it, maybe vegetables also fell and needed a savior, and they got good broccoli, and we just never heard about it, because members of the Brassicaceae family are illiterate?

Regardless, the broccoli served as a nice baseline; it whet the palate, preparing us for the next item, an upside-down mushroom, by its lonesome on a wide plate, seared and blistered, like Anakin Skywalker on Mustafar.[4] Our server described it as "natural mushroom, from that day." This baffled Shawn; aren't all mushrooms natural? Isn't every mushroom from today? Imagine you went to a department store and you saw a blouse advertised as "real clothing, where it is". Wouldn't you be baffled too?

I wasn't, because I have a somewhat unusual deficiency. When someone says something to me that is even the slightest bit ambiguous between two or more meanings, I choose the less likely meaning a shockingly high percentage of the time. Like, if my American, German-speaking actor friend Trevor looks over at my wife next to a table and says, "what she's standing there for?", there's a 50% chance I'll ask, "who ... Shawn or the table?" At which point we'll have the following dialogue, which I promised never actually happened, but which I also promise basically always happens:

Trevor: uh ... your wife. Why would you think I meant the table?
Me: well, I thought maybe you were using German genders.

---

4. I don't remember the scene I'm talking about either.

Trevor (incredulous and confused): but, uh, ... I was speaking English ... ?

Me: I know, but you recently did a role where you spoke German. I figured it was subconsciously entering into your vocabulary.

Trevor (pausing, and then suddenly remembering): ... but the German gender for "table" is masculine!

Me: I know, but I figured you made a mistake.

I don't know why I'm like this; I suspect it's because I spent the first eight years of my academic career interpreting Kant, and if you want to make your bones as an academic who publishes papers interpreting the third-most interpreted philosopher in the history of the west,[5] you have to come up with novel, *i.e.*, incredibly unlikely, interpretations.[6] So, my interpretive license is either an occupational scar or the scar that got me into my occupation.

But at that moment, in that restaurant, my penchant for maddeningly implausible reads on straightforward utterances came to our rescue. Right after Shawn asked me, "what is she talking about?" I said, without missing a beat, "oh, 'it's natural' because someone picked it from the forest, and it's 'from that day' because it was picked today." Shawn was impressed,

---

5. I honestly don't know who is the first-, second-, or third-most studied western philosopher ever, but I was relying on this unscientific poll: https://leiterreports.typepad.com/blog/2009/05/the-20-most-important-philosophers-of-all-time.html .

6. I owe the point about how historians of philosophy have to indulge increasingly unlikely interpretations in order to get published to a blogpost by the philosopher Michael Huemer called "Against History." For some reason, though, his post has been taken offline, leaving no historical trace. I guess that means he practices what he preaches!

while I sagely nodded and, with a fake modesty, tilted my head and shrugged my shoulders, as if to communicate, "what can I say? I'm just good at this sort of thing." Inside, though, I felt like I had just kicked the game-winning grand slam from half-court.

Oh, also, the mushroom was fine.

The next dish was daikon, a giant white radish. They gave us three pieces, lightly fried, and stacked together so that they looked like stones you'd collect from the beach. The dish harkened back to a similar dish we had at the Shōwa-era diner on our trip with Gourmand Tours. This was more beautifully presented, wasn't as thickly breaded, and the pieces, rather than cut into thin strips, were instead carved into thick, hardy nuggets, so that the flavor of the vegetable could speak for itself.

Again, it was palatable, but at the end of the day, it's a mild-tasting vegetable. Unless there's some special paradisiacal vegetarian restaurant I've missed out on—a possibility I'm both completely open to and rather hopeful for—I just think the ceiling of flavor for vegetables is low. Like a delivery truck for Aramark, they are vehicles for sauce, salt, butter, or breading.

Now it was time to prepare the steaks. I saw them there, sitting on blue-and-white fine china. The wagyu filet and the wagyu sirloin, hanging out, a team. The filet was tall but stout, with two large veins of fat coursing through the red meat, and, off each vein, myriad white capillaries. Next to it lay the sirloin, wider but flatter, with just as much white as red, such that it wasn't clear whether it was marbled with fat or speckled with meat. The two steaks reminded me of myself and Shawn: I was the wide, flat sirloin, while the tall, stout filet was Shawn's butt.

The chef took the plate of uncooked meat and presented it to us like a beef-sommelier. Were we supposed to touch them? That seemed wrong. We didn't do that. In fact, we didn't know what to do, so we just smiled and nodded, like I do when I talk to my mom. I guess this was the right answer, because he then put the plate right back where it was.

Both of the steaks looked more substantial than 3.5 ounces. Based just on sight alone, I would have put the filet at six ounces and the sirloin at eight. But not only did the menu read "100 g" (which translates to 3.5 oz.), but there was also a food scale right next to the steaks! Yet what's weird about the food scale is that, although it was right between us and the steaks, I never saw him use it. It's like it was there in case the feds raided the place.

Before he put the steaks on the large grill, he gave each of us a cup of light brown soup. I have no recollection of what this soup was, or what it tasted like. In my almost five full minutes of researching what broth this was, I found only an unlabeled photo on tripadvisor, which shows the soup in the cup, as well as some weird puppet thing. We were not given a puppet thing. I would have remembered. Not only would I have remembered, I would have never forgotten.

Anyway, the soup was the last event before the main event began. Now, I'm something of a steak aficionado, not to mention quite good at grilling the things, so from this point on I looked closely at his technique.

The chef first seasoned the beef with a salt-and-pepper mixture—rather lightly, by my reckoning, and just on the top—and pressed the seasoning into the flesh with his fingers. The steaks seemed rather unyielding, giving me the impression that they hadn't been out of the fridge for long.

Next, the chef oiled the grill and placed the filet, salt-and-pepper side up, on the hot surface. For a little while, he just looked at the steak intently. No doubt, he had a very precise eye, alert to any minor changes in the filet's complexion, like a hawk searching for a prairie dog from 10,000 feet above.

The chef pulled out a long knife and a thin, wide spatula, the kind you could use to penetrate the interstices of plate mail armor. It was sharp enough to be a battle spatula. Using the battula, the chef alternately moved the steak around or pinned it in place while cutting off tiny pieces, for reasons that were unclear to me. Did he remove them because their spindliness would make them burn to a crisp? Were they significantly tougher than the rest of the steak? Or did they simply interrupt its symmetry?

I'm guessing it was the last one, but who knows? He did lots of things that I didn't understand, *e.g.*, speak in Japanese. Another example: there was a bronze ... cloche, I guess? ... that was on the grill at the same time as the steak, but nothing seemed to be under it. I thought maybe it was there, like a low-ranking racketeer, to catch heat, but he kept on moving and lifting it with his dangerous spatula, for no obvious reason. Part of me thought his seemingly whimsical movement belied hidden depths. Another part of me thought he was just banging it around to keep us entertained. A third part of me thought he was simply fidgety.

Once the filet turned from pink to gray, he placed the thinner (but still thicc!) sirloin on the grill. He moved it around a bit, this time with two spatulas, but again, I didn't know why. I know this is anti-growth mindset, but I was starting to think that trying to figure out how to cook as well as a trained Japanese chef with five decades of experience might not be something I could pick up by casual observation.

Nevertheless, ever the optimistic American, I continued to observe. He turned over the filet, and it had a nice, crispy top to it, but it didn't look like I expected, to the point that it shocked me. I swear to you that the cooked side of the filet, rather than looking like charred filets normally do—possessing a black, flat, top—looked like a charcoal-grilled hamburger. This was wild: a filet is fundamentally a pile of organically glued-together flesh strands, whereas a hamburger is a bunch of ground-up beef pressed together through human artifice. Somehow, he re-textured the meat!

And to further throw me off, while he was cooking it, he took a towel, wrapped it around his right hand, and pressed down on the top of the cloche, pushing into it a bit with his whole body. Only the cloche was partly on our raised counter and partly on the grill, so his force caused it to fall off the counter and land on the grill, making him somewhat lose his balance. He looked like a high school boy who leans against the wall, trying to be cool, but then falls into a broom closet. Yet while he did this, he wrought some kind of minor Jesusian beef-miracle, turning a filet-ceiling into a hamburger-roof.

At last, both steaks were done. He carved the filet while it was still on the grill, slicing it into six pieces. He did the same thing to the sirloin, except cutting it into eight pieces. Next, he splashed some watery substance (I think it was water!) onto both steaks, creating a cloud of steam. Then came a surprisingly small spread of butter atop both steaks, a squirt of lemon juice, and a drizzle of a dark sauce that I assume was soy sauce. Finally, he slid his spatula under each of the segmented slabs, and plated them.

I tried my steak.

I've seen movies where someone achieves some great goal that he's been striving to reach for the whole movie, only to get immediately shot in the face (*Uncut Gems*), impaled (*Serenity*), or eaten by a shark (*Deep Blue Sea*; *Kramer vs. Kramer*). I fully expected that to happen to me, because I believe that the flavor of this steak was what my whole life was leading up to. It was why I was put on this earth. God destines some people to create great art, and others he destines to enjoy, like, a really good game of Mario Kart. I fall into the latter category.

The flavor of my A5 wagyu filet opened up vistas I didn't know existed. It was a hallucinogenic gustatory experience, awakening papillae that had never been used, but that had nonetheless stuck around in the hope that victual extraterrestrials would beam down and ask for our tastebuds' leader.

My mouth involuntarily creased into a smile, and my head reared slightly back and slightly to the left, as though Lee Harvey Oswald had attempted to kind of assassinate me. All of me was in flavor country.

For a long time, I have asked people what their favorite animal flesh was to eat. Usually, the answer is beef. Occasionally, some people will say "chicken" or "pork", presumably because they wanted to be contrary, or because they had suffered a traumatic brain injury. But I always had a surprising, plausible answer in my back pocket. Yes, perhaps beef. But you know what? Maybe fish.

Fish comes in so many varieties, and this is if you just restrict yourself to fin-fish. Not only can you cook it in lots of different ways, but you've also got sashimi. So I've never known what my answer to this question was.

It was just my luck that I had had, but two days prior, the best sushi meal I'd ever had in my life. Moreover, it included my favorite kind of raw fish, mackerel. On top of that, it included my favorite part of any fish, crispy fish-skin.[7]

So I was in a unique position to answer a question that I have long pondered: which is better—the epitome of beef or the apotheosis of fish? Steak.

---

[7]. People who have salmon filet and eat everything but the skin are no better in my mind than people who have children merely for the pleasure of abandoning them.

Shawn asked me what I thought of my steak. I told her that our marriage was in danger, as I might leave her for perfectly cooked psoas major. She acknowledged the necessity of my potential decision, but staved it off by offering me a taste of her steak. I tried her sirloin. It was similarly excellent, and it was different, but it is beyond my powers as a writer or recollector of things to explain to you its ins and outs.

As chary as I was of doing this, I offered Shawn one of the five remaining pieces of my filet. She declined. It shocked me. "Why??" I asked. She slurred that she couldn't really appreciate the steak in the same way I could.

It was then I realized: my lady was stone-cold drunk.

This whole time, our server had been plying us with alcohol. I had been having my fill of sake and whiskey, while Shawn had been drinking sake and wine. But here's the thing about me: I am a very large man. I am an inch taller than six feet and I weigh 210 pounds.[8] And I have a surprisingly great tolerance for alcohol, beyond what my mass would suggest. Shawn, by contrast, is absolutely no taller than five feet, five inches (and definitely not shorter than 5'5"!), and also weighs a lot less than I do. Besides the two drinks we had earlier enjoyed at Café Hassui, we had drunk somewhere between three and five drinks each during this dinner. That's fine for me; not only am I large, but I'm as twitchy as an anthill in a hurricane, so I burn off alcohol like a French chef making crepes suzette for Wade Boggs. Shawn, on the other hand, is deliberate, still, regretless. So when she drinks alcohol, the booze has nothing to do but corrupt her. Her liver

---

8. At this point, you may be surprised that someone who has repeatedly described himself as the fattest man in Japan would be only 210 pounds. But I'm right, and you're wrong, because I have body dysmorphia.

says, "GO TO BRAIN. Go directly to brain. DO NOT PASS LIVER. DO NOT FORGET TO PAY $200."

Normally, when she's drunk, Shawn takes a leave of absence and gets a lady to cover for her. We like to call this lady "Chatty Kathy." However, despite Shawn's having shown up to this restaurant tipsy, Chatty Kathy had yet to be subbed in. I think this was because of the deference both Shawn and I offered to Japan, as well as the fact that we were the only customers in the restaurant (the family had left by the time we received our broccoli). Consequently, I did not know Shawn was drunk until she declined my offer of steak. I wheeled around, astonished, and my eyes locked with a pair of heavy-lidded eyeballs in the skull of an idiotically smiling, gently swaying federal employee.

This is why I love my wife.

She remembers zilch about the night. The pictures I took and videos I recorded triggered nothing except a proud satisfaction at her past life choices.

The night ended with dessert. They gave us three kinds—a cake topped by Stracciatella-looking tendrils of cream, a slice of tiramisu covered by a fistful of cinnamon, and some kind of custard cake. It was nice, but, like the vegetables, not worth describing in any great detail. Perhaps if we hadn't been so full, I would have more to say. But we were full, so I don't.

If you ever go to Kyoto, you really should try Boruta, if for no other reason than to make Hiromi happy.

# JANUARY 4, 2023

# 30

# You Can Notice a Lot of Stuff if You Just Read about It Months after You See It

We toddled home after our steak dinner and then went to sleep the sleep of the just-having-eaten. In other words, we felt too bloated to lie down, looked at our phones, found it difficult to fall asleep because of the blue light, and then enjoyed a fretful, shallow sleep. 21st-century America, folks, right in Japan!

Our first major task, upon waking on January 4, was to get some breakfast at the hotel. This is what happens on vacation: you consume to where your eating is positively calisthenic, which burns so many calories that you want to eat when you wake up. Those constantly vomiting Romans I've heard so much about (but never investigated because: gross) apparently knew how to live after all.

The restaurant we were dining at this morning was called Kyo-Suiran. According to Suiran's website, Kyo-Suiran was "[c]onstructed as a summer residence during the Meiji Restoration," and so it "invokes the feel of a bygone era, while embracing modern Japan." The Meiji Restoration,

I later learned, was a time between 1868 and 1872, when the emperor of Japan—Emperor Meiji, coincidentally—decided to consolidate all political power under himself, the emperor. At least when it came to restaurants, the Meiji Restoration apparently manifested as ridiculously low ceilings, presumably to represent the floor restoring the ceiling to itself, thereby collapsing the restaurant into a ball of pure emperor.

Regardless of whether I'm correct about that bit of architectural trivia, I noticed the ceiling in time before bonking my head, because a joist was hanging down so far that it obstructed my field of vision. I had to duck down just to see the rest of the dining room in front of me, which gave away the location of the low-hanging beam trying to concuss me.

Kyo-Suiran had a central(ish) table functioning as an island holding all manner of china within, carafes of coffee and hot water, shooters of juice, and glasses for cold water on top. Above it hung a spectacular lamp comprising three interlocking circles, making it look as though the rings of Saturn were having a fight while the planet took a powder.

Suiran's website described the food at Kyo-Suiran as "washoku cuisine prepared in the French style, using the freshest local ingredients." The denotation of "Washoku" in Japanese is, apparently, "Japanese food," but the connotation is that it's a traditional style of food emphasizing harmony, not only of the dishes with each other, but of the whole meal with the season in which it's offered.

I'll get to the food at Kyo-Suiran in a second, but I would not describe it as Japanese cuisine prepared in the French style. Instead, I'd describe it as "a mostly Western breakfast that got a little Japan on it."

The breakfast came in three waves. The first wave was a large tray with a lot of stuff on it. There were four small glasses of juice: red (watermelon), orange (orange), yellow (pineapple), and green (your typical thick, green, sweet spinach slurry or whatever). Those four juices stood in a row on the part of the tray that was farthest away from me. In the middle row of the tray were three small boxes of solid fare: a pile of sauteed, leafy vegetable; a small helping of prosciutto; and next to that, sliced peach with herb sprinkled atop. The third row on the tray—the row closest to me—began with some kind of gray beet-like thing covered with a white sauce and green herbs. It looked unappetizing and I don't remember how it tasted, but I'm guessing it was actually passable, for if it weren't, I would regale you with a rather heightened tale of my time in Japan eating what I think was marinated bark. Next to it was a bowl of yogurt with a float of chia seeds atop it. Rounding out the third row, a transparent box offered candied nuts and white currants. Finally, on the right-hand side of the tray, taking up the slack of the middle and closest rows, was a large white bowl holding some underwhelming slabs of pineapple and a pair of red grapes.

This was a fine start to breakfast, although the flavor was, compared to previous breakfasts, unremarkable. But, after learning about Washoku cuisine, I noticed that there was a lot of harmony that escaped the eye if you were oblivious to beauty and focused only on self-fattening.[1] The color of the orange juice perfectly matched the hue of the peach slices; the coloration of the leafy vegetable coincided with the green smoothie; the shade of the prosciutto was the tone of blanched watermelon; and the pineapple juice corresponded to the pineapple (that last one felt phoned in). As for the third row comprising the yogurt, the beet-stuff, and the candied currants: well, I'm not entirely sure what they were going for, but if you squint you can see various off-shades of white and gray among all the offerings. Perhaps a nod to winter?

---

1. My ears are burning!

The second wave was more restrained than the first, but also, I believe, more Japanese. We got only two things: first, a bowl of white rice and orange pork broth. Both its presentation and its preparation intrigued: the rice was beginning to mix with the pork broth, but it wasn't fully stirred together. It seemed that they had stacked the rice high on the right side of the bowl, and low on the left, and then poured the pork broth onto the left side of the bowl, making the rice on the right side appear to be an iceberg of rice (a riceberg, obvs.). I should add that the pork broth had big, delicious chunks of pork in it, and the rice was dotted with finely grated green herbs.

The second part of the second wave was a small bowl of orange-yellow curry. There wasn't much to say about this wave, except that the yellowness of the curry reminds me now of the pineapple, the orangeness of the pork broth recalls the orangeness of the peaches and the orange juice, and the white rice with green highlights brings back the whiteness of the yogurt, etc., and the greenness of the sauteed kale, etc.

The final wave was classic Western breakfast: a bread plate next to an egg plate. The bread plate held a picture-perfect croissant, a piece of Japanese milk-bread, and a hearty multigrain roll. My egg plate had two fried eggs (over easy), cooked so as to meld into a single white, flat, eggy circle, and next to that were orange tater tots, reddish ham, and a sprig of green watercress. White, orange, red, and green, again. Shawn chose the scrambled eggs, and they came out bright yellow, flecked with bits of cooked red tomato. Besides that, she had her orange tater tots and her reddish ham, and everything was accented with watercress. Orange, red, and green. But no white in her food, save for the plate itself which, like mine, was white with the occasional streak of green. In retrospect, I think that means Shawn was supposed to eat the plate.

# 31

# Traduttore Traditore

After we settled our business with Kyo-Suiran, we looked around the premises more closely. There were parts of the grounds we hadn't explored, so I decided to look at a novel nook next to the river.

It was beautiful, of course, but it was at about this time that I had had my fill of beauty. This was perfect timing, because I believe that I, as a writer, have also run out of ways to describe the natural and artificial beauty that we were seeing everywhere around us in Japan. That said, the experience of enjoying too much beauty is an odd one. My mind knew that what I was seeing was wonderful and, because I was soon going to leave and (maybe) never come back, fleeting. But it didn't matter; there was nothing I could do to appreciate the serenity, the harmony, the prettiness any more than I had already done. The distinctions I saw were ones I had already noticed. My meditations on them became infinite loops, recurring to the same themes after only a couple of cycles. The powerlessness I felt in crafting new observations was like the paralysis I endure when I have a great joke in my head: until I offload that joke from my mind onto some external medium (even another person), I can't think of any more jokes. It's like my joke-making facility is an amusement-park ride that can only have one rider at a time; until she[1] disembarks, no one can have any fun.

However, a difference between beauty- and joke-overload is that I can find more things to say about aesthetic excellence simply by changing the kind of thing I'm looking at. I had seen many river- and garden-scenes in Japan by now, including, thanks to the Silver Pavilion, probably the best garden I ever would see. But I had only seen one bamboo forest, and that was last night, and not for very long, so Shawn and I returned to it in the daytime, when it would be less mysterious, less crowded, and, *ipso facto*, more accessible.

After a short walk, we reached the main entrance to the Arashiyama Bamboo Grove. There were two differences between the bright version and the dark version of the bamboo forest that struck me.

First, in the morning light, the trees didn't seem as close together. I could see through the clumps of trees to other parts of the path, making the forest seem more controlled, and less like something that simply happened to one part of Kyoto.

Second, the trees didn't seem as high as before. Because of the great and powerful sun, the trees were generally unable to provide any patches of shadow for bandits to hide in, fearful only of RICO prosecutions.

Because we had just enjoyed both breakfast and a postprandial stroll, we were energized to map the forest more thoroughly than before. We discovered a cemetery marked by the sign, "It is off-limits of the graveyard this ahead excluding parties concerned." Now, of course, part of me wanted desperately to make fun of the grammar of the sign, but the greater part of me was impressed by the sign. Someone decided to translate a fairly complicated phrase from Japanese to English despite having only

---

1. All my jokes are ladies. In particular, debutantes.

a limited grasp of English. It may have required a lot of courage for that person to make that translation, though just as likely, the person was simply voluntold to do the work, and then sadly complied.

The effect of all these experiences, however, was to dampen the mystery of the forest and to make it more like an ordinary part of the neighborhood. Not only was there a graveyard here, there was also a Zen temple, and several paths out of the forest to other parts of town. Indeed, we left the forest and, after hiking for about ten or fifteen minutes, we ended up behind Suiran, looking at it from above a protective wall. It was like when I was a kid in my neighborhood growing up, and I realized I could get to places faster by just cutting through my neighbors' yards, which, as a young teenager, I did, many times.[2]

The sense of prosaicness that I felt about the bamboo grove, coupled with my inability to get any metaphorical blood from the pretty stones near Suiran, made me think the magic of Kyoto was wearing off. I felt like Cinderella noticing that it was 11:55. I feared Kyoto was becoming, in the words of the podcast *S-Town*'s John B. McLemore, a site of "proleptic decay and decrepitude."

I didn't want Kyoto to become ordinary, not only because the more familiar you are with something, the harder it becomes for you to notice its standout features, but also because I worried that its ordinariness would extend its tendrils forward into my memories of it. It was definitely time to leave Kyoto.

---

2. In retrospect, I'm not sure whether I feel guilty about that. As a homeowner, I would probably be quite alarmed if I saw unfamiliar teenagers walking through my backyard to get to school. But as an extrovert, I would enjoy the sense of vibrancy I would feel from living in a neighborhood full of children secure enough to do that.

Realizing that we probably shouldn't just jump Suiran's guard-wall and show ourselves to our room, we took the long way back. We packed our things and told the concierge to hail us a taxi to take us to the train station. After a brief wait, our chariot arrived.

Our taxi driver didn't speak English, but he was quite conversant with Google translate. We communicated little, but at the start of our drive, he noticed the morning sun shining brightly upon us through the windows, and proceeded to his phone. He dictated something into it, and after a beat, his phone told us, "if it's dazzling, you can raise the blinds." I really enjoyed this turn of phrase, so much that I wrote it down verbatim.

This leads to a theory of translation I've had for about twenty-four years now: when you translate words from one language into English, you shouldn't make that language sound like the way we Americans speak English. I developed this theory when I lived in Germany for a year, from 1998 to 1999. I noticed that Germans would use the construction, "ich hätte gerne" to say that they would like something. For instance, if you would like to eat something, you would say, "ich hätte gerne etwas essen." In a German class, this would be translated as, "I would like to have something to eat," but literally, it means, "I would have happily something to eat."[3]

Regardless of whether my more literal translation is technically accurate, I certainly thought (and think) that it's accurate, and it gave me the idea that German is just a more polite, formal language than English. Now, that was only one example, but thanks to the power of confirmation

---

3. At least, I *think* that's the literal translation. If you know how to speak German, and this doesn't sound right to you, then I would have happily you to tell me.

bias, after I concocted that theory, I saw evidence for it all throughout German.

I'm not the only person who thinks this way about translation, by the way. The Notre Dame theologian, David Bentley Hart, wrote this in the introduction to his translation of *The New Testament*:

> Again and again, I have elected to produce an almost pitilessly literal translation; many of my departures from received practices are simply my efforts to make the original text as visible as possible through the palimpsest of its translation. I cannot emphasize this too starkly: I have not chosen to fill in syntactical lacunae, rectify grammatical lapses, or draw a veil of delicacy over jarring words or images ... Where the Greek of the original is maladroit, broken, or impenetrable ... so is the English of my translation.
> (xvii-xviii)

When he produced this kind of translation, he got a surprise:

> What perhaps did impress itself upon me with an entirely unexpected force was a new sense of the utter strangeness of the Christian vision of life in its first dawning—by which I mean, precisely, its strangeness in respect to the Christianity of later centuries. ... most of us would find Christians truly cast in the New Testament mold fairly obnoxious ... Or, if not that, we would at least be bemused by the sheer, unembellished, unremitting otherworldliness of their understanding of the gospel.
> (xxiv-xxv)

I think that, if you want to be a faithful translator of any text—and I say this as someone who has done a bit of translation of contemporary German philosophy into English—you have to commit a balancing act of highlighting differences without overemphasizing them, while also ensuring community with your own language. In slogan form: people are different, but people are people.

The car ride was uneventful, though there was something romantic about being able to sit in the back of a car and look at the sunny sky through the sunroof. I haven't been able to look through the sunroof in our car for a while, because I'm often driving it. Also, the sunroof is broken.

# 32

# The Pre-Show

The taxi driver dropped us off at the main train station in Kyoto, the Kyoto Station, so that we could take a Shinkansen (a.k.a., bullet train) to Tokyo. That we were returning to Tokyo made me realize that my trip to Japan was almost over. We had stayed at the two most luxurious hotels we would stay at—the Ritz-Carlton Kyoto and Suiran—and were now on the way back to Japan's capital. Despite my preservative need to leave Kyoto, I was nonetheless sad that it had come to this: I was moving from pummeling poshness to gently slapping splendor. Still, there was one last highlight of the tour: Wrestle Kingdom 17.

Now is about as good a time as any to beat you over the head with my in-depth involvement with professional wrestling. (Don't worry, I won't be really hitting you; I'll just make it look like I am.)

I'll be honest: the original draft of this day involved a long disquisition describing the trajectory of my pro wrestling fandom from 1985 to the present day. However, that version, as is my wont, was both dilatory and myopic, to the point that just covering 1985 to 1990—the Hulk Hogan part of my story—took up seventeen pages.

If you've read this far, there's a chance you actually would read seventeen pages that could just as well be entitled "My Dinner with Hulk" as "January 4, 2023."¹ But in a book called *The Most Awkward Man in Japan*, there's a much greater chance that you'd be interested just in the Japanese part of my walk with wrestling rather than the whole journey. So I'll give you just enough backstory to focus.

I've been a fan of professional wrestling since 1985. As a kid, what I loved was the fighting (I didn't know it was entirely fake until around

---

1. Spoiler alert: "My Dinner with Hulk" would involve my having dinner with Hulk Hogan to the same extent as *My Dinner with Andre* involved Wallace Shawn's having dinner with Andre the Giant. And don't make fun of me for thinking that *My Dinner with Andre* involved a comedian who starred in *The Princess Bride* making a movie about hanging out with Andre the Giant, because *that actually happened, and it was called* My Giant. You'd never make fun of me if I thought the same thing about a movie called *My Dinner with The Mega-Powers*.

1987[2]) and the zany characters. In the 80s, in the World Wrestling Federation (WWF), wrestling was straightforward: there were good guys ("babyfaces") and bad guys ("heels"), and the good guys would follow the rules and be good examples for the kids, while the bad guys would cheat and be object lessons in what to avoid. The babyface standard-bearer was Hulk Hogan, who told his little "Hulkamaniacs" to say their prayers, eat their vitamins, and love America, while the prototypical heel was "The Million Dollar Man," Ted Dibiase, who bragged about his wealth and used his riches not only to get fans to degrade themselves in exchange for

---

2. In 1986 or so, I and my brother saw what the wrestling business calls a "house show"—a non-televised, live performance—at Hara Arena in Dayton, Ohio with our "Uncle" George (he wasn't really our uncle; he was our dad's friend, a fellow business professor, and a very loud Greek). I don't remember any of the matches I saw, though I do remember that the main event was Hulk Hogan against King Kong Bundy for the WWF World Heavyweight Championship. Earlier in the night, Uncle George told us that all the wrestling matches have predetermined winners – except for the championship matches. This confirmed my suspicions about the unreality of professional wrestling, though it had the (intended) effect of making me more invested in at least the championship matches. Then, just as the championship match between Hogan and Bundy was about to start, Uncle George told us that we had to leave, so as to beat the traffic. The fact that we were leaving before seeing the allegedly only real fight on the show was something of a tell that Uncle George didn't think the championship matches were entirely on the up-and-up. Being a ten-year-old, though, I never put two-and-two together. Until I was, like, eleven.

payment (which Dibiase always found a way to weasel out of paying), but also to bribe his way to the WWF championship.[3]

As I grew older and more studious, the rigors of high school forced me to direct my attention away from professional wrestling and towards studying ... *Friends, Seinfeld,* and *The Kids in the Hall.* Happily, this was when pro wrestling was in one of its cold periods. By the mid-nineties, though, wrestling got hot again, entering what the WWF called "the Attitude Era."

In the Attitude Era, the good guys went from being aspirational to relatable. In the time of NAFTA, declining union membership, and independent movies, wrestling fans didn't want someone who told them to straighten up and be a good boy. No, they wanted someone like them: a beer-drinking working man who didn't like being told what to do and stuck it to the boss (typified by "Stone Cold" Steve Austin); or a taciturn, white-faced, fun-hating clown who would stare at you for hours from the rafters and then suddenly drop down and try to murder everyone around him with a baseball bat (typified by Sting).[4] The bad guys, by contrast, were either the boss who set the rules (Vince McMahon) or the people who buttered up the boss to get special treatment (Dwayne "The Rock" Johnson and ... Hulk Hogan, with the new nom-de-guerre, "Hollywood" Hulk Hogan).

---

3. In real life, Dibiase and his three sons started a Christian ministry that they used to direct taxpayer dollars—earmarked for anti-poverty efforts—to their own personal enrichment. That's what wrestling fans would call "living the gimmick."

4. The wrestler, Steve Borden. Not the musician. Though, maybe the musician.

# THE MOST AWKWARD MAN IN JAPAN

I, like every male college student, got really into the Attitude Era, with its compelling storylines, over-the-top violence, and rampant sexism.[5] By 2003, though, Stone Cold Steve Austin quit, Sting had left for the indy wrestling scene,[6] and the Rock started his movie career. So, like every male college graduate, I quit watching wrestling and started some really intensive reading of Kant.

Between 2003 and 2014, I barely followed wrestling. I mean, I followed it closely enough to have heard of John Cena, CM Punk, and, um, Chris Benoit, but I don't think I watched many, if any, matches. In 2014, though, WWF, now called WWE ("World Wrestling Entertainment") because they lost a lawsuit to the World Wildlife Fund (how did they lose that?!), started its own network, where you could watch almost every episode of almost every wrestling show, and every pay-per-view, past and present, for only $9.99 a month. By 2014, I had a good income, so I had money to burn. I plopped down ten of Shawn's dollars every month and got back into wrestling.[7]

I returned to wrestling at the perfect time because things started changing a lot, and for the better, in the wrestling business in the 2010s. These

---

[5]. During this time, in about 2000, I ran into Eric Bischoff, the guy who ran WCW—WWF's main competitor—in an airport. On TV, Bischoff was the little con artist, who hung around big, tough guys and used his mouth to get himself into and out of trouble. In real life, he was taller and bigger than I am, and I was then 6'2" and 180 pounds. Since then, I have gained thirty pounds and lost an inch, presumably because my heft is literally compressing my spine.

[6]. "Indy" stood for "independent", not "Indiana". Though, maybe Indiana.

[7]. I never said the good income I had was *my* income.

changes were partly driven by the success of the independent and Japanese wrestling scenes.

WWE's recruitment of Daniel Bryan and CM Punk in 2008 marked the beginning of independent wrestling's influence on the company. There were then two key differences between independent wrestling and mainstream wrestling. First, the wrestlers in independent wrestling did not look like mainstream wrestlers. McMahon's most successful period of booking wrestling ranged from 1984 to 2003, so his idea of what a wrestler should look like drew entirely from what the wrestlers of that period looked like. And, though many of those wrestlers couldn't wrestle very well, by God they were big: big muscles if they were male, and big bolt-on boobs if they were female. Bryan and Punk were both short (by WWE standards) and possessed of little muscle definition. While Punk had a roguish appearance, Bryan resembled a surprised goat, something the WWE commentators, undoubtedly following McMahon's guidance, frequently pointed out to viewers.

The second big difference was that indy wrestlers did not *wrestle* like WWE wrestlers. McMahon mandated that his wrestlers use a limited range of moves to minimize injuries and establish distinct wrestling styles. This was not a problem for much of McMahon's talent, because many of them, like McMahon himself, didn't particularly like wrestling; and they especially didn't like the people who liked wrestling. Sure, doing the same five moves every match is dull, but if you don't care about wrestling anyway, it's all part of the job. And sure, maybe some people in your audience will soon tire of a product that is indistinguishable from one year to the next, but if you think they're dumb marks who'll accept anything you do, you won't care about not giving them their money's worth.

By contrast, wrestlers in independent wrestling were there because they loved wrestling. The work was dangerous, the pay was low, and you performed in front of 300 drunk Alabamans; but it was all worth it because it let you feel like a superhero (with a painkiller addiction).

Despite McMahon's distaste for both Punk and Bryan, they both gradually got the audience behind them after they joined the promotion. Indeed, the more successful Punk and, to a greater extent, Bryan became, the more agitated McMahon got. Sure, he wanted to make money, but he wanted to do it on his terms. The fact that a scrawny, scummy-looking, tattooed asshole and a hideous, shrimpy, bearded environmentalist were becoming the most popular and best-selling wrestlers in the company made him furious, to the point that he tried to undermine both their successes.

McMahon failed, though, and soon enough, there was an invasion of independent wrestlers into the WWE,[8] showing off their small-bodied, hard-hitting acrobatics and their fourth-wall-breaking, self-referential, eye-winking mic work. However, McMahon channeled most of the indy horde into WWE's developmental league, known as NXT. Soon enough, dedicated wrestling fans were revering NXT as the place where you could watch the best televised wrestling in America.

OK, that's how the independent wrestling scene was changing American wrestling: by making the in-ring product more diverse, more entertaining, and more postmodern. While this was happening, though, another pincer was penetrating the heart of wrestling and transforming it from an organ that predictably, rhythmically pumped blood, into a gun that shot entertaining wrestling instead of bullets. That pincer was Japanese wrestling.

---

8. Let's be clear: this was an invasion that McMahon hired. As much as he hated thinking about things in a different way, he loved making money even more. Sometimes.

The most prominent Japanese professional wrestling promotion, New Japan Professional Wrestling (NJPW), distinguished itself by seeming more realistic than WWE. Their storylines were less fantastical; they broadcast improvised press conferences before and after events; and the in-ring style was more impactful. In the USA, when a wrestler makes like he's punching another wrestler, he'll try to come as close as he can to punching him in the face without actually punching him in the face. In NJPW, though, the wrestlers would simply strike each other as hard as they could in the fleshy parts of their bodies, which, given the angle from which chops are thrown, usually meant the chest. This is known as "strong style" wrestling, and you will know it by the trail of dead pecs it leaves in its wake.

Japanese wrestling started a while ago, becoming popular in 1951. NJPW started in 1972. Given this storied history, what was it about the 2010s that led to Japanese professional wrestling changing wrestling? As usual, the Internet.

Truly hardcore wrestling fans had been trading tapes of Japanese professional wrestling since the 80s, if not earlier. But not only was I not that dedicated to wrestling, the existence of tape-trading was something I didn't even know about until the 2000s, by which point I wasn't much of a wrestling fan anyway. And even if I had known about tape-trading, I was like the overwhelming majority of fans in lacking that particular degree of fanaticism. I was willing to join Heaven's Gate, but I wasn't going to cut my balls off.

In the 2010s, though, Japanese wrestling was on YouTube. And by 2014, NJPW debuted their own streaming wrestling service, NJPW World, where you could peruse their entire catalog at the low, low cost of understanding Japanese. Consequently, the Internet wrestling community became steadily more aware of Japanese wrestling, and by 2016, its biggest stars—Hiroshi Tanahashi, Tetsuya Naito, Kazuchika Okada, and Kenny Omega—were pretty well known in the USA as well, at least among hardcore wrestling fans.

Japanese wrestling was distinctive not only in its realism, but also in its awesomeness. There would occasionally be really good wrestling matches in the WWE, mostly in NXT, but starting around 2012—and reaching its peak in 2018—the wrestling matches in NJPW were epic, pushing the boundaries of what we thought wrestling could do. Going to watch the best New Japan Pro-Wrestling matches after watching average WWE matches was like getting electric light after having to live on candlepower. You mean I can see better and I don't have to spend $3,600 a month on candles? Sign me up!

To give you a sense of how good Japanese wrestling was in those days, it helps to know the match rating system of professional wrestling's most successful journalist, Dave Meltzer. Meltzer marries an autistic man's passion for ranking and categorizing things to a cocaine addict's impatience for editing. Every week, he produces a 40,000-or-so word newsletter that not only documents the biggest stories of the week, it also includes capsule summaries of the sixteenth match of the fourth biggest Mexican wrestling company's sixth worst show. In short, Meltzer has probably seen more wrestling matches, of more different kinds, than any person who has ever lived. And although he has his quirks, I, like many wrestling fans, take his evaluations very seriously.

Meltzer's scale runs from 1 to 5 stars. 1 star means bad; 2 stars means nothing special; 3 stars means good; 4 stars means very good; and 5 stars means incredibly great. To provide a perspective on the improvement in wrestling during the 2010s, WWE, as a promotion, only had five 5-star matches from 1983 to 2011. By contrast, between 2012 and 2020, NJPW had forty-eight matches that were five stars *or higher*. That's right: some of the wrestling NJPW produced in the 2010s was so good that it broke Dave Meltzer's scale, forcing him to give some matches 5.25, 5.5, 6, or even more stars.[9]

Several of these matches had taken place at NJPW's premier event, Wrestle Kingdom. Always held in the Tokyo Dome on January 4, this event is a major attraction for wrestling fans, and Shawn's first trip to Japan was primarily to attend Wrestle Kingdom 12.

At the beginning of 2023, when we saw Wrestle Kingdom 17, four wrestlers from NJPW were worth singling out:

Kazuchida Okada, a six-foot-three, blonde-haired, lanky Japanese technician who can get great wrestling matches out of anyone;

Kenny Omega, a super-athletic, over-the-top, frizzy-haired Canadian whose love for video games led him to wrestle like a video game character whose stats have all been set to maximum;

Jay White, a deliberate, perfectly muscled, villainous New Zealander; and

Will Ospreay, a British wrestling genius and real-life dumbass.

---

[9]. In the song, "Yeah!" Usher sings "'Cause on a one-to-ten, she's a certified twenty." He sings this, presumably, because he wants to compliment the sexiness of the woman he sees in the dance club. And look, if he sang that "on a one-to-ten she's a twenty," I'd roll my eyes and chalk it up to artistic license. But Usher goes too far—way too far—when he claims that she's a *certified* twenty. If the scale goes only to ten, then only a madman would *certify* her as a twenty. For years after hearing "Yeah!" I cursed Usher's name, wondering why he couldn't be better-behaved, like P. Diddy or Drake. But when Meltzer did in real life what Usher only sang about, I never recovered. On a one-to-ten, if burning your tongue is a one and what Usher did is a ten, then what Dave Meltzer did is also a ten!

Okada and Omega wrestled a quartet of matches that were rated, out of 5 stars: 6 stars, 6.25 stars, 6 stars, and 7 stars. Meltzer gave that last match—which lasted sixty-nine minutes—7 stars because not only was he immediately convinced that it was the best match he had ever seen, but he concluded that it would probably remain the best match he would ever see for as long as he would live.

That's Okada and Omega. While they pushed each other to advance the art form, Will Ospreay was following in their footsteps, amassing more five-star matches than anyone in history. In the 2010s, he put on seven 5-star matches and two 5.75-star matches; from the beginning of the 2020s to the start of Wrestle Kingdom 17—a four-year period—he had performed in seven 5-star matches, one 5.25-star match, three 5.5-star matches, two 5.75-star matches, and one 6-star match. Finally, there's Jay White. Though he doesn't have either the highs of Omega or Okada, or the output of Ospreay, he's an outstanding wrestler in his own right, having wrestled three matches in his still-young career that Meltzer rated higher than 5 stars. That's two more than Ric Flair has, and he's arguably the greatest American wrestler ever.

Anyway, I give you this very long backstory because at Wrestle Kingdom 17, the co-main event was a match between Kenny Omega and Will Ospreay, and the main event was a match between Kazuchika Okada and Jay White.

Needless to say, I was excited.

# 33

# A Very Small Part of My Life Has Been a Lie!

Wrestle Kingdom 17 (henceforth WK 17) was taking place in the Tokyo Dome, also known as the "Big Egg." Now, a long time ago, I had heard about the Tokyo Dome, and what I had heard was that it was a stadium shaped like an egg, but it was held up by fans or magnets or something. This was in the 90s, and back then, people didn't have mobile phones. So, we didn't develop the habit of looking up everything that we didn't understand.[1] Even if I had wanted to investigate further the idea that the Tokyo Dome was a big, floating egg in which baseball games took place,

---

[1]. You have to realize, a common discussion people would have in the 80s and 90s was, "hey, who was in [insert movie here]?" We would sit there, and just, *remember*. And then we would *argue* about it. Like, we would have a fight about whether it was Viggo Mortensen or Michael Biehn who was in *The Abyss*. I'm not even sure how we were even *able* to argue about this, but we did! People complain about mobile phones and social media cutting off face-to-face communication, but remember: *these were the kinds of conversations we used to have.*

# THE MOST AWKWARD MAN IN JAPAN

I would have had to go to the library and look to see whether they had any books on the Tokyo Dome. But I wasn't about that life. Also, even if I had, momentarily, formed the intention to do that, I would have later forgotten that I had ever wanted to do that, and then I would have found myself in a library, puzzled about why I was in a library, leading me to wonder whether I had finally fallen into one of those fugue states people were so het up about back then.

I confess, I didn't know how to interpret "floating, egg-shaped stadium" any other way than literally. So, whenever I imagined the Tokyo Dome (which was more often than you'd think), I imagined what looked like a 100-foot-tall, white, oblong object floating about ten feet off the ground, completely inaccessible to the masses of people who wanted to enter it. Then my imagining would come to an end, satisfied that that was basically the idea.

As we got closer to the Tokyo Dome, and I began to reconsider my image with greater realism, it slowly dawned on me that what I imagined was a complete crock of shit, and that I actually had no idea what it looked like.

This has happened to me before, by the way: once, when I was a little kid, someone told me that you shouldn't swallow pumpkin seeds, because if you do, a pumpkin will grow in your stomach. As an elementary school student, I didn't remember any facts about, say, social studies, but of course I remembered this, because this was a matter of life and death (I assumed).

One day, when I was about seventeen, someone offered me pumpkin seeds. I don't remember the context surrounding the offer, but I assure you, I furiously declined, justifying my decision with the remark, "of course I'm not going to eat those, because if I do, a pumpkin will gro ... ohhhhh ... for years, I have been had. I'll try one."

Anyway, because I had no idea how to visualize the Tokyo Dome, I was intrigued to approach it and find out how this thing would appear. Well, it looked like a perfectly nondescript stadium. I mean, we had to cross a bridge to get to it, and next to the bridge, there was a roller coaster (called, I just learned, "Thunder Dolphin"), so that was kind of cool. But I guess my intrigue was misplaced; I mean, what else could it have been but a stadium?

Still, if it's just a stadium, why call it the Big Egg? On January 4, 2023, I didn't try to look that up. I'm not sure why, but either I was just too interested in seeing Wrestle Kingdom, or I felt kind of embarrassed that I even had the expectation that I was about to see a wrestling show in a flying metal watermelon. But I just now (as I write this) looked it up, and I actually get how I arrived at the image I did.

Although the Tokyo Dome is a stadium, it has a pale, white color, and so, to that degree, it is in the egg family, in the same way that a painting of a cat is, to that degree, a cat. But more than that, it has a thin membrane roof. The membrane roof has two layers: an inside layer that is 0.35 mm thick, and an outside one that's 0.8 mm thick. That is very thin! It is so thin that, according to the Tokyo Dome website, "about 5 percent of the sunlight goes through" the membrane roof. Also, despite being barely thicker than ten sheets of letter-sized paper, the roof weighs 400 tons. 400 tons is 800,000 pounds, which is very hard to imagine, so if it helps, realize that the roof weighs about as much as 4,500 kangaroos.[2]

OK, it's got a membrane roof, but what's the relationship between this and eggs? Eggs don't have membrane roofs, do they? This answer

---

2. See this website for the proof, so long as you don't mind equating bare assertions with proof: https://weightofstuff.com/11-things-that-weigh-about-400-tons/

may shock you, but: no, they don't. However, the Tokyo Dome has a network of pressurized ventilation fans that shoot air into the stadium and, if the powers-that-be want to, they can inflate the roof of the Tokyo Dome, making the whole stadium appear oblong, like a big, white egg. Hence, in the words of the Tokyo Dome website itself, "Tokyo Dome is an air-supported structure."

This is why I came to think that the Tokyo Dome is a giant floating egg: because even Mr. Tokyo Dome himself calls the stadium an "air-supported structure" that looks like an enormous egg! No wonder I thought what I thought back when I was twenty.

Never have I been so justified in being a credulous idiot.

We entered the Tokyo Dome, walked down some stairs, and migrated to our part of the stadium. Like every other stadium I've been to, the action was in the center, with a variety of eateries and bathrooms along the perimeter. I showed up hungry, so I was excited to see what my options were. Alas, I didn't record all the diverse possibilities, but I remember this much: my decision about what food to purchase was agonizing, a certified twenty on my ten-point pain scale. First, I was hungry, so I wanted to eat well. But second, none of the options looked significantly better than any of the other options. I'm pretty sure there were things like noodles, hamburgers, German sausages, and fried chicken. I went back and forth from food wall to food wall, patrolling the area like a highway cop on the last day of the month. Nothing was grabbing me, but after about fifteen minutes of indecision, I concluded that I had to pick something, lest I die of starvation à la Buridan's ass.[3] So I told myself that I should pick based on novelty. I selected something that I've never had the opportunity to purchase in an American stadium: steak with corn and a thin, brown sauce. Look, I wasn't in the mood for beef, but as I said earlier, if I didn't pick something, I would eventually die. Quite literally, my life was at steak.

As bad as that pun was, it didn't stop me from returning to my seat with a steak for myself and a sausage for Shawn.[4] True to form, Shawn had purchased excellent seats for us. We were in the floor seats near the wrestling ring, in the seventh row. We had an excellent view of whatever action would take place in the ring, and were fortunate enough to be seated in the midst of Japanese fans.

I should explain why being seated among the Japanese was such a boon. Buckle the fuck up, because I'm going to generalize like hell.

I've been to many wrestling events in the United States. With one exception (an ECW show in Dayton in 1995), most of the crowd is respectful, albeit quite loud, and often not paying attention to the show.

---

3. Buridan's ass is a philosopher's thought-experiment. The idea goes like this: if you place a donkey equidistantly from two identically sized bales of hay, the donkey, not having any basis for picking one bale rather than another, will be paralyzed and will eventually starve to death. The whole thought-experiment is extremely unrealistic, though, because donkeys are terrible judges of distance. I realize that I already described this in chapter 19, but I wanted to see whether my description of it in this chapter was precisely as appealing as the earlier description, to test whether I can kill you with words.

4. Not a double entendre! I didn't even think of that until you brought it up. Oh no, that's a double entendre too!

That said, no matter how peaceable are the bulk of the fans, there's always a contingent of shock troops sent in by bad taste itself to ruin everyone's fun. This is just the nature of the beast: wrestling attracts a lot of young men who publicly want to appear too cool for school while secretly wanting to be part of the show, in the same way that K-Pop attracts a lot of ~~young women who publicly want to tear anyone who criticizes them or their favorite artists limb from limb while secretly wanting to tear anyone who criticizes them or their favorite artists limb from limb~~ great people.

Even when you're lucky enough not to be near the 120 pound drunkard repeatedly SHOUTING the name of his favorite wrestler with the rapidity and inexorability of a hummingbird's heartbeat, there's still the problem that fans in American venues are tall. I don't mean to say that American pro wrestling fans are giants (well: not vertical giants) but when you're seated within a predominantly male fanbase and you are, like Shawn, only 5'5"—admittedly, every inch of 5'5", and definitely not half an inch shorter than that—then nine times out of ten, most of your live wrestling experience will be looking at the back of the head of a twenty-something-year-old man who, if pressed, will claim that his mullet is ironic, but who secretly doesn't know what "ironic" means.[5]

Japanese wrestling experiences are, mercifully, nothing like that. Although people will regularly check their phones—Japan, like America, is also a nation of self-made slaves—most of the time, they will quietly and intently focus on the wrestling match: oohing and ahhing at appropriate moments, silent and short the rest of the time. As a result, in Japan Shawn can actually enjoy the wrestling show, and I don't have to hear her bitchy complaints.

OK, that's a lot of build-up. How was the show?

---

[5]. I also have no idea.

# 34

# A Sad Ending, an Embarrassing Beginning, and an OK Ending

When I first heard about the line-up for WK 17, I was excited about three things, and very excited about one thing. The first thing I was excited about was the last New Japan match of Keiji Muto, known in my childhood as "The Great Muta." The second thing was the Japan debut of top-flight wrestler Sasha Banks (formerly associated with WWE) under the new moniker, "Mercedes Moné." Third was the main event match between Kazuchika Okada and Jay White. But the thing I was most anticipating was the co-main event match between Kenny Omega and Will Ospreay.

Since Wrestle Kingdom is the biggest show New Japan puts on every year, there were lots of other matches; looking at the lineup a year later, I was rather surprised about some of the bouts on the card, as I had no memory of them ("I've always wanted to see Master Wato wrestle. Wait. I did?"). As a result, I concluded that if I, an actual wrestling fan, had no

# THE MOST AWKWARD MAN IN JAPAN

recollection of these matches, then there was no need to inflict even brief descriptions of them on you, who is (I'm assuming) not a wrestling fan.

Let me quickly sketch the three storylines that intrigued me before getting to the main event: the co-main event.

Storyline #1: Keiji Muto vs. Father Time. When I was a kid, I first saw The Great Muta at Starrcade '89, which was the Wrestlemania of NWA wrestling, at that time the biggest competitor to the WWF. Muto was really cool: not only was he an excellent in-ring performer, but he wore eye-catching face-paint and spat eye-blinding green mist at his adversaries. As far as I knew, Keiji Muto was the man who brought "spitting green mist at your enemy" to America.[1] And also as far as I know, the only wrestlers who continue to spit green mist at their adversaries are, by tradition, Japanese wrestlers (the most recent Japanese wrestler to spit green mist at her opponents is the wonderful WWE wrestler, Asuka). I thank Muto for delivering this bit of circus magic to America in 1989, but in 2023 the man was sixty years old. Although he was really good at wrestling for being sixty, he was not really good at wrestling for being a human. Not only was he too old to be wrestling to begin with, but he had sustained so many injuries over his career that by this point his husk was tied together with horse-floss and twine, his knee joints permanently poised to explode out of his body at the merest prompting, as though he was a villain who had been punched in the legs by an off-brand Ken, Fist of the North Star.

Storyline #2: Sasha Banks vs. Herself. I love Sasha Banks as an in-ring performer: although she is extremely slight, she takes crazy risks, and she

---

[1] Up until just now, that was my belief. But according to the Internet the first wrestler to have done this was not The Great Muta but The Great Kabuki. You learn many important things by reading this book.

has that intangible "it" factor that the best wrestling stars have—you just want to watch her when she's doing a match. However, I had three problems with Sasha Banks's debut for New Japan.

First—and this is just me—though I like the name Sasha Banks, "Mercedes Moné" does nothing for me. Mercedes is her real-life first name, so I can't begrudge her that, but "Moné" (to evoke "money") makes it feel like she's trying too hard. That said—and I just realized this—it's a natural evolution of "Banks" which, in case you don't know, refers to financial institutions (not bodies of water). Still, I would have preferred it if she changed her name from "Sasha Banks" to "Mercedes Gotenyama Trust."

Second, when you listen on the NJPW rebroadcast of the event to the crowd's reaction to her not-officially-announced-but-everyone-knew-it-was-coming-anyway appearance, the crowd seems quite stoked to see her. But ... I'm pretty sure New Japan sweetened (a wrestling term for "loudened") the crowd's reaction. You see, I was actually in the stadium when she showed up (complete with video package and super-cool dye job), and the crowd reacted like my students do when I tell them they've driven me to contemplate retirement: mostly indifference, some clapping.

Third, the manner of her debut was unfortunate. Right after the women's champion, Kairi (who had previously wrestled for WWE), defeated her opponent, Tam Nakano, Moné's music hit. The Japanese crowd's politeness dragged them against their apathy to look to the entrance ramp. Then, she got to the ring and did a maneuver on Kairi called a "DDT."

Don't worry if you don't know what a DDT is, because that night, neither did Kairi or Mercedes. There must have been some miscommunication, because Mercedes pretty much missed the move and then Kairi just fell over. In wrestling, that's called a botch. When it happens in a match,

## THE MOST AWKWARD MAN IN JAPAN

the performers can accommodate it or even use it to their advantage—it can give their match heightened realism, depending on what the botch looks like. But when it happens as the very first move that you do in your big debut for a new promotion, it's very oof.

To make matters worse, Mercedes had to cut a bad-ass promo immediately afterwards, one that was supposed to announce to the crowd that she was now here in Japan and would soon rule over the women's division. However, Mercedes is a shaky promo at the best of times. So, coming out to an uncaring crowd and then messing up your very first move must have shot her confidence straight down to the stink-o-sphere (which is what airline pilots call the part of the sky right under the plane bathroom). I couldn't hear her that well at the time, but I could hear enough to politely look away while she was talking.

Storyline #3: Jay White vs. Kazuchika Okada. For a few years—say, from 2016 until 2020—Kazuchika Okada was the best wrestler in the world. Indeed, he had such a good career, with so many legendary matches, that Shawn and I (following the lead of wrestling journalist Dave Meltzer) would routinely tell anyone who asked that he was the best wrestler of all time.

By 2023, I would deny both claims. The best in-ring performer of 2022 (and remember, we were only four days in 2023 by the time Wrestle Kingdom happened) was Will Ospreay. Ospreay has been having such an amazing 2020s, and Okada has cooled off enough, that I no longer felt comfortable describing Okada as the best wrestler of all time. He was still a first-ballot hall of famer, and perhaps the greatest wrestler of his generation, but it seemed (and still seems—he's only thirty-five) that his time at the tippity top has passed.

Jay White, because he works a pretty safe style, is a young thirty-one and is, I think, entering the prime of his career. He wrestles very deliberately, which perfectly suits the Japanese fanbase's appreciation of careful excellence, but unfortunately it's one that often leaves me cold. He has a big move-set, and his ability to execute any individual move is, perhaps, nonpareil, but he rarely chains his moves together, meaning that for much of his matches, he just hits one move, laughs, hits another move, mugs to the crowd, hits another move, vamps, and so on. As an in-ring performer, he's a pot-shot artist. On the mic, he's like Starscream, the irritating transformer who could turn into a jet, but who always whined about dumb stuff until Megatron killed him.

White and Okada had a good match that night. Unfortunately, owing to White's unhurried villainy and Okada's mimetic versatility—he can emulate any style of wrestling—we ended up getting a match where White worked slowly and Okada paralleled that slowness. I guess you were supposed to focus on the silence between the notes rather than the notes themselves?

This is my polite way of saying: it was boring.

It's possible that, in a vacuum, the White-Okada match would have been quite exciting, a slow burn of a psychological thriller. But, we weren't in a vacuum: we were in a world where White and Okada followed Ospreay and Omega.

And that night, no one could have followed Ospreay and Omega.

# 35

# I Went to Wrestle Kingdom 17, and All I Got Was One of the Most Thrilling Nights of My Life

To fully appreciate the match between Will Ospreay and Kenny Omega, at Wrestle Kingdom 17, on January 4, 2023, you had to know four things.

First, both Omega (Canadian) and Ospreay (British) are big fans of a wrestler named AJ Styles (American). From about 2013 to 2016, AJ Styles was probably the best wrestler in the world. He was so good at wrestling that he kept getting better and better at it as he moved from his mid-thirties to his early forties. He was so good at wrestling that the top babyface of New Japan, Hiroshi Tanahashi, called AJ, a foreigner then working in NJPW, the best wrestler in the world. He was so good at wrestling that he could even have good matches in the WWE.

That last compliment might sound weird, but as I said in Chapter 32, wrestlers in WWE have constraints put on them that wrestlers in other promotions don't have. Their move sets are limited, their ability to lay out their own matches is restricted, and they have less time to perform the matches they couldn't take part in designing in the first place. But AJ was so good that he could rise above all that and have, not just the best matches in WWE, but some of the best matches in worldwide wrestling—and this, during a time when NJPW was regularly putting on the best matches in the history of wrestling.

AJ's in-ring excellence is why Ospreay liked him so much. Ospreay (age, as of January 4, 2023: twenty-nine) is considerably younger than the forty-five-year-old Styles, so when Ospreay was growing up, AJ was his idol. Despite Ospreay's no-bones-about-it idiocy (a fellow British wrestler, Zack Sabre, Jr., said of Ospreay that he "is one of the stupidest people I've ever had a conversation with"[1]), he has excellent taste in wrestlers.

Omega (age: thirty-nine) isn't so young that he grew up idolizing Styles. However, when Kenny first started in wrestling, back in 2006, he was unsure whether to devote his considerable athletic gifts to professional wrestling or to mixed martial arts. After deciding that wrestling wasn't for him, he nonetheless had a match with AJ Styles (which he thought would be one of his final matches), and after the match, AJ, upon hearing of Kenny's plans, told him that, no, he's incredibly good at professional wrestling, and he should absolutely continue doing it. Getting such a compliment from a wrestler as manifestly awesome as AJ Styles convinced Kenny to stick around, much to the benefit of wrestling fans everywhere.

OK, that was the first thing. The second thing you should know about is another wrestler, Kota Ibushi.

Kota Ibushi is an immensely talented, extremely handsome, very eccentric professional wrestler. Many of the things he says sound off-kilter

---

1. https://x.com/njpwglobal/status/1222263077023952897 (the actual interview appears to have been disappeared off the internet).

or unrelated to the conversation he's in, and he has strange ideas about how the world or his body works, leading many fans to think of him as a mysterious, tortured artist. Shawn and I, however, have a much simpler theory: he is just very, very stupid.

Kota had a long tag-team partnership with Kenny when they were both wrestling for DDT. Because they were such good friends, even roommates, Kota and Kenny called their tag team the "Golden•Lovers." From 2009 to 2016, confirmed bachelors Kenny and Kota were one of the great tag teams in Japanese professional wrestling.

From 2016 to 2018, Kenny was the boss of the biggest bad guy faction in NJPW, "The Bullet Club." During that time, he and Kota had a falling out, because Kota did not truck with bad guys. The Bullet Club, being a group of heels, would periodically replace their bosses by literally (as in: not figuratively) kicking the old one out. The Young Bucks did it to Prince Devitt (now known as Finn Balor) replacing him with AJ Styles; Kenny did it to AJ; and, most relevant to this match, Cody Rhodes did it to Kenny Omega. But, while Cody and his goons were beating the crap out of Kenny, Kota ran to his rescue! The Golden•Lovers reunited, and fans all around the world cheered these two longtime companions.

From 2016 to 2021, Kota Ibushi was the uncrowned champion of New Japan. He was definitely a good enough performer to be the champion at the top of the card, but he just wasn't being given that opportunity. The more time passed, the more people worried that he'd never win their most important title, the IWGP ("International Wrestling Grand Prix") Heavyweight Championship. Happily, in 2021, Kota managed to win it from tranquil scoundrel Tetsuya Naito at the overripe age of thirty-eight. Unfortunately, Ibushi would hold the belt for only a month, losing it to none other than Will Ospreay.

You'd think Ibushi's spaciness and Ospreay's very public battle with stupidity would make them like each other. Game recognizes game, and all that. But it was not to be: in a January 2019 match between him and Kota, Ospreay brained Ibushi with a move he debuted in that match called "the Hidden Blade." In the storyline, it gave Kota a concussion. It turned out to be a very believable story, though, because during the match, Will botched a different move called "the Cheeky Nando" (about which more anon), such that he gave Kota a real-life concussion. Fortunately, Kota pretty much always acts like he has a concussion, so the stars were aligned.

After Kenny's final match for NJPW in 2019, Kenny knew that Will Ospreay was going to take up his banner and become the standard bearer for the company. Per Dave Meltzer, Kenny had a long talk with Will that night, advising Ospreay not only about how to be the face of a company, but also going over the evening when Will hurt Kenny's very, very close friend Kota. We don't know exactly what was said during that meeting, but we do know that in his press conferences leading up to this match, Will said that he was going to do to Kenny what he did to Kota.

Thing three: for a while, the contest between who would end up having the most 5-star matches of all time was between Kenny Omega and Kazuchika Okada. Because he had a plausible case to be the best in-ring performer alive, and because, unlike Okada, Kenny was generally a heel, Kenny hubristically called himself "the best bout machine".

Soon enough, though, Will Ospreay surpassed Kenny in terms of the number of 5-star matches he wrestled, despite being ten years younger. So Will started calling himself the best bout machine, presumably because he didn't realize that the name was already taken and he didn't make it up.[2]

---

2. This is like how I often confuse what happens in George Plimpton's life for what happens in mine.

Well, Kenny wasn't having this, especially not heel Kenny. So Omega had his manager, the despicable Don Callis, kayfabe[3] sue Will Ospreay for copyright infringement. Going into this match, then, both Kenny and Will had something to prove: that he was the true best bout machine, and the other guy was a pretender.

Fourth and final thing, Kenny left NJPW in 2019 to join an upstart American promotion, AEW (for "All Elite Wrestling"). This, despite the fact that Kenny was NJPW's champion at the time. For a while, NJPW was pretty mad at Kenny for leaving them—they were an important promotion, and they had gone all-in on making Kenny their face, but Kenny rewarded their generosity by turning heel on them and going all-out for another promotion.

But time and money heal all wounds, so by February 2021, AEW was partnering with NJPW, making it safe for Kenny to return to NJPW to wrestle after a four-year absence. Not only was he back to performing for New Japan, though—he was competing for a (minor) title, the IWGP United States Heavyweight Championship, the belt whose inaugural holder was none other than a young Kenneth Omega, way back in July, 2017.

I wasn't the only one in the building who was more excited for the Omega-Ospreay match than for any other match. When "Devil's Sky," Kenny's "Night on Bald Mountain"-meets-"Carmina Burana"-meets-Al-

---

3. You should know what "kayfabe" means by now, if you are a person who has lived in the United States since 2016, as various political observers invoke "kayfabe" to both explain politics in the Trump era and burnish their working class street cred. If you have not been living in the USA since 2016, though, it's just a corruption of how you say "fake" in pig Latin ("ake-fay" becomes "kayfabe").

ice-Deejay-style theme song hit,[4] and Kenny "The Cleaner" Omega came out, the crowd exploded, cheering more loudly for the entrances to this match than they had for any moment of the show up to this point. This Kenny vs. Ospreay match was finally about to happen.

When Omega first emerged, rising on a hydraulic lift from below the stage, he was clad in a black trench coat with steel plates over the shoulders, his profuse hair gathered in a cascading ponytail, his back to the audience. Shortly after his music started, he thrust out his left arm, and on the left side of the Jumbotron, a giant black wing shot out in parallel, representing Kenny's finishing move, the One Winged Angel.[5] The cameraman rounded toward his position, and Kenny slowly turned to the camera. Widening his eyes, he broke into an evil grin and mouthed, "I'm back."

Once in the ring, Kenny was joined by his mouthpiece and manager, the deplorable Don Callis. Callis paired rose-patterned pants with a matching rose-patterned blazer rounded out with rhinestone-studded loafers, a dark gray fedora, pink-tinted sunglasses, a big gold Rolex, and a silver necklace, like he had been shot out of a cannon and landed in the wardrobe section of the auction for the Dennis Rodman estate. He looked exactly like the

---

4. This is how it landed on my ears. It turns out it was just a slightly altered version of the song, "Advent: One-Winged Angel," which is one of the songs in the video game, *Final Fantasy VII*.

5. This is another reference to *Final Fantasy VII*. Spoiler alert: in the final battle of this (twenty-six-year-old) game, the character Sephiroth grows a single black wing from his back, becoming Safer Sephiroth, the one-winged angel. I did not investigate any deeper than this, so I don't know if he can fly. If the standard bird is any guide, though, all he can do is flap helplessly in a circle.

kind of person whose carcass would be stuffed in the trunk of a Cadillac after mouthing off to Big Vito in Las Vegas.

After Will "The Assassin" Ospreay's music and video package played, Will, wearing an elaborate cloak that made him look like a feathered knight, purposefully marched down the ramp, while The United Empire, Ospreay's four-man team of supporters, accompanied him to the ring.

I thought for a while about how to do this next part, which is describing the match they had. I could do an adequate job of describing the match if you allowed me the indulgence of using terms like "Sky Twister," "V-Trigger," "Apron Oscutter," "Aoi Shoudou," etc. to refer to the moves. I could even link to webpages full of GIFs that you could switch to in order to understand my shorthand.

But I decided that that would be like giving you an impassioned description of a dream in which I somehow had $28 million, but concealed it from my wife, and she reacted by complaining that now she had to disclose this source of outside income to her employer, and this would be a whole *thing*.[6] This was a real dream, a real dream that my wife had, and I can't imagine anything crueler for a writer to do than inflict a description of such a thing on his audience, even if he supplemented what he wrote with photos of his W-2.

So instead, I'll say this: when the match first began, the anticipation bubbling through my body nudged me to the edge of my seat, but as the match carried on, I was finding myself a little disappointed. And then, out of nowhere, Ospreay did this kooky maneuver where he did a backflip while simultaneously kicking Kenny in the face, like Guile from *Street Fighter 2* flash kicking Blanca. And then, I was in.

---

6. The fact that Shawn's first reaction to a giant pile of money was, "BUT THE DISCLOSURE!!!" tells you a lot about her character.

The match was well laid out: as it started, Ospreay, full of manic anger, attacked Kenny, leaving Kenny largely powerless to stop him. After a couple of minutes, Ospreay telegraphed a move, allowing Kenny to take control. Kenny then disciplined Ospreay like the wayward student he undoubtedly once was, back when he attended Sir Marcus Thugwell's Academy for Ambitious Chavs.

Due to Ospreay's mistake, Kenny gained the upper hand and targeted Ospreay's middle back, continuing the attack for five minutes before Ospreay had a brief moment to recover.

Ospreay again lost the thread, and then Kenny took over. Because this is wrestling, when Ospreay was outside the ring, wounded, unable to stand, Kenny smashed a folding table across his back. (In kayfabe convention, Japanese folding tables are particularly well-made, difficult to destroy, and painful to be hit by.) Kenny jumped from the top of the ring post and stomped Will's back through the table, disintegrating the table and further damaging Ospreay's middle back. Picking up the table, he thrust his head through the hole he had made, and shrieked, in an homage to *The Tonight Show with Johnny Carson* (and maybe even *The Shining*), "Heeeeeere's Kenny!!!"

Unfortunately for Kenny, his abiding love of make-believe cost him, as changing focus from smashing Ospreay's back to impersonating Jack Nicholson's face allowed Ospreay to briefly get the upper hand, and Will used a wrestling move called a "suplex" to flip Omega's back onto the underside of the folding table, a move that no doubt hurt very much in real life.

Now in charge, Ospreay dragged himself and Kenny back inside the ring, and after doing a couple of successful moves, he realized he was calling the shots. Realizing things has always been Ospreay's weakness, though: the time it took for his poorly wrought ball-and-socket brain to convert confusion into understanding was just the fourteen seconds Kenny needed to get back in the saddle. Once again, Kenny wrested the reins from Will, who in this analogy is, I guess, a horse who wants to ride a man?

It went back and forth like this for a while: Kenny dictated the action for two or three minutes, only to get overconfident and lazy, and then Ospreay took over until his zeal caused him to make a mistake.

Speaking of mistakes, about thirteen minutes into the match, Ospreay performed a series of three "Cheeky Nando"s. Here's how this move works: Will draped Kenny over the middle ring rope. Kenny's face pointed to the ground and his arms went limp. In this defenseless position, Kenny's hindquarters were exposed to Ospreay, while his head remained tucked between his legs, resembling a football ready to be hiked. So Ospreay kicked Omega in the face as he precariously rested in this position. That's the Cheeky Nando.

Now, to perform the Cheeky Nando correctly, you slap your thigh as you kick your leg out, just missing your opponent's face with the heel of your boot. Since your victim is bent over and his face is shrouded by his legs, the audience can't easily see that your foot isn't actually making contact, and since you loudly slap your thigh, to an onlooker it really feels like you're kicking the shit out of the other guy's noggin.

As I've highlighted, Will is an absolutely phenomenal in-ring wrestler. So, he did the first two Cheeky Nandos perfectly. And the third one he did more than perfectly, because he actually kicked Kenny extremely hard, right in his orbital bone. While he didn't break it, he sure as hell hurt it, because after the hit, Kenny shot up from prone and grabbed at his face, after which blood began to ooze from a cut next to his right eye, which in turn started to swell almost completely shut.[7]

I'm sure that Will's mistake caused both men to mentally time-travel from 2023 to 2019, to the moment when Ospreay not only botched a Cheeky Nando, but botched Kota's smooth brain. I think Will was rather upset at himself for messing up, because after his mistake he turned away from Kenny, affected a pained look, and felt at his middle back which, remember, had been the focus of Kenny's malicious efforts for the whole match up to this point. In other words, Will expressed his real psychic pain as very believable (fake) physical pain.

As for Kenny, well, this was one of those moments where a wrestler makes use of a botch, because instead of calling to the ref for a time out (which wrestlers can do), he rolled off the ring post, stumbled onto the apron of the ring, and woozily opened his eyes. He leaned into it with his facial expressions, his contorted features revealing the pain he was enduring. Very much like how I tell my students, "yeah, good point," when they spitball me with one of their typical inanities.[8]

Regardless of how either man felt, shortly after his mistake, Ospreay would get a receipt. After pummeling Kenny a bit more, Will dragged Kenny to the top of the ring post to do a "superplex" from up top (about twelve feet up, if you figure the men's heights into it) to the mat below. Will's luck ran out when Kenny thwarted his move and smoothly

---

7. You can look at video of Kenny after this match and he has a literal footprint on his face. It was only one footprint though, meaning this was one of the times when the LORD was carrying him.

8. You may think this shows that I'm a bad professor, but if I were a bad professor, would I lie to my students?

transformed it into a top rope DDT, causing Will to tumble out of the ring onto the ground below.

When Will emerged from this brutality, his face was drenched in blood, a "crimson mask" as wrestling enthusiasts say.[9] For the next five minutes, Kenny had his way with Will, and he may have worked a bit "stiff" (as they say in wrestling), in retaliation for Will's face-kickful mistake. Kenny completely annihilated Will in this part of the match. The point of this section of the match was not only to make Will's defeat look assured, but also to make Kenny seem sadistic, and Will's comeback feel more inspiring.

Will's resurgence started with not one, not two, but five Hidden Blades (three of which were done to the front of Kenny's head, rather than the back; so: Revealed Blades?). Will was trying to bruise Kenny's frontal and occipital lobes, not only to induce color agnosia, but also to remind us of the time he used it to cause a kayfabe concussion in Kota four years prior. But this time, rather than associating it with malevolence (in-story) and negligence (out-of-story), we cheered for Will. Because of Kenny's relentless and unanswered (Don-) callousness throughout the previous, fairly long, segment, the crowd and I—but especially I—hungered for blood. So when Will landed that Hidden Blade, the crowd cheered and I

---

9. Will wasn't bleeding from the DDT gone haywire, but instead from "gigging." "Gigging" (or "blading" or "juicing") is what wrestlers call their practice of slicing their own faces open with razor blades in order to raise the stakes in their matches. The razor blades are usually hidden somewhere on their bodies—sometimes, even in their mouths—and then when they're done, they oh my goodness I just realized why Will Ospreay's finisher is called the Hidden Blade

joyfully shouted, "TBI!"[10] Not only did Will slice and dice Kenny's brain with all manner of Hidden and Obvious Blades, but he also performed AJ Styles's finishing maneuver, the Styles Clash, on Kenny, as if to say, "you dared to advise me about how to carry your torch, but I am a student of AJ Styles, not Kenny Omega!"

If Omega did get a traumatic brain injury, it didn't much affect his performance. Color agnosia or no, Kenny could at least see the outlines of Ospreay's body well enough to get the final upper hand of the match. Right before finishing the match with a One-Winged Angel, Kenny pulverized Ospreay's face with the "Kamigoye," which is Kota Ibushi's finisher. It was as if Kenny told Will, "Mr. Ibushi sends his regards," before pushing Ospreay's nose into the void where his brain should be. The match was not only a fight for the IWGP United States Championship (which, to my surprise, Kenny won), but also a fight for the honor of Kota Ibushi. And Kenny, despite being the bad guy, successfully defended the honor of his Golden Lover.

Even though the Okada/White match that followed the Ospreay/Omega match was a comparative disappointment, Shawn and I left the arena on a high, giddy like high school kids who ran at full tilt from their friend's party because someone called the cops after finding an upper decker in the bathroom. Shawn and I had seen the best wrestling match in our lives, one that not only had incredible action, but an emotionally complex storyline where your allegiances constantly changed thanks to your memory of the past and your appreciation of the present.

Alas, seeing this artistic display didn't reignite Shawn to her past love of wrestling. For her, it served as a satisfying valediction rather than a

---

10. TMI?

dramatic return, one last night of fun with your man before kicking him out and burning his clothes.

As for me, I was quite eager to learn what Dave Meltzer thought of the match. Mere hours after the match, Meltzer was interviewed about the match by his podcast co-host, Bryan Alvarez. Alvarez said, "maybe it was, actually, the best match I've ever seen in my whole, entire life" and Meltzer said, with some hesitation, "I would not say it was the best match I've ever seen, but I would certainly say it's top five, top three ... top five I'd say, easily, easily. ... one of the best matches of all time." In the *Wrestling Observer*, Meltzer gave the match 6.25 stars, making it the second most highly reviewed match in the history of Meltzer.

I didn't get to see Woodstock, but I did get to see Altamont.

# 36

# Above It All, Except for Drinking Alcohol, Which I Was Not Above, Except for When I on the Second Storey of a Bar, at Which Point I Was Above It All

My bloodlust (briefly) satiated, Shawn and I returned to our hotel. I haven't told you about this, our final hotel, the Prince Gallery Kioicho.

The two hotels we stayed at in Kyoto—the Ritz Carlton and Suiran—both felt like respites. Suiran was sheltered by a large wooden gate that protected the guests within from onlookers' prying eyes, while the Ritz Carlton stood next to a gentle river, giving it a somnolent dignity. Prince

Gallery Kioicho, by contrast, shot out of the ground like a bloody splinter stuck into the thumb of God.

That's something of an exaggeration, but it was definitely tall. Like, 700 feet tall! And while the Ritz and, especially, Suiran, seemed designed to induce meditation or relaxation, the Prince Gallery is where I would hold a convention for cocaine enthusiasts: it was gigantic, modern, and shining.[1]

I realize that the picture of the Prince Gallery I've given is very Las Vegasian. I don't mean to say that it was gaudy, transient, and disgusting, like Las Vegas or anyone who likes Las Vegas (no offense). Maybe this comparison will draw the contrast better: when I'm in a Las Vegas hotel, I feel dissolute, judgmental of all around me, and loathing of myself; but when I was in the Prince Gallery Kioicho, I wanted to crash a seven-horse chariot into a 1,200-person carnival. I felt important and invulnerable.

Part of this must be the contrast effect;[2] if I had been in Tokyo this whole trip, the Prince Gallery wouldn't have been very distinctive. But when you spend most of your time in fancy auberges, being in a hotel room on the 32nd floor of a coruscating skyscraper feels like moving from spa day to knife-fight day.

I'm being serious when I tell you that when I was in this hotel I forgot how to do simple things. I couldn't figure out how to open some doors, I got lost when I left my room, and I didn't trust the elevator.

---

1. I've never injected cocaine, or whatever it is people do with it.

2. Normally, I use the footnotes to explain technical terms like "contrast effect". So you're probably expecting me to do it again. How rude it must seem for me to now tell you: look it up yourself! It's actually not that rude. But it feels super-rude because my previous politeness makes this bit of rudeness really stand out. That's the contrast effect!

But, like Deadpool, let me go back to the beginning and explain how I got here.

The hotel was located in Kioicho, which the Prince Gallery Kioicho website describes as "a town embraced in luscious greenery and a rich history, where Japanese traditions and Western culture intertwine." This is a nice description, but I'm pretty sure it describes most of Tokyo? Other than its convenient access to a subway stop, the only thing that really stood out to me about the hotel was the breathtaking sculpture outside of it of enormous flowers and butterflies, geysering from the earth and reaching a height of thirty feet. It may be a kind of artsy district, but five minutes of Internet sleuthing turned up nothing, and five minutes is my limit for research.[3]

The hotel reception occupied the thirty-sixth floor of a vertical mall. Separating the reception desks from the rest of the floor was a massive black marble wall containing an active fireplace. Shawn handled the unpleasant business of exchanging money for goods and services, so I didn't catch whether any of the exchange was noteworthy. But what was really different was that, even though the reception area was on the thirty-sixth floor, all the hotel rooms were below it, on the thirtieth to the thirty-fifth floor. It made me feel like I was a guest in a top secret bunker the US military will use to house the president whenever he helps to precipitate a nuclear war.

Before we could access our room, though, the hotel treated us to champagne and a high-tea-style setup of desserts. There was a strawberry cookie, a tiny slice of chocolate cake, a small slab of strawberry shortcake, a glass of yogurt topped with a layer of lemon-yuzu compote, and a

---

3. You might think that, because I'm a philosophy professor, I'd actually be good at research. But really, we just make shit up.

thumb-size piece of sticky gluten that tasted strongly of toffee. That was my favorite, but they were all good, and drinking the champagne was a nice bit of pregaming for going to Wrestle Kingdom 17, which we were going to do as soon as we dropped our stuff off in our new digs.

Aside from the topsy-turvy reception, the hotel's interior layout was probably the most standard of any of the hotels I stayed at in Japan. Just like the typical American hotel of my experience has long, carpeted hallways and anonymous walls, so too did this one. However, the hallways seemed longer and more mazelike than the usual American hotel. Moreover, glass doors separated the elevator lobby from the rooms. You could *see* through them, but unless you had your authorized room card, you couldn't *get* through them. I imagine those doors must have made the hotel rooms quite tantalizing to any hobo who accidentally wandered too far from the train track and found himself here. Finally, the room itself was, compared to the rooms in Suiran and the Ritz-Carlton, rather small. But there was an unbelievable view of the city below. Small room, big view.

The last and most remarkable feature of the hotel was its bar, known as "Sky Gallery Lounge Levita." We didn't visit it until after WK 17, but Shawn knew to save it as our place to decompress post-show.

It was a striking, majestic sight. Double-height panes of glass showcased a view of glittering Tokyo. A dramatically-lit bar stretched across the vast vitrine. Even though they had an impressive array of fancy cocktails, I decided to keep it simple with a personal pizza and a beer. The pizza was fine, but the beer, although just a normal Japanese lager, had the Prince Gallery Kioicho logo printed on the foam. I asked them how they did that, and the bartender pointed to a machine behind him that looked a bit like a SodaStream but whose only function was to imprint pictures into beer foam. Like my cat Avon, it was extravagantly useless, but unlike Avon, I loved it.

On the walls framing the bar hung wavy emerald-colored glass sculptures, which individually looked like single, cooked strands of spaghetti, but that collectively looked like a lot of cooked strands of spaghetti. As per the Prince Gallery Kioicho website, the glass artworks were designed to convey the image of a waterfall. But I still like my spaghetti idea.

Finally, Sky Gallery Lounge Levita was itself two storeys high. That is, moving away from the bar, you and your drinks could take a spiral staircase up to the second storey and then drunkenly fall to your demise in front of everyone.

The length and monotony of the walk from the elevator to the room, combined with the glass doors slicing the hotel up into segments, spiced with the relatively small room and absolutely high-up views, made me feel like I was in a spacecraft voyaging to Alpha Centauri. My fellow earthlings were taking this trip with me, but because we'd be here together for 1,000 years, there was no rush to return to Sky Gallery Lounge Levita to fraternize and have space beer.

Also, I had already gone to the bar; I was leaving tomorrow, and I didn't know anyone except Shawn. So, rather than linger in the cantina, we tucked in and got ready for the last part of our Japanese adventure: ending our Japanese adventure.

# JANUARY 5, 2023

# 37

# Fancies Don't Let Me Down

Today was my last day in Japan. Yet I wasn't sad to go. Not because I didn't enjoy my time, but rather because ahead of me lay my flight back to the States.

See, one of the many things that Shawn had planned properly about this trip was having us fly to Japan in business class and then fly back in first class. Since I enjoyed business class a great deal, I couldn't wait to see how good the first class experience was. Moreover, the excellence of Japanese service in general made me eager to see the degree to which first-class Japanese attendants would outdo their earthling counterparts.

Still, before getting to the flight, I had to, like, get out of bed, eat, wander, and arrive at the airport. The getting out of bed part wasn't particularly noteworthy: I did it. That said, the view from our room in the daytime was quite lavish. If I recall correctly, I could see bullet trains flit hither and, arguably, thither. Looking at the passengers, I thought, "that will be me one day. I will be someone who is not in a hotel room!"

We went up from the 32nd floor to the 35th floor for breakfast. The chamber where we ate breakfast was a spectacle of grandeur. The moment we stepped into the dining room, our attention was divided between the state-of-the-art kitchen on our left and the magnificent view of Tokyo stretching out before us on our right. Continuing, we passed a gigantic wine rack, and then we were seated at our table. The whole place felt like a fancy train car designed for rich acrobats.

Like many ritzy places in Japan (*e.g.*, the Ritz), this hotel offered both Japanese and Western breakfast. Now, while I won't be so bold as to say that Western breakfasts are strictly better, I will say that Japanese breakfasts are stupid and they should be ashamed of themselves. Obviously, both Shawn and I picked the Western breakfast.

The Western breakfast menu page was wonderfully crafted. On the one hand, it had lots of options, but on the other hand, next to some options only the names were written, while others included the dishes' names along with recommendations that effectively read, "GET THIS UNLESS YOU ARE A COWARD."

I was no coward. If I were a coward, why would I do exactly as I was told? So, although I could have gotten one of "grapefruit juice," "tomato juice," "mixed vegetables" (juice, presumably), "apple juice," or "whole milk," I instead opted for the "UNSYU Mandarin orange juice," which floated above the other drink options like Patrick Swayze floating to his reward at the end of *Ghost*. And similarly, though I could have gotten one of "EGG BENEDICT," "FRIED EGGS," "SCRAMBLE EGGS," "OMELETTE," or "SWEET TEMPTATION FRENCH TOAST w/Fruits," I chose to get the "TRUFFLE SCRAMBLE EGG ESPUMA STYLE" which not only was the first dish listed, but the only thing on the whole goddamn menu to have a picture next it, as though the menu was saying, "*This* is food; everything else here is just *words*."

I also got a bunch of other stuff—coffee (a whole cup!), a "wellness shot" smoothie (it looked like strawberry gravy), thick, lustrous yogurt, some pineapple and strawberry pieces to mix into said yogurt, various breads, some sausage, and the now-classic Japanese take on bacon, which apparently they think you should boil.

Shawn got the French toast, because she is an agent of chaos. I didn't try it, but she said it was fine. I would have tried it, but unlike Shawn, I'm not dripping with contempt for my host country and their gustatory counsel. As for my food, it was very tasty, but most important, it tasted of truffles, respect for Japanese culture, and disdain for Japanese breakfast, which could only be the product of a backwards culture.

After finishing our food, we went back to our room, got my stuff ready and onto my person, and then headed out to Shibuya Mark City to do some last-minute gift-buying. Now, if you'll recall way back to Chapter 5, Shawn screamed to the heavens about the fact that there was allegedly a Tokyu Food Show in Shibuya Mark City the last time she visited Tokyo, and that now there wasn't one. Well, it turns out there was a Tokyu Food Show, and Shawn, being unable to find it, convinced herself that it no longer existed. Shawn gaslit herself. As usual.

(In case you read this, and you know Shawn, and she tells you she doesn't gaslight herself, I want you to listen to me, right now: convince her that she gaslights herself all the time. And if she says she read that I told people to say that to her in this very chapter, tell her that she's making that up.)

Anyway, the Tokyu Food Show was pretty neat. Japan doesn't really have street food, but if they did, it would be the kind of food they sold in this place. It was stall after stall of delicious-looking bread, meat, fish, and fried everything. (There is some overlap there.) Alas, I was still full from breakfast, else I would have guzzled down some pollock. At the food show, we bought a few gifts for my mother-in-law, and then went to the train station so that I could get a train to the airport. Shawn was going to accompany me as far as she could before we would part ways. She was going to remain behind in Japan for another week (which ended up being nine days)[1] while I returned today to America. Before we parted, I had three thoughts: (1) would I cry when we said our goodbyes? (2) Would she cry when we said our goodbyes? And (3) would I be able to find my way to the airport?

When we finally arrived at our final stop, I proceeded through the next turnstile while she remained behind. I teared up a bit as I saw Shawn turn around, jump and click her feet together, raise her hands in the air and scream "FREEEEEE!!!!!!"

We all grieve in our own way.

Well, despite my nervousness—and I really was pretty nervous that I would mess up and miss my stop—I managed to get out at the airport. The next task was to pick up Briscoe's toys from somewhere within (see chapters 10 and 11 if you don't remember what I'm talking about). I looked on the map, which of course had a lot of English on it, and quickly realized that, despite knowing what the place I was looking for was *called* (the Black Cat), I had no idea *what* I was looking for. Was it a locker? A storefront? A Japanese cemetery, but for mail? So I went to the information desk and the lady quickly set me straight: it was a counter, it was over there, and no, it wasn't staffed by cats. I went to the Black Cat, picked up Briscoe's toys, and then moseyed to the Japan Airlines (aka JAL) desk to get my ticket and be pointed to the first class lounge.

After a surprisingly long time—the person working with me was a trainee—I finished up at the first-class check-out and got a map to the first-class lounge. I was on pins and needles about what I would discover.

Why so nervous? Because this was one of those relatively rare times in life where I would see whether Atlas could lift the weight of ages of hype.

---

[1]. You'll learn why in chapter 39.

Don't get me wrong: I was not someone who knew much about first-class lounges, let alone the JAL first-class lounge. Rather, I was someone who believed in the great chain of being.

The great chain of being, in case you don't know, is a hierarchy of beings that runs from God down to inanimate matter. It has God at the top, angels are beneath, rational animals (humans, intelligent space aliens, and maybe, in the future, AI) are on the level below angels, non-rational animals are below us rational ones, then plants, and in the end it finishes up with inanimate matter. As I understand it, it was a largely western, Christian, medieval idea that allowed people to make sense of everything's proper place. Despite the six coarse divisions I listed, at least some thinkers—Leibniz comes to mind—think of the chain as having an infinite number of links arranged into six broad kinds; on this view, there are an infinite number of kinds of angels, all arranged hierarchically, and so on with rational animals, non-rational animals, etc.

I don't know that I've always thought of the great chain of being as being infinitely fine-grained, but I have always thought that it had a seventh link. Below angels, and above humans, there are the "fancies": luxurious hotels, fine dining, first-class international travel, and, most pertinent to now, first-class airline lounges.

Before and during this trip, I had been to several fancy restaurants; and on this trip I went to several fancy hotels. But I had never had a first-class international flight, nor had I ever been to a first-class international lounge. It promised a novel experience, but one I had built a raft of expectations for. The first time I went to a really fancy restaurant—let's say, The French Laundry—I had expected the chefs to be so skilled that they could make the food literally jump into my mouth. That didn't happen, but what did happen was close enough to satisfy me.[2] So, I knew the fancies could do things I hadn't even dreamed of.

Consequently, before going into this lounge, I had been walking around, ever since I first learned that there were fancy airline lounges, hobbled by the weight of expectations. Those heavy expectations had been haunting me for the last fifteen years, like the specter of a dead sommelier who had constantly been offering me "spookignon blanc," "monstertrell," or even "hunchbec." Just before I could taste one of his spectral pours, though, he would vanish, leaving me frustrated and thirsting for whatever unearthly vintage I had missed out on.

So, after rounding a corner and going up an escalator in the Haneda airport, I found myself staring at the entrance to the Japan Airlines first class lounge. There were black tiles on the floor, meeting a beige wall with an arrogant goose that is the JAL decal (it might also be a proud duck, I don't know from birds). Under the decal were the words, "First Class Lounge." In front of the sliding glass doors that made up most of the entrance was a stand reading:

*****

5 STAR AIRLINE

SKYTRAX

[Skytrax logo, which is a circle with three lines going through it. This is meant to represent a tri-plane flying right at you, but instead it looks like someone is doing strike-through on the moon]

This is to Certify that

---

2. After asking us which of their desserts we wanted, they said screw it, and gave us all of the desserts they make! And we had a menu that had Shawn's name on it! And they gave us a tour of the kitchen afterwards, with a really cool guide!

> Japan Airlines
> is ranked as a 5-Star Airline

Next to that was a lectern with a golden page describing the delights you'd find in the lounge ahead of you. And next to that was a nondescript hand-sanitizer dispenser. The last bit of the decoration outside the entrance was two trios of large bamboo shoots standing in some kind of thatch pottery that sprouted flowers and other plants from below. They looked unmistakably Japanese.[3]

I don't know if this was intended, but this display dampened my expectations. The font of the JAL sign was pleasing but discreet; the sign for Skytrax looked chintzy, but Skytrax is a UK company, so that tracks. The hand-sanitizer dispenser looked like every other dispenser you've ever seen. And while the bamboo shoots were appealing, standing next to that crowd they looked out of place, like the ghost of a sommelier in a story about an airline lounge.

I should say, I didn't spend as much time ogling the display as this description may suggest. As I've mentioned elsewhere in this book, the space you live in influences your mood, but it's often so subtle as to be observable only in retrospect, which is to say, I was likely confabulating. Nevertheless, I think my first encounter with the JAL lounge was slightly deflating.

Going through the sliding glass doors took me face to face to face to face with the three ladies womaning the computers in the lounge. I showed them my passport and my boarding pass and they gently admitted me to their garden of earthly delights.

---

[3]. Shawn later informed me that they were, in fact, Japanese. They're called "kadomatsu," but to me they'll always be three bamboo thingies in pots.

Past the foyer was a hallway. Once you entered the hallway, to the left was a sushi bar, Sushi Tsurutei, and to the right was the rest of the lounge.

Some people have a taste for desert landscapes; others are drawn to florid jungles; as for me, I like menus. Looking at the appetizers, the mains, the secondi, the desserts, the drinks, all of it—I linger over the fonts, I game out the various combinations like it's fantasy football, and I project myself into the darkest or the brightest timelines based on culinary possibility. I may not have any idea where I put my Airpods, my wallet, my keys, my smartphone, or my laptop but I can remember what Shawn thought of the Dover sole at Republique.[4]

Naturally, I was quite eager to go to Sushi Tsurutei—a restaurant! In an airport lounge!—to see its offerings, all of which would be free. I was stingingly disappointed when I learned that it was closed, either because of remodeling or the discovery of an unexpected waste bin. Still, I was cheered because, at one point, a restaurant *was* there. Just knowing they once had a restaurant in an airport lounge is like finding cave paintings on Mars. You'd rather meet a Martian, but it's still cool to know that there once were Martians, and that, like us, they were born, they buried their dead, and they painted pictures of themselves Eiffel-Towering some broad.

Disappointed, I walked down to the other end of the hallway. To be honest, this hallway *by itself* would be something to write home about. It was bright and shiny, to the point where I wondered if JAL, in peak Japanese style, laminated the whole thing. At the end of the hallway was a red, lightly smoked pane of glass, behind which militated battalions of glassware, so organized as to appear threatening. In front of the red pane of glass was a map of the lounge.

---

[4]. "Good! For fish. I'm not having any more."

I'm not going to let a dumb map tell me what to do, so rather than look at the wordless guide (whose services I did *not* ask for), I hung a louie and found myself in the center of what was, far and away, the largest lounge I've ever visited.

The lounge didn't feel long, but it did feel extraordinarily wide, as large as the first floor of my university's library. There was a spectacular view of the tarmac, a view almost as expansive as the lounge itself. The lounge had sections, but they weren't divided; instead, the end of one section and the beginning of another was marked by the arrival of different furniture. I later learned that this was intentional, and not just them running out of Arhaus tables. To quote the website: "Each area within the lounge is uniquely styled, creating an all-encompassing space for every guest."

It was true. The first visible section was a spacious area comprising sets of ivory-colored leather chairs set up to face each other, three to three, as if to inspire spirited conversation or to simulate a British quiz show. Call this section "the Symposium."

On that same side of the lounge, a long bar abutted the window. This area seemed like it was meant to accommodate single business-people who wanted to plug in their laptops and write PowerPoints about how to induce travelers to look at the airport itself rather than the PowerPoints on their laptops. Call this section "the Workbench."

If the Workbench was to the north, and the Symposium was just south of it, then just south of the Symposium were several carrels that would allow for an adult to work in dark privacy, or a child to win hide-and-seek. Call this section "the Cavern."

As you proceeded further, you saw the bar area, which the red pane of smoked glass had been obscuring. If memory serves, in front of it were two-tops and four-tops; the kind of tables you'd eat at if you were a normie. Following the map's own designations, I'll call this area "JAL's Table."

As I kept going down the lounge, there were more tables and stuff, but what really caught my attention was the booze selection. Several bottles of liquor and sake stood at attention, allowing you to feel them up and sample their wares. In addition, there were lots of taps that were cooling white wine, sake, beer, or sparkling wine within them. The effect of presenting good alcohol in this format was discomfiting, like serving caviar in a cafeteria. Still, seeing all these kinds of hooch, available and free, made me want to gluttonously try them all. Call this section "Hemingway's Prostitute Shop."

I realize that I'm really objectifying these bottles of alcohol, but it did occur to me, months after I pigged out on this booze, that, although alcohol is, more or less, everywhere, I noticed it is definitely more prevalent in airline lounges than any other places I've been, save for weddings, philosophy conferences, and the part of my home office devoted to crying, which I call "sniffle-nook." Writing this book, during which I have been thinking of how my American-ness affects my experience of Japan's intense Japan-ness, has also made me look at many things in what I fancy is the anthropological mode, and one of those things is alcohol.

Why is alcohol so ubiquitous in airport settings? The first explanation is that alcohol is a relatively cheap way to make people feel catered to. Paying for bottles of fancy alcohol is actually not that big an expense when you consider that, even when the good booze is free, most travelers will, like me, limit themselves to three drinks. And yet they tell themselves they've gotten a really good deal by paying $400 a year to secure access to the airline lounge that gives them, at most, $25 worth of alcoholic value each visit. It's like how my cat thinks I'm a hero for letting him explore the backyard, when really I'm just trying to feed the coyotes.

This explanation isn't fully satisfying. The problem is, even people who don't buy memberships to airline lounges will sidle up to Applebee's during their layover and have a couple of libations. There's no reason for them to think they're getting a good deal when their two Dollaritas and Riblets come out to $39.57.[5]

The second explanation of alcohol's ubiquity is that people are terrified of flying, and they need intoxicants to steady their nerves. I think this is also pretty unlikely; of the many people I've met who have flown on airplanes, very few of them are so scared of flying that they have to take to drink.

Although this second explanation isn't right, it's close to the true explanation. It's not that people are afraid of air*planes*: they're afraid of air*ports*. All people, in all airports, at all times of day, are perennially six hours into *The Purge*. You know that someone, somewhere near you, is going to transform from a human into a spiteful pile of knees and elbows, ready to shoot a harpoon of bone into you so that he can take your overhead space, snag the last open seat near the gate, or beat you to the information desk. And not only do you know that; everyone knows that. And not only does everyone know that; everyone knows that everyone knows that. Anyone who has read Hobbes' *Leviathan* and doubts Hobbes' claim that, in the state of nature, life is a war of all against all, has never been to an airport.

Historically (and contemporaneously), when men are about to do violence, whether in a military or a criminal setting, many of them take drugs to remove their inhibitions so they can do what they need to do.

---

5. I cannot believe that in 2023 Applebee's offered one dollar margaritas. To me, this is as good an idea as ten-cent beer night was in 1974. Does Applebee's really want to be known for its riots?

This is why alcohol pervades and fuels life in the airport: it is that which allows us to put on our warpaint, a helpmeet for our lycanthropy.

Not for me, though. I actually don't mind being in airports. I still drink, but that's just because there's no better deal than free alcohol!

Back to the JAL First-Class Lounge: having these five different places—the Symposium, the Workbench, the Cavern, JAL's Table, and Hemingway's Prostitute Shop—to decamp to made me experience an uncomfortable abundance of choice. In normal airport lounges, I just try to find a place where I can sit down and write on my laptop.[6] But this place wasn't crowded at all. There was space for miles. I could sit in pretty much any place I wanted. After a uselessly long period of time, I opted for the Workbench, so that I could purposely fixate on my laptop right in front of the stunning view of whatever-it-was.

I sat down, took out my laptop, and, well, wrote some of this. However, I also wanted to try some food. So I looked at the online-only menu and ordered some sushi. They brought me three pieces. It was really neat to get sushi in an airport lounge, but while the sushi was better than the sushi in an American all-you-can-eat sushi buffet, it was resolutely not great.

While I was eating my sushi, drinking my sake, and playing my video games, I overheard a middle-aged American woman sitting in the Symposium talking loudly at her white, white-haired, harried husband. She was holding forth about how entitled the younger generations are:

---

6. Now that I think about it, I don't think I've ever gone to an airport lounge without having it in mind to do some work. This means one of three things: (1) I'm a workaholic; (2) I'm a procrastinator; (3) I don't pay much attention to what I do in airline lounges.

"Why can't they eat out just once or twice a month? Why do they have to do it so many times a week?! And why do they bring their problems with them wherever they go and expect us to care about them?"

She went on in this manner for a while. I couldn't help but notice that she was doing this in the first-class lounge at JAL, at what must have been the end of a (presumably) luxurious trip to Japan from (presumably) America.

Bitch.

But as I sat there, drinking my Hibiki whiskey, eating my Japanese mackerel, and ignoring my exclusive view of the well-manicured Haneda tarmac, my judgment softened. Yes, it's unseemly for someone who is obviously well-heeled, and probably (though not necessarily!) lazy and demanding, to complain about the softness of the youth. But after a trip to Japan, where people are polite but non-intrusive, and the service is both excellent and restrained, your mind can't help but to turn to the failings of your fellow citizens (though a fair mind would also look inward at its own imperfections). You wonder: why can't America be as well-oiled a machine as Japan?

In chapter 40, I will try my hand at answering that question.[7] For now I'll simply note my ambivalence about this woman's probable hypocrisy.

---

7. Spoiler alert: not really.

# 38

# Mate for an Hour

When you go to a grocery store, it's a bad idea to show up hungry. Not only do you end up buying more than you need, you also end up buying stuff you don't need. Two boxes of Captain Crunch is three boxes too many.[1]

I feel the same way about shopping for alcohol. So whenever I go to a liquor store, I make sure to show up drunk. I'm much less likely to make an impulse buy if my reaction time equals that of a poisoned moose.

After three drinks, then, I was lubricated enough to leave the first-class lounge and buy some expensive alcohol, for both myself and the people back home who either took care of Briscoe or watched him while he was having playdates with his friends: Shawn's mom; Lon, the father of Briscoe's friends Tucson and Francis; Musk, the father of Briscoe's friend Hyruss; and Scotty, the father of Briscoe's friend Annie. Heroes, all. The good news, from my point of view, was that my mother-in-law and Lon were teetotalers, which not only freed me up to not get them anything, but also to blame them for thinking they're better than me.

---

[1]. I make sure to destroy a box of Captain Crunch every time I visit the grocery store.

In graduate school and after, there were famous philosophy professors I could have taken classes with—Allan Gibbard, Peter Railton, Elizabeth Anderson, David Velleman, Peter van Inwagen, Alvin Plantinga—but I didn't, because I felt bad for the less famous professors who I feared weren't getting any students. So I selflessly, condescendingly, but, more importantly, stupidly didn't take classes with them. It could have really helped me to have one or more of their letters of recommendation.

I made a similar mistake at the duty-free store. I would see bottles of Japanese whiskey with signs reading, "limit one per customer," and I would think, "I should leave those for people who need them more." Little did I know, the reason for that sign was that the resale value of these bottles was extremely high. I could have bought a bottle of Nikka Whisky's single malt Miyagikyo Grande for $100 and sold it in the USA for $585. More important, I could have justifiably said that I tried a $600 bottle of whiskey, so I could lord it over my friends: Musk, who's always trying to get me to join him in defending his mulish behavior while doing handstands in public; Scotty, who's constantly bouncing around from one bandwagon to the next; and Lon, given that pseudonym because he looks like the wolfman. Villains, all.

Anyway, I got Scotty and Musk some whiskey; I got Shawn's mom nothing because I had already gotten her tea in a different store; and I got Lon some silly samurai bobble-head because he's not into anything except maybe Jimmy Carter hagiographies.

Now loaded down with gifts like a genuine Japanese tourist, I returned to the JAL First-Class Lounge. I still had about an hour to kill, so I explored the lounge a little more thoroughly, and what did I find but a somewhat inconspicuous entry to a sixth part of the lounge: an area called "The RED SUITE."

When I entered The RED SUITE, I let out a pained yelp. No, the floor wasn't covered with LEGOs. Instead, my pain stemmed from the fact that this was the best room I've ever entered in my adult life, the grown-up equivalent of when a kid first enters Chuck E. Cheese's.

Let me explain.

A lot of people talk about soulmates. "When I saw him, I knew he was the one," and all that business. Look, I'm not sure that I even believe in soulmates. Shawn and I have a happy marriage, but I don't think we're "soulmates"; instead, when we met each other, we each had the same philosophy: marry the first person you meet whom you regard as barely acceptable.[2] We did that, and now all I do for her is take care of her when she's sick, try to brighten her day, conspire with her about how to raise Briscoe, learn from her, and let her take me on life-changing vacations. And all she does for me is inspire me to believe in myself, try to get me to improve myself, inform me about what's going on in the world, pay the taxes and bills and make a baller Thanksgiving dinner. If that's all it takes to be soulmates, then hell, even penguins could qualify.[3]

---

2. I owe this observation to my brother, who had the good sense to put it in his best man speech at Shawn's and my wedding.

3. Upon reading this, Shawn told me that this was extraordinarily thin praise for her. When she told me that, I blanched; I really was trying hard to be flattering! In my defense, I'm bad at praising people. I always fear that any idealized description will pressure them to live up to what I've said they are, when really they'd rather spend time playing Slime Rancher. But she loved how feckless my love-poetry is, which is one of the things I most love about her: her willingness to play the fool, at least in front of me. This is possibly why, after marrying Shawn, my taste in women changed from "Catholic saints" to "sexy oafs."

I think when people talk about soulmates, the simpler ones have in mind something that the 1980s comic book series, *Elf Quest*, called "*recognition*" (if memory serves, it was always italicized). This was a magical effect, where, upon locking eyes with a particular other elf, both you (who are also an elf) and the other elf would realize that you now *had* to mate for life with each other. Elves who *recognized* each other always made perfect couples, and so *recognition* was usually a positive thing. But sometimes, it could be a horrifying realization. For instance, you might *recognize* someone whose life was going in a very different direction from yours, meaning that either you or they would have to uproot everything they were devoted to, or you'd have to spend your lives apart, permanently bereft.

If soulmate-theory requires something like *recognition*, then I'm skeptical of soulmate-theory. But, after experiencing this room, I now believe in the interior design equivalent of *recognition*, for, upon setting my eyes on The RED SUITE, I *recognized* it as my forever-room.

It was my roommate.

The RED SUITE was divided into four zones: the Library, the Gallery, the Retreat, and the Bar.[4] I'm not going to describe them—by now, you should know that my physical descriptions are as faithful to the real McCoy as a photo of a Carl's Jr. hamburger is to whatever it is that place serves—so, if you want to read about them, just read about it on the website. I will say, though, that it had all the elements of everything I think I need in a living space: bookshelves with glass panels; dark cherry wood

---

4. You can disbelieve me—be a prick, why not—but I swear to you that I separated the rest of the lounge into five named sections ("the Symposium", etc.) before reading that The RED SUITE was divided into four similarly named sections.

everywhere; desks spilling out from the walls; chess boards; huge bowls filled with ice with champagne bottles chilling within; old Italian shoes; a typewriter, presumably no longer operational; and loving retellings of the history of Japanese aviation. The only thing it was missing was a fireplace with a lit fire in it; an ice storm outside, along with gale force winds; and no grading.

I said before that when I first saw The RED SUITE I let out a pained yelp. The yelp was an involuntary cry of *recognition* of my roommate; and the pain, far more acute, was the almost instant recognition that I could have spent the previous two hours in this room, but didn't; and that I probably would never see The RED SUITE again.

After spending an hour cavorting over all the furniture in The RED SUITE, it was time to go on my flight. I grieved that I only got to spend one hour of my life living in the area for which God designed me. But if nothing else, The RED SUITE showed that fancy airline lounges really were above us humans in the great chain of being. Sometimes Atlas can hold those heavy expectations.

It was in that mindset that I boarded my first-class flight home, ready to enjoy the divine fulsomeness of a higher mode of existence.

# 39

# The First Rule of Flight Club Is That You Brag to Everyone about Flight Club

It was time to walk the last leg of my tour: the flight. Not just any flight, though: a first-class flight on Japan Air Lines (JAL) from Tokyo to Los Angeles. For the next twelve hours, I would live like a sultan in an airy castle: I would have every need catered to, and I would destroy all my political rivals through subterfuge.

Though I would like to report to you that I was carried on a palanquin from the gate to the airplane, I unfortunately had to hoof it on the jetway like the riff-raff. At least I was entitled to be one of the first people who boarded.

When I got onto the plane, I recall walking through a door directly into the first-class cabin. I was seated near the front, in row 2, in the middle part of the row, but on the left side of the plane. I couldn't see the other passengers when I stood up, but, save for one, I didn't dwell on them. The only thing that surprised me was how young my co-cabiners looked. I'm not saying they were teenagers, but they seemed to be in their thirties.

I suspected that these were successful businesspeople, which is to say: they were all hitmen, I'm sure of it.

The one passenger who periodically drew my attention throughout the flight was an older Japanese man. He looked to be in his sixties, and his belly told me he was prosperous. He seemed to elicit special treatment from Oyabu and Ideta, the two flight attendants stationed in our cabin. The fact that these extremely professional and polite women appeared to be extra-interested in him, as opposed to me, led me to believe, certainly on insufficient evidence, that he was a JAL bigwig. This thought pleased me: I convinced myself that they would try to impress him by very visibly treating the rest of us well. More importantly, if both of the engines failed, they would try extra hard to prevent the plane from exploding.

I was amazed by the extravagant setup of my first-class seat. It was, of course, a lie-flat seat, and in front of it was a large screen. Next to it was a panel that offered an incredible number of opportunities for plugging things in, pulling things out, switching things off and on, and opening and closing little cabinets. Not to brag, but I suffer from an impressive variety of tics and twitches, so I found this to be a promising start. "I love toggling things!" I yelled as I took my seat, to everyone in particular.

Whenever I imagine first-class flights (which is surprisingly often), I fantasize about what the menu will be. I realize now that if I had wanted to, I could have simply looked this up on the Internet, but I've been dreaming about three-star sky-food since the 90s, so it never occurred to me that I could concretize my reveries by Googling this. In case you're like me, though, and you're all about food, I will write out for you what was on the menu that day.

There were two sides to the menu; a Japanese menu and a western menu. Since I had already tried a JAL Japanese menu on the business class trip to Japan, and as I had already had top-tier sushi and wagyu beef in

Japan, I decided I didn't want to try the Japanese food; the best Japanese fish and beef still sat conspicuously on my tongue, like powdered sugar on a freshly fried donut, so I opted for the western menu.

Don't worry, I will tell you what was on the Japanese menu. But first, I want to register some outrage. The older Japanese man—I had some evidence that he worked in the C-suite of JAL, if you'll recall—was served caviar and a tin of champagne before he received any portion of his dinner. I, on the other hand, was not. I was offered champagne, and I drank it, but I didn't appreciate it, as my rage must have clouded my appreciation. How dare that man get a bowl of beluga caviar when I, who paid no money for this flight, wasn't offered anything! Just because he probably runs JAL!

I don't complain, even if a pushy, middle-aged Indian man puts his head right next to my head as I type, imperiously correcting my diction,[1] so none of this happened out loud. And to be frank, I don't remember feeling angry. But I do remember seeing that guy's caviar and wondering, "hey, will I get caviar too? ... Eh, I'd better not ask."

Nevertheless, I must have been extremely angry because the champagne was not memorable to me. Yet when Shawn had her own first-class flight

---

1. This really happened. I could hear his rapid, snorting breaths. He was a professor at my institution and I had the misfortune of writing a grant application with him. He was highly directive but also completely unwilling to do anything, which was so galling that I actually enjoyed him. I remember comforting myself at the time, "oh, this is going to be a good story one day," but I literally forgot his name and that is the extent of the story. In retrospect, that son of a bitch totally made me.

home, on January 14,[2] she was given champagne as well. Apparently, she and, I guess, I(?), were offered something called "Champagne Salon 2007." During her flight, she wrote to me: "I had the salon. Easily the best champagne of my life." Since I had no recollection of this, it must be the case that a sudden infusion of rage—rage because the definite owner and founder of JAL was dancing around the cabin, throwing caviar everywhere—caused my tongue to break.

I know what you're thinking: maybe you just didn't notice how good the champagne tasted? Or maybe you did notice, but you forgot?

No, that's impossible. I'll tell you why.

First, Shawn doesn't even like champagne. But I quite enjoy it. There's just no way that she would appreciate a fine champagne and I wouldn't.

Second—and this is more important—I have an excellent memory for tastes. Shawn, on the other hand, does not. If you haven't noticed by now, she suffers from many ailments.

Ailment #1: she has terrible insomnia; she couldn't fall asleep if she flopped down onto a $6,000 mattress on a houseboat after a nine-hour hike. If she were asleep, the footsteps of a ghost would wake her up, even

---

2. In Chapter 37, I promised I would tell you why Shawn headed home on January 14 (nine days after me) instead of January 12 (seven days after me, as originally scheduled). Well, the reason is that she couldn't get a first-class ticket home if she had traveled on January 12; this is because she could upgrade her business class ticket to first class only if (a) she did so one day before the flight and (b) a seat in first class was available. On January 11, we had the following tearful exchange over text: Shawn: hey I can't take a first-class flight home until January 13 or 14, so I think I'll just take business home on January 12. Me: DON'T!!! If you don't take the first-class flight, you'll miss the best flight of your life! Shawn: ok

though ghosts don't exist. Something she regularly asks me and Briscoe is, "have you guys seen my ether?" Point is: bitch can't sleep.

Ailment #2: she is, as I have already mentioned, beard blind; she has seen ZZ Top, but she describes them only as "those white guys who do music." I once showed her a photo of Rock Hudson with Phyllis Gates and she didn't realize that Gates was even in the picture! She can't even see metaphorical beards!

Ailment #3: although she is capable of tasting and enjoying food, she has no recollection of anything she has eaten, ever. I mean, she knows she has eaten things, but she doesn't know what things she has eaten, what anything tastes like, or what she likes. When I go to a restaurant with her that we've been to before, I have to act like I'm an aide to the President at a state dinner: "President Rob's Wife, that's called a hamburger; you enjoy those, but you find that the cheese makes you feel bloated. Yes, that's right, smile at it. No, don't eat that, that's a plate." I call this last condition "gustatory dementia."

The point is, given her numerous and manifest defects (I haven't even talked about how poorly put-together her feet-bones are!), there's no way my wife appreciated a delicious glass of champagne that I failed to notice. Hence, I must have been mad at the immortal founder of JAL, a paunchy Japanese vampire who has survived only on caviar and gloating.

Anyway, the Japanese menu was as follows (keeping in mind that I can't make it as pretty or as sleek as the actual menu was):

*The menu is created by chef-owner ISHIKAWA Hideki of "KAGURAZAKA ISHIKAWA" and chef-owner KOIZUMI Koji of "KOHAKU" Kagurazaka, Tokyo*

**Seasonal five colorful delicacies**

Snow Crab & Savoy Spinach with Crab Sauce <ISHIKAWA>

Grilled Blowfish Milt Flavored with Yuzu Citrus & Miso Garnished with Turnip <ISHIKAWA>

Hard Clam with Thickened Clam Broth Topped with Sea Urchin with a hint of Yuzu Citrus <ISHIKAWA>

Prime Taro & Garland Chrysanthemum with Mullet Roe <KOHAKU>

Grilled Blowfish & Lotus with Skin with Truffle Sauce <KOHAKU>

**Soup**

Scallop Dumpling, White Radish, Kyoto Carrot & Mitsuba Herb in our Masterpiece Dashi <ISHIKAWA>

**Sashimi**

Ise Lobster, Lobster Innards & Canola Blossom Covered with Lobster Broth <KOHAKU>

White Sesame Tofu Topped with Caviar, Wasabi & Thickened Soy Sauce <KOHAKU>

### Simmered

Free Range Duck from Yamagata Prefecture, Bamboo Shoot & Green Onion <ISHIKAWA>

### Rice

Steamed Rice with Seasonal Greens <ISHIKAWA>
or
Steamed Rice

### Miso Soup

Nameko Mushrooms & White Leeks <ISHIKAWA>

### Pickles

Cucumber Pickles with Shiso Herb, Kelp & Yam <ISHIKAWA>

### Dessert

Japanese Traditional Confection of "Matcha Flavored Arrowroot Cake" <ISHIKAWA>
Strawberry Ice Cream & Strawberry Sauce with Rum Jelly & Roasted Pine Nuts <KOHAKU>
Green Tea

Obviously enough, I can't tell you what this Japanese menu was like, as I just told you that I didn't pick it. I will say I was pleasantly surprised to see someone in Japan finally make use of blowfish milt, whatever the hell that is. And I'm sad to say that I, once again, missed out on my once-lifely portion of mullet roe. Still, I did a bit of research into chef-owners Ishikawa and Kohaku, and I discovered that they both run three-star Michelin restaurants, that their websites are eerily similar, and that, whereas Ishikawa seems to specialize in shellfish, Kohaku's passion seems to be for piles of things. Like, almost every photo of Kohaku's food seemed to be of a small bowl, filled with a small pile of food, topped with a smaller pile of shavings of something. Now that I think about it, that's kind of perfect for airline food.[3]

The quality of the in-flight dining serves as a nice segue to discussing how good the service was in JAL first-class. My goodness, I'm a talented writer. I mean, did you see that segue?! Segues are really underrated tools in the writer's arsenal. Honestly, I think someone should write a whole book just about segues. But how would it start? And how would it end? This is probably why no one has ever done that. Oh wait, I know! It would have to start *in media res*, where you don't quite know what's going on, and then the ending would give the context of the beginning, allowing you to see that the ending was an excellent segue to the beginning!

Well shit, now I've lost my place. What was I talking about? Oh yeah, the service. Shortly after we took off, they offered us some in-flight casualwear. You'd have to be crazy to turn down an offer of sky pajamas, so I took them, incredulous that we were even given the option to decline. Honestly, I wouldn't have objected if they had forcibly stripped us to our skivvies and then aggressively pulled our new, beige, drawstring

---

[3]. I've written a bonus chapter describing the first-class meal on this flight. You can get it emailed to you by visiting robgressis.com/japanbonus.

sweatpants and matching long-sleeved jerseys over our bodies like we were helpless two-year-olds.

After eating my dinner and drinking three libations, I was ready to sleep, and started fiddling with one of the panels to transform the chair into a bed. Oyabu instantly noticed thanks to (what I assume is) her internal panopticon, so she came over and told me to stand up. I did so dutifully, curious about why this was happening, and she then added a mattress and comforter to my set-up. I settled under the covers and attempted to tipsily fall asleep.

This being Japan, the cabin temperature was a bit hot for me, and adding a blanket to that just made things worse. I couldn't help it, though: sleeping without a blanket, especially in a public place, just makes me feel vulnerable and rude. So I split the difference by taking off my jersey and lazily hurling it at my feet. Very quickly after that, I fell asleep.

When I awoke, I found my overshirt neatly folded and placed in a very accessible place right next to me. Not even my mom ever did that for me, and she regularly tells me that she'd die for me!

Impressed by this, I tried to do some writing for this book on the plane, and to help me in this task, I did some reading first. I wanted to get another set of foreign eyes on the Japanese culture of service, so I went back to Pico Iyer's *A Beginner's Guide to Japan*. The book consists mainly of aphorisms, so I took out my pen to underline those that seemed most relevant. However, while I was doing this, I dropped the pen into a pocket of my first-class pod, and I couldn't reach it, so I asked Ideta for some help. I should say that earlier, because I'm myself, I had dropped my glasses into a different tiny abyss. That time, Ideta had reached her slender hands into the crevice and retrieved my glasses. This time, though, she couldn't do it, so she probably internally cursed her fat, FAT hands. She asked me, quite sincerely, whether I wanted her to fetch a mechanic to get my pen after the plane landed. I told her no, I didn't need to interrupt at least three different people's days to recover my sixty-cent Bic pen. But I thanked her for her supererogation.

Last bit about the service: near the end of the flight, Oyabu approached me and asked, "do you want to use the bathroom?" This came out of nowhere, so I wondered whether I looked like I had to go to the bathroom. Was I making the pee-pee dance? After a beat, I concluded that I wasn't, so I looked at her with eyes full of perplexity and said, "why are you asking me this?" Without missing a beat, she said, "because we expect some turbulence soon."

Pleased by this unique (though it shouldn't be!) reminder, I introspected, asking myself that age-old question, "can I pee right now?" I could!

I went to the bathroom and did my business, and when I opened the door after finishing, I found Oyabu waiting outside the door, holding both a bag to carry my pajama pants as well as my going-around pants. She also pointed at a drop-down floor latch near the door that she wanted me to use, but the device was completely inscrutable. After ineffectually fiddling with it, I gave up. Knowing this flight, I'm guessing it was some technologically clever way of allowing me to put on my pants two legs at a time.

When I finished taking off all my casual wear and putting on my slacks, I noticed that I didn't have my button-down shirt. She forgot to put it in the bag! I would have to have words with Oyabu once this door was open, words like: "where is my shirt?"

When I opened the bathroom door, Oyabu was standing before me, holding up a coat hanger with my shirt on it, presumably so it didn't get wrinkled. She probably ironed it too.

I sheepishly thanked her and closed the door again. I quickly put on my shirt and when I opened the bathroom door for the last time, she was standing outside of it. Again. She asked me whether I wanted to keep the pajamas. Of course I did. I looked at the other customers. I didn't notice any of them wearing JAL's comfortable clothes. Savages, all.[4]

During the voyage, I enjoyed one bit of in-flight entertainment: a movie called *Smile*. This was a horror movie, and it was the scariest one I'd seen since *The Grudge*. When I watched it, I could feel the hair literally raise on the top of my head. I didn't know scalps did that! I had to pause it several times, too, to prepare myself for whatever dreadful event was about to occur. Part of me wondered whether it was so scary simply because of the contrast effect between the frightening events in the movie and the impeccable comforts of my flights. However, when I got back to Los Angeles, I was scared for days that Briscoe was actually a terrifying monster under his skin. So: not the contrast effect.

Speaking of the contrast effect, soon enough it was time for me to be fully finished with Japan and to reenter the United States. The plane landed without a hitch, and after a very polite goodbye, I deplaned.[5] As soon as I got on to the jetway, I took off my mask. That is almost certainly a double entendre.

Since I was flying in first class, and therefore more important than everyone, I got to be at the front of the line for customs. Despite the

---

4. Another bit of bathroom business. Earlier in the flight, when I wanted to go to the bathroom, it was occupied. Ideta noticed this and immediately informed me that there was another bathroom available, but that "it is smaller. Is this ok?" I wonder what would have happened if I had said no?

5. I half-expected either a mechanic to be there to break open my seat panels, or at least for one of the employees of JAL to hand me a royal pen in recompense for my clumsiness. It didn't happen, but it was only half of an expectation, so I didn't mind.

fact that I live in America and read English, I found it difficult to figure out where the signage was telling me to go. All I saw was a sign reading "visitors." I didn't see any sign reading "residents." Confused, I looked for authorities to solve my problem. There were lots of guards, laughing and joking with each other behind the customs, quite multi-ethnic. I approached, and asked, "is this the line for US citizens?" He responded, "it's for anyone."

Then why have a sign at all?

I walked up to a small shutter door (it reached up to my knees), by about 5:50 AM. It was locked, so I waited. According to the signs, the customs lanes were supposed to open at 6:00, but in America, I was coming to realize, signs were just for show. At 6:03, the door still hadn't unlocked, so I asked the guard, "when will you open?" He said, "in a bit. The system is booting up."

If only they had some sort of apparatus that would tell them when passengers are arriving! I'll drop something off at the suggestion box that is not there.

Finally, after a gigantic five-minute wait, the doors unlocked. He told me to push the door open. I tried. It didn't budge. He exclaimed, "oh, my bad!" and then pulled it open from his side.

He asked me if I had anything to declare. I said, "whiskey, candy, some art."

"Oh," he said. "Art's cool. Welcome to America."

# 40

# My Master Theory of Japan: No Masters!

The philosopher Immanuel Kant invented a novel philosophical position he called "transcendental idealism," which he articulated and defended in his magnum opus, the *Critique of Pure Reason*. Unfortunately, no one knows what transcendental idealism is.

Oh, don't get me wrong: a lot of decorated, erudite scholars *claim* to know what transcendental idealism is. But no one has landed on an interpretation of it that satisfies most of the scholarly community. In other words, every Kant scholar is a failure.

One of these failures was named Wilfred Sellars (1912-1989). Robert Brandom, the George R. R. Martin of philosophy (in that he looks like an old-timey sea captain), dubbed Sellars "The Sage of Pittsburgh,"[1] and thought of him as one of the two greatest philosophers of his generation. Although Sellars didn't convince all Kant scholars (including me) to read Kant in his way, I find Sellars's interpretation, adumbrated in his "Philosophy and the Scientific Image of Man,"[2] interesting as a novel philosophical position in its own right, so I offer the following, helpful-because-intelligible misreading of it.

In enunciating his transcendental idealism, Kant claimed that reality consists of two "worlds": the world as it appears to us and the world as it is in itself. In Sellars's terminology, people have both a "manifest image" of reality (this is the world as it appears to them) and a "scientific image" of reality (this is the world as it is in itself, supposedly revealed by natural science). If you describe humans in the terminology of the scientific image, we're just bodies that are caused to move in certain ways because of forces we can't sense or even imagine, but can mathematically represent. But if

---

1. Quoted from https://www.utimes.pitt.edu/archives/?p=45850. I love this appellation because it marries an archaic title with a location that neither amplifies nor dampens it, but rather confuses it. It's like "the tyrant of Omaha" or "the oracle of South Burlington". Whereas I'd be laughing at the Tyrant of Woonsocket (population: 43,000) and be petrified of the tyrant of Moscow (population: Russians), I guess I'd be *somewhat* scared of the Tyrant of Omaha (population: 485,000), but I would expect his main flex to be giving me lots of parking tickets. As for the oracle of South Burlington, I imagine she'd give me *some* insight into the future, but it would be about stuff like whether I'm going to get more than a 5% pay raise in two years.

2. Wilfrid Sellars, "Philosophy and the Scientific Image of Man", *Frontiers of Science and Philosophy*, ed. Robert G. Colodny (Univ. of Pittsburgh Press, 1962), pp. 35-78.

you describe us in the language of the manifest image, we're people who perform particular actions on the basis of reasons.

I'll elaborate on both images.

The manifest image is the world of human experience. In Sellars's somewhat speculative telling,[3] the manifest image has a history (here, Sellars goes Hegelian rather than Kantian): people first experienced the world as consisting only of people—bees, trees, and breezes were full of spirits, though to be beings that did things of their own free will, often for inscrutable reasons, but for reasons nonetheless—but gradually, we pruned away the intentionality from more and more things, e.g., reconceiving of a volcano's eruption as a natural process determined to happen because of plate tectonics forcing magma out, instead of as an earth god's diarrhea.

One branch of philosophy, which Sellars dubs the Platonic conception, after famed Greek wrestler Plato, sees carving out the joints of the manifest image as philosophy's primary job. However, there is another branch of philosophy that follows in the footsteps of bad-boy lens-grinder Baruch de Spinoza (also a philosopher on the side). According to the Spinozists, philosophy's job is to show how the scientific image can not only explain everything in the manifest image, but might even be able to get rid of the manifest image altogether.

The Spinozists think like this: science predicts really well. Not only can it tell you that a solar eclipse is coming on April 8, 2024, but it can create a device that allows you to look at it without hurting yourself. It would take a miracle for science to be so exactly correct all the time, unless the

---

3. That said, it does have some empirical support, such as Pascal Boyer's *Religion Explained: The Evolutionary Foundations of Religious Belief* (Basic Books, 2001).

postulated forces underlying these predictions really existed. What can the manifest image offer compared to that? Only a bunch of people foolishly looking at what they think is a black sun, and suffering burnt out eyeballs as a result. Heck, they don't even have cool names for their injuries! I mean, which sounds more impressive to you: "my ophthalmologist says I have solar retinopathy" or "my eyes hurt and I can't look good no more?"

The problem with adhering to the scientific image is that, at the end of the day, you lose people and reasons. The Spinozists say, "hey, according to science, all things, at the end of the day, are just fundamental forces and subatomic particles. Those things that you call 'people' just consist of those, too. Well, since electrons don't act for reasons, and since 'people' just consist of electrons, then people don't exist either. So, you Platonists should really stop revering this silly manifest image."

Against this, the Platonists will say, "what do you mean, 'should,' mother fuckers?? I thought you assholes thought that 'should's aren't even real?!" And the Spinozists will retort, "classic manifest imagers, making everything personal."

Sellars is neither a Platonist nor a Spinozist. Instead, he's in a third tradition, the Kantian one. He thinks he can have his manifest cake and eat his scientific one too. This is because he thinks neither the manifest nor the scientific image can be privileged over the other one. According to the scientific image, tables are just arbitrarily selected parts of larger energy continua and are mostly empty space, whereas according to the manifest image, the gaming table in my office takes up so much space that I constantly ram my mammoth butt into it because God has cursed me for my gluttony. Both claims are true, but each claim is made from a different perspective, and the philosopher's challenge is to "stereoscopically" merge the two perspectives into one single view on the world. How to do exactly this is very hard, but if philosophy were easy, we wouldn't get paid like store managers at Walgreens.

I give all this throat-clearing because I'm going to offer my master theory of Japan. However, I'm not saying it's true, *tout court.* It's not a scientific image of Japan, the kind that careful social scientists would construct. Nor is it anything close to a robust manifest image of Japan, the sort of image you'd piece together through a lot of anthropological research, interviews with people, and living there a long time. No, it's Japan as it appeared to *me, my* manifest image of Japan, Japan as seen through a keyhole. It's *my* answer to the age-old question, "what's Japan feel like?"

Despite how common this question is, it isn't well-posed. I mean, surely the answer to it depends on what part of Japan I'm grabbing at the time. But I don't mean this as a question about haptics, but instead about phenomenology, "the study of structures of consciousness as experienced from the first-person point of view."[4] "What's Japan feel like?" was really the question, "is there something that stands out to me about Japan that separates it from other places I've been to?"

This question occurred to me four times: when I walked to Boruta in Kyoto, when I watched Wrestle Kingdom at the Tokyo Dome, when I looked down on Kioicho from my skyscraper hotel room, and when I rode the subway in Tokyo. And my answers to the question changed each time.

---

4. See the first line (thank goodness) of David Woodruff Smith's forty-two page long article, "Phenomenology," from the *Stanford Encyclopedia of Philosophy*. You can read all the other lines at: Plato.stanford.edu/entries/phenomenology/.

Walking through the dark, empty, concrete-laden backstreets on the way to Boruta, my mind judged Japan to be discomfitingly safe, even though my body associated such scenes with camouflaged scallywags. While watching Wrestle Kingdom, I found that Japan felt subtly excellent – not only was there a high level of athleticism and thoughtful in-ring psychology in most of the matches, but the audience was paying close attention and knew what to clap for.

Looking upon Tokyo 700' below me from my hotel room in the Prince Gallery Kioicho, I thought, "wow, there are so many people here, all living their own lives, yet none of these lives seems appreciably bad from my extremely limited exposure to them." Contrast this with Twitter, whose denizens seem miserable enough to move St. Francis of Assisi to strangle a Eurasian Jackdaw. Save for the two homeless people I saw, everyone appeared able to have enough to carve out a satisfying living: they were safe, and they had homes.

Finally, on my first subway trip in Tokyo, I looked around and saw lots of advertisements, with loud colors and smiling faces, but I saw no celebrities. Where was Steve Harvey? Kim Kardashian? Kevin Costner? How do I know what to buy or think without celebrity guidance? Whom am I supposed to look up to?

See, in America, I know who my betters are. They are the rich people I've heard of. But in Japan, on that train, I felt adrift. Never have I felt more anomie than the time I was on that train, in a foreign land, unsure of the customs, and with no Richard Kind to turn to.

I think this lack of celebrities is the key to my manifest image of Japan. On the one hand, I've heard that Japan is a very hierarchical culture, more so than the USA (that would be, I suppose, the scientific image of Japan). I don't know how to measure that, but let's say it's true–it wouldn't be the biggest shock in the world to learn that some cultures are more hierarchical than others according to some metric. And yet, the most famous person I saw while I was there was a dog statue.

I'll put all these observations together to build my manifest image of Japan: Japan is a safe place where most of its citizens can make an honest living by contributing to and appreciating excellence, but despite all this, it has very few world-famous celebrities.[5] You know the proverbial bucket of crabs where, just as one crab is about to climb out, the other crabs pull it back down? Japan is like that, but where most of the crabs are already very high in the bucket, and the crabs who are about to get out just pull themselves down.

I can now pay off the two promissory notes I offered, back in chapters 9 and 37. In chapter 9, I noted that the German-Japanese cheese-and-herb sausages I tried in Schmaltz had a strong umami flavor while also being understated. This is like Japan: lots of unobtrusive greatness; the crabs are high in the bucket, but they're not *too* high in the bucket.

In chapter 37, I wondered why America can't be as well-oiled a machine as Japan. The answer is that our crabs are at a much greater distance from each other. Whereas some crabs are at the bottom of the bucket, others have reached escape velocity, and have reached outer space, veritable crabellites. A lot of things are messed up in my country, but what, you thought you could have Benny Blanco for free?

In many ways, Japan is as a country what I'd like my career to be: rich but not famous.[6] But it's also why I left Japan not wanting to be Japanese. You'd think that with as much praise as I've heaped on Japan

---

5. Or Nobel Prizes! See the penultimate footnote of chapter 12.

6. If I were a superhero, I'd be like Batman, only I wouldn't save anyone. Instead, I'd just sit in my cave and read books about how to save people.

in this chapter that I've become a full-blown weeaboo. But not only do I not want to, the thought never even occurred to me while I was there. I'm American through-and-through; when I wrote above that I felt lost without being able to rely on Peter Dinklage as my North Star, I was only half-kidding. Maybe it's bad that I've been socialized like this, but I like having celebrities around to tell me that no matter how high I climb, and no matter how much I succeed, there's always more to go, so I'll always have something to strive for. And no matter how far I fall, and no matter how much I fail, well, all I have to do is read any tabloid to learn that even having all the status and success there is won't save you from ragging on your co-stars from *Charmed* while you're dying of cancer.

One thing you may be wondering after all this is: why did he have to bring in Wilfrid Sellars in the first place? Was it all just a fancy way to justify ragging on Shannen Doherty?

I have three answers. First, no, I don't think as much about Shannen Doherty as you'd think. Second, indifference to *Charmed* aside, I nevertheless amuse myself by imbricating "Philosophy and the Scientific Image of Man" with a show about witches from the WB. My third answer is that I involve Sellars's essay because its animating attitude is a twin to the attitude I take to all my own beliefs.

Above, I gave the impression that the manifest and scientific images are static. But they're dynamic. Not only does the manifest image have a history, but so too does the scientific one. While there are constants in both images—the manifest image forever revolves around people and their experiences, while the scientific one always postulates unseen forces and entities—they are always changing, using their own previous versions to detail themselves in ever-increasing depth and breadth.

That's the vantage point I take on my own beliefs: they feel final while I inhabit them, but after times passes, I look at them like they're rough drafts sorely in need of edits, written by someone who clearly didn't do the reading.

So my manifest image of Japan is the first image of it I developed. I hope to make more in the future, ones with greater resolution. Whether I do or don't, I'm glad I have this one, reminding me there once was a time when I knew Japan just as that place with ancient shoguns, delicious mackerel, and lamination for days.

# APRIL 1, 2024

# Coda: Answering the Question

During my vacation, Shawn and Scotty repeatedly asked me whether I liked Japan. Scotty would do this via text, while Shawn would do this via hopeful gazes. At least, I think that's what she was doing; she could have just been fantasizing about reaching Executive Platinum status on American Airlines.[1]

Regardless: the question, in either form, irked me. At the time, I didn't understand why it irked me; all I felt was pure irksomeness, like gazing upon the Platonic form of irk. As I reflected on and deconstructed the feeling, though, it turns out that the question bothered me for five reasons!

First of all, I couldn't answer it honestly. Imagine I had *not* liked Japan; would I have really communicated that to Shawn or Scotty? Shawn had spent many hours and a small fortune on ensuring that this would be the trip of my dreams. For me to tell her I didn't like it would be like when the Joker set all that cash on fire: think about the air pollution! Similarly, Scotty had given me several assurances that Japan was better

---

[1]. This is the highest tier available to consumers without an invitation. Foremost among its several benefits is getting free alcoholic drinks in the main cabin. And all you have to do is spend $20,000 on flights!

# THE MOST AWKWARD MAN IN JAPAN

than the rest of the world, and their people proof that at least some racism is true. Could I really, in good conscience, go against Scotty's pro-Japanese racism?[2]

Thus, regardless of how I felt, I'd have to say I liked Japan, lest I insult both Scotty and Shawn. But that means that there was no point in them asking me! I'd say "yes" no matter what, making my answer completely uninformative.

And that leads me to the second reason I didn't like the question: because if Shawn and Scotty had just thought, a little bit, before asking it, they would have realized all of what I just described above. I mean, they're adults. And if there's one thing adults do, it's second guess literally everything they say and think and always figure out a way to treat an innocent question like a possible insult, because the entire world is a Jewish mother.[3]

Yet despite their being cognizant, highly intelligent adults, Scotty and Shawn nonetheless, and repeatedly, asked me the question. So—and this is the third problem—I felt pressure to offer them an inauthentic yes.

---

2. Of course, I grotesquely exaggerate. Though Scotty indeed thought that Japan was, in many ways, a more well-run country than the USA, he has nothing but contempt for the Japanese people. No, I have to come clean again. Scotty has no problem with the Japanese people, though he has said, on several occasions, that he thinks that Okinawans aren't *really* Japanese. You got me, I was being untruthful. Scott didn't say, on several occasions, that Okinawans aren't really Japanese. It was only on two occasions. OK, I'm leaving out some important context. He was talking about Oklahomans, not Okinawans. Also, he never said any of this.

3. Nothing is wrong with the other sweater!

But that would have felt non-comedically dishonest,[4] so had I lied in response, I would have experienced both a loss of integrity and a gain of resentment towards Scotty and Shawn for doing me like that. It's like when I was younger, and my brother would ask me if he could have a bite of my steak: if I said "no," then he'd be mad. If I said "yes," then I'd be mad. Spoiler: I always ended up mad. It would have been much better if he had just never asked me the question, which is probably something Shawn thinks about me from time to time.

The fourth problem was that saying, "yes, I like my luxury trip to Japan that my wife has been planning for months!" seemed almost to denigrate it. "What do you think of heroin?" I ask my friend Andy. Imagine he replied, "I like it."[5] Wouldn't just liking heroin feel inapposite for such an excellent drug? When asked about what heroin was like, the comedian Harris Wittels—who literally loved heroin to death—said, "you feel like there are a thousand dicks all over your body and they're all coming."[6] That feels significantly more apt than "yes, I like heroin."

But now this takes me to my fifth problem. I can't just say I liked Japan, but I have to say *something*. But that means that I have to ruminate ardently about what I thought about it. And now I've got a dilemma: to respect my time in Japan, I have to think hard. Yet the longer I think,

---

4. This is the only kind of bad dishonesty. Tricking people because it's funny is actually morally obligatory.

5. Andy has tried every drug, so I did once ask him that question, but that's not how he responded. However, his answer was so resolutely pro-heroin that I felt including it would have been unfair to MDMA.

6. https://www.vulture.com/2016/02/on-the-anniversary-of-his-death-inside-harris-wittels-final-intimate-revealing-discussion-with-pete-holmes.html

the better my answer has to be. After a while, so much time has passed that you practically have to write a book. And, well, here we are.

Now, if you have, for some reason, been wondering about this as well, I don't want you to feel guilty for having wondered it. I'm not irked when *you* ask it. First of all, I haven't been hearing *your* insistent, whiny, self-serving questions over the course of a year. Second of all, if you're reading this book, then you probably paid me money, in which case: thank you, you are my everything.

Unfortunately, I never directly answered the question about whether I liked Japan in this book. I just wrote a book and talked about my experiences. However, over a year has passed since Shawn and Scotty peppered me with their jabbing query. So I guess I have to finally get to it: did I like Japan?

As is my wont, my answer to the question begins with a deflection, namely a jaunt through an article by the contemporary philosopher Agnes Callard. On June 24, 2023, Callard published an essay in *The New Yorker* called "The Case Against Travel."[7] I get the sense that this piece caused outrage among its readers, just like everything else that Callard does near the public. But I didn't want to read whatever commentary it generated both because I wanted to peruse her piece in an uncontaminated fashion, and also I find that outraged commentary, about almost anything, is usually overwrought. So I figured that, since I was here, writing a book about touring Japan, and she was there, writing an essay against my

---

7. Agnes Callard, "The Case Against Travel", *The New Yorker* (June 24, 2023), https://www.newyorker.com/culture/the-weekend-essay/the-case-against-travel.

behavior, I should read it, to see whether I should have called this book *Sorry I Went to Japan*.

Again, I don't know whether this essay made people mad, because I didn't look, but I am also 100% sure that it made people mad. This is because she writes like a philosopher, which is a discipline whose practitioners publicly defend infanticide, argue that people don't exist, and get into heated debates about whether we should say "I perceive a green thing" or "I am perceiving greenly."[8] In other words, philosophers defend positions that are both absurd and immoral, and then get all snippy about diction.

Here's the problem, though: she wrote this essay for *The New Yorker*, not *The Journal of Aesthetics and Art Criticism*. But the people who read *The New Yorker* are reading it because (a) they like to gaze at ads for Loro Piana; (b) they're in the mood for dinner, so they've digested the recent review of Foul Witch; and (c) they want to find another reason to hate Republicans, so they've already read the latest dispatch on Matt Gaetz's possibly illegal plan to fly a wide-body freighter full of hippos into Nancy Pelosi's Napa Valley estate. In other words, they're coming to her article angry, hungry, and in the mood for expensive clothing. This is a volatile audience! They don't want nuance, they want foliage print scarves and arctic char!

To top all this off, Callard's public brand is "notoriously quirky." She has, um, a lot of look. Speaking of look, her office looks like a paint store fell on a Kindergarten. She asked her friends not to defend her if she were ever to be the victim of an attempted cancelation. That bit of advice came in handy, because she infamously threw away her kids' Halloween candy, causing a Twitter mob. And she agreed to be profiled

---

8. Anyone who thinks we perceive greenly is a fucking idiot.

in a way-too-revealing portrait of her divorce and remarriage. In other words, what we have here is a known weirdo arguing to a bunch of hangry, well-heeled status-chasers that they're bad people for wanting to go to Parma.[9]

Enough throat-clearing. What is her case against travel?

The first thing to note is that Callard does not make a case against all travel, but rather a particular kind of travel. She has no problem with going to a place because you must, say, on account of work or war. And she has no problem with pleasure-seeking tourism, *i.e.*, traveling to a place just for a good time. Instead, her problem is with what you could call "transformational" tourism, *i.e.*, voluntarily going somewhere because you think going so will change you for the better, either by giving you a deeper appreciation of the world's cultures, or by connecting you to other people whom you wouldn't otherwise meet.

However, she doesn't think transformational tourism changes you for the better, in either of these ways. What's her evidence for this claim? It's observational: think of someone you know who travels to a different country and then comes back gushing about the place. How often have you ever known such experiences to actually change such a person, at least for longer than it takes for him to show you his photos of Hadrian's Wall and to revert back to his normal pronunciation of "aluminum"? Callard bets you have seen this kind of person change for the better approximately never.

But if it doesn't happen to other people, why think it happens to you? After all, you're not so special. You may say it happened to you because you've experienced it happening to you. But if you say this,

---

9. Technically, she's saying they're delusional, not bad. But remember my stance on comedic dishonesty!

you're deluding yourself, because it's a lot harder to notice an important change happening in you than it is in someone else.[10] If you say, "no, I introspected, and I detect the change!" Well, that's also the protest of the other tourists, the ones you had such disdain for just a minute ago.

Let's say this evidence convinces you that transformational tourism doesn't change people for the better. If it doesn't, why doesn't it? Callard's theory is that transformational tourists won't let it change them. She claims that when you decide to tour a place to get a deeper appreciation of the world's cultures, your companions on that voyage aren't just your spouse, friends, and children, but also your prior assumptions: *e.g.*, you arrive hoping to breathe in the grandeur of the Grand Canyon, enjoy the awesomeness of the Great Wall of China, or suffer one of the Pyramid of Giza's many curses. Once you get there, the destination either lives up to your expectations or it doesn't. If it does, you say "good," and you check it off your bucket list of "things that I expected to happen to me that did"; if it doesn't, you just assume that something was off that day. Hence Callard's assertion that the transformational tourist "outsources the vindication of his experiences to the ethnologist, to postcards, to conventional wisdom about what you are or are not supposed to do in a place."

Assuming all that is right, it explains why transformational tourism doesn't enrich your aesthetic faculties. But remember, people justify tourism not merely on aesthetic grounds, but also for ethical reasons: they claim it connects you to others in the world, people whom you wouldn't have normally met, which in turn expands your moral horizons.

Callard dissents. Her reasoning is that going into a land trying to appreciate its people for the ethical benefits of meeting them is actually a

---

10. Except, apparently, for whether I have a beard.

way of objectifying them. Travel, she pronounces, has a "dehumanizing effect, which thrusts [the traveler] among people to whom he was forced to relate as a spectator."

If there's no good evidence that transformational tourism is edifying, and we also have good explanations for why it's not, then why do so many people invest it with such significance? Here, Callard goes out on a limb. She claims that without travel, our lives would come across as much more monotonous. She asks us to imagine how we'd feel if we knew that we'd never travel again. Were we bequeathed that terrible foreknowledge, many of us would taste bitter absurdity in carrying out the rest of our lives. "More and more of this and then I die," is how Callard summarizes it.

But travel "splits this expanse of time into the chunk that happens before the trip, and the chunk that happens after it, obscuring from view the certainty of annihilation. And it does so in the cleverest possible way: by giving you a foretaste of it." Consequently, travel does deserve veneration; just not for the reasons we venerate it.

This last point is weird and it confuses me. What I think she's saying is this: when we travel, we don't really do anything. We go somewhere with greener grass, we pantomime epiphanies, and we return unchanged. And yet for all that, we think we have done something. But the only thing we did was a nothing abroad that makes the routines we habitually execute at home more bearable. Like death, then, travel is a doing nothing that gives significance to life. Hence her essay's last paragraph: "Socrates said that philosophy is a preparation for death. For everyone else, there's travel."

This is mostly horseshit. I've already mentioned that, despite her article's title, she's not really arguing against travel in general, but rather against one kind of tourism. Now, I won't hold that too much against her, as authors often don't get to choose the titles of their pieces.[11] Nevertheless, it's worth bringing up again, because the overreach of her title characterizes the argumentation of her whole piece.

First, her observational evidence that travel doesn't change people isn't very strong. If the standard for something's changing you for the better is "must produce a noticeable, positive change, almost immediately," then almost nothing changes us for the better, other than, say, near-death experiences, cracking your back, or reading this book. But I wager that things that change us for the better usually take a while to gestate, like when I realized that playing chess every day not only made me better at chess, but gave me a stock of metaphors to convey my general confusion about everyday interactions, like when someone responds to the Caro-Kann Defense with the Fantasy Variation.

A second problem is that when Callard is trying to explain why people don't actually get anything out of enjoying another culture's treasures, she goes way too binary. I don't think the only options are, "this is what I expected" or "something went wrong because it wasn't what I expected." Other options are, "I don't know how I feel," "it turns out *Lonely Planet* was wrong; the Mona Lisa sucks," and "it was just a trashcan?!"

A third problem lies in Callard's brief against tourism's ethically uplifting qualities. She writes that going to a place wanting to encounter new kinds of people requires us to observe them, which forces us to maintain our distance, which dehumanizes them. Although she enlists other authors to support this claim, her personal experience seems to be doing the heavy lifting: "During my Paris wanderings, I would stare at people, intently inspecting their clothing, their demeanor, their interactions. I was

---

11. The original title of this book was *Land of My Rising Dick*. My wife told me this was offensive and inaccurate, but I don't know, seems fine to me.

trying to see the Frenchness in the French people around me. This is not a way to make friends."

If I were mean, I would say that it's not her observing people that explains why she didn't make friends. But I don't think that's the problem.[12] The problem is that she seems to be saying that because observing people is not a way to make friends, it follows that it's not transformative.

I disagree. One day, a month after I moved to Los Angeles, I was walking down the street. A man in a nice sportscar found himself waiting behind a bus that had stopped to pick up passengers. He furiously tried to merge into the lane on his left, but it was too late—the traffic was unyielding. Finally, after an eternity that must have occupied seconds, the driver saw an opportunity to merge and he took it. As he sped away, he yelled at the boarding passengers, "GET A CAR!!!" I didn't make friends with either that man or the indifferent passengers, but I learned a lot about LA that day, namely, that it wasn't as chill as I was led to believe, that public transportation is not particularly popular among the car-owning classes, and that you can capture the spirit of a city just by watching its impatient assholes.

Finally, what do I make of her last point, that the reason that people valorize travel, despite its ineffectiveness, is that it breaks their lives up into

---

12. I was actually in a days-long seminar with Callard. We chatted a few times. She seemed very nice, and I enjoyed all her contributions. I have nothing against her! If my response to her piece seems mean, keep in mind, first, that, despite (jokingly) calling her arguments "horseshit", I actually think her piece is very good. It revealed to me an outlook that I didn't know was out there, and it made me think about my own travels in a new way. Second, the kind of grilling I do in this chapter is how philosophers interact with each other's work in general. This is what we're trained to do. Unrelatedly, many of us have drinking problems.

bearable chunks and prepares them for death? To be honest, I think she just came up with that so she could write her punchline, about how while philosophy prepared Socrates for death, for the rest of us, there's travel. It's a good last line! But I think she's stretching to come up with some reasoning to fill it in, as evidenced by the fact that I, a diagnostician of argumentation, couldn't even find the bones of an argument underneath the fatsuit of rhetoric.

Don't get me wrong: I'm not the world's best philosopher, but I am good enough at philosophy to be a professional philosopher. And this is supposed to be breezy pop philosophy for educated laypeople, not Hegel's *Science of Logic*. If *I* can't render her last point intelligible after trying really hard, then I'm guessing it will leave no marks on the understanding of *New Yorker* readers who glance over it on their way to the Frick's exhibition of trophies from Jeffrey Epstein's sex island.

So no, I'm not convinced that I did anything wrong by going to Japan, and I will not apologize for it. But despite the failure of Callard's article to convict me of wrongdoing, it did make me reflect on the attitude I took when I was in Japan, and it allowed me to figure out why it was so difficult for me to determine what I thought of the place.

My comportment while I was in Japan was observational: I was looking very hard at Japan, not because I thought doing so would elevate me, but initially because I wanted fodder for jokes. Then, the more I wrote, the more I wanted to write, not just to make my intimates laugh, but so I could remember what I went through. And finally, the more I wanted to write, the more it became an obligation to write, not only because I wanted to make lots of people laugh, and not only because I wanted to retain this adventure, but because I wanted to understand myself. I not only wanted to understand what I thought of Japan, but I wanted to understand how I thought, in general.

And here Callard is right: while you observe people, you have to distance yourself from them, but in doing this you make yourself unable to have a second-personal relationship with them. It's like you're reading about them in a book rather than sharing feelings with them. And this is all the weirder when the person you're doing this to is yourself.

If I hadn't written this book, and I had tried to stay more in the moment, I would have lost track of most of my memories, but I would have been left with an overall impression. I probably would have known immediately how to answer whether I liked Japan. I would have said, "Japan was great!" If you had asked me why, I would have said, "um ... good food, competent people, lots of beautiful stuff."

However, because I wrote this book, I memorialized many more things, but I lost my emotional connection to my general impression. I have a three-hundred page explanation for my answer, but I can't find my answer.

But then I realized: that's my answer. The fact that I can't find the answer by introspecting means I shouldn't look inside, but outside. And when I look outside, what do I see? On my desk I see a drawing of the rock garden from Ryōan-ji Zen Temple that I occasionally look at to give myself peace. In my garage, I see a box for an unassembled toy that Briscoe will never play with. And, most important of all, on my computer I see my draft of this book.

Never before have I gone to a place and then written a book about it. Never before have I gone to a place and thought "I should go to places for a living!" And never before have I worked so hard to keep something a part of me.

So did I like Japan?

Yes. It changed my life.

# About the author

Did you enjoy this book? Tell your friends or leave a review on Amazon, it helps this independently-published book reach more discerning readers like you. Want more from Rob? Follow this link for a bonus chapter and to stay updated on the next book from Rob.

Reading on paper? Sign up for bonus material and a newsletter at robgressis.com/japanbonus.

Robert Gressis is a professor of philosophy at California State University, Northridge. His research interests include Immanuel Kant's philosophy of religion, the epistemology of disagreement, and professional mediocrity. He enjoys Cincinnati Bengals football, *Dungeons & Dragons*, and professional wrestling. He lives in Los Angeles with one wife, one son, and one cat. The cat's interests also include professional mediocrity.

Made in the USA
Middletown, DE
08 December 2024